CNN互动英语系列

STEP BY STEP 听懂

CNN名人专访

Master Listening with CNN News
—Interviews with Celebrities

LiveABC 编著

科学出版社
北 京

图字：01-2010-3279 号

本书原名《Step by Step 听懂 CNN——名人专访》，原出版者 LiveABC Interactive Corporation，经授权由科学出版社在中国大陆地区独家出版发行。

图书在版编目（CIP）数据

Step by Step 听懂 CNN 名人专访/LiveABC 编著．—北京：科学出版社，2010

（CNN 互动英语系列）

ISBN　978-7-03-028038-1

Ⅰ．①S…　Ⅱ．①L…　Ⅲ．①英语－听说教学－自学参考资料　Ⅳ．①H319.9

中国版本图书馆 CIP 数据核字（2010）第 115587 号

责任编辑：张　培 / 责任校对：张林红
责任印制：赵德静 / 封面设计：无极书装

联系电话：010-6403 9074 / 电子邮箱：zhangpei@ mail.sciencep.com

科学出版社 出版
北京东黄城根北街 16 号
邮政编码：100717
http://www.sciencep.com

北京佳信达欣艺术印刷有限公司 印刷
科学出版社发行　各地新华书店经销
*
2010 年 9 月第 一 版　　　开本：B5（720×1000）
2010 年 9 月第一次印刷　　　印张：16
字数：360 000
定价：**58.00 元**
（含 DVD 互动光盘 1 张）
（如有印装质量问题，我社负责调换）

序

中国的英语教育长期以来都处于学生英语听力能力较弱的状态，"说英语"还"操之于我"，"听英语"则是"操之于人"。比如在公司用英语作简报，准备好内容上台演讲，也许可以勉强应付，但讲完以后，如果有外国客户在场提出问题，也许就会出现窘困的局面了。

你，准备好了吗？

我们先从英语听力较弱的原因说起，接着谈谈有哪些可行的方法及策略来消除大家的英语听力差的心理障碍，再解释这本《Step by Step 听懂 CNN 名人专访》跟一般听力课本有何不同、它的着力点在哪里。

一、英语听力差的几种原因

1. 母语发音与英语发音相差较大，无法"进行配对"。
2. 英文单词量小，或是无法正确理解某一单词在某一情境或上下文中的正确意义。
3. 不懂词组（即"短语"或"短句"）——绝大多数词组的正确意义无法仅凭借单词猜出，而英文中的词组使用极为常见，光靠英汉词典里的单词意义来理解，可能会完全"摸不着头脑"。
4. 懂单词及词组意义，但跟不上英语正常说话速度。
5. 懂单词及词组意义，但对于情境或背景文化很陌生，无法"进入状态"。
6. 知道字面意思，但听不出字里行间的幽默、隐喻、言外之意等。

二、解决之道

1. 多看英文杂志、多听英文歌曲、多看英语旅游节目、Discovery、国家地理、CNN、BBC World 等频道、多听 CRI 广播等。

   a. 有规律地阅读大量英文材料：上网或看纸质杂志，先从阅读材料中的相关报道熟悉热门话题的关键词句、用法以及了解背景知识，然后再听材料便会有事半功倍的效果。

   b. 有规律地听大量英语材料：开始先要求自己听出主题，熟悉英语平常说话的速度和语调，然后努力听细节。这样练习，久而久之会发现即使漏失一些词，仍能掌握重点。

2. 重视发音。中国的英语教育普遍存在发音问题，发音不佳的教师比比皆是，结果变成：听到原本认识的单词也听不懂了。

三、练习方法

1. 听写英文：利用如《Step by Step 听懂 CNN 名人专访》这种提供英文字幕、可重复播放收听的实用听力书籍。练习的方法有两种：

   a. 先看英文字幕、熟读字幕，学习其中词汇、短语，然后再看影片，换言之，先了解背景知识，会很容易进入听力最佳状态、逐渐完全听懂，换言之，在头脑里先构筑整个事物的结构，再配上影像、声音，将三者合而为一。

   b. 先看影片、不看英文字幕，把听到的内容写下来，一次次反复聆听，直到将自己能听出的所有单词写出来，之后核对英文字幕，这时便很容易了解到自己原来的弱点。如此练习一段时间以后，便能逐渐掌握一段完整的听力材料。

   第一种是"舒适"的学习方法，第二种是"挑战性"的学习方法，两者可以交替使用。如果读者对于自己不太熟悉的题材，建议使用第一种；对于自己比较熟悉的题材，可使用第二种。

2. 借用口译训练的技巧

   a. 跟述／影子练习（shadowing）：不中断录音，紧跟录音后进行重复，即重复听到的每一个音节。

   b. 复述（repeating）：听到一个完整句子之后重复该句子。

   c. 延迟复述（lagging）：隔一个句子重复之前的句子，甚至隔两个句子重复之前的句子。

   d. 听写（dictating）：听一句，写一句。

   e. 笔记（note-taking）：边听边写重点。

   f. 摘要（summarizing）：听完一个段落以后写出重点。

   g. 换述（paraphrasing）：听完一句子，用自己的话表达出来。

   h. 快速联想（brainstorming）：听到一个关键字／词，在短时间内写下联想到的所有事物。

   i. 预测（anticipating）：听完一个句子，想像下一句可能会是什么。

   j. 推论（inferencing）：听完一个句子，判断其在该情境或上下文中适当的含义。

四、可选择的材料与工具

1. 收音机广播、MP3、电视新闻、电影 DVD 等，都是容易获取的材料与工具，可依照自己的偏好、生活习惯以及作息时间来选择，也可以全部尝试之后再决定最适合自己的方式。此外，最重要的一点莫过于要持之以恒。

2. Podcast（播客）是苹果电脑的 iPod 与 broadcast（广播）组合而成的，iTunes 上有免费的 Podcast。Podcast 是练习英文听力的很好的方法，因为：

a. 题材包罗万象，如：时事、科技、社会、医疗、商业、体育等等，包含各类的信息。

b. 覆盖以英语为母语的国家和地区、包含各种年龄层的口音以及说话方式。

c. 可以看影片，也可以只收听广播。

但 Podcast 没有字幕，对于缺乏相关的背景知识与词汇的学习者而言，本书更可以说是收听 Podcast 必要的"前奏"。

五、注意事项

1. 关注自己感兴趣的题材

   为什么很多人都知道前面提到的方法，但英语听力能力强的人却仍然凤毛麟角？其中一个原因在于，大多数人不懂得如何利用听力材料来配合自己的兴趣。譬如，喜欢英文歌曲的人自然对歌词有所研究。当学习与兴趣相结合时，学习效果便能事半功倍。这也是了解英语社会文化的最佳途径。

2. 了解材料内容的难度

   超出个人水平太多的内容，听一百遍也不会懂；太简单的材料即使听了很多，进步也很有限。由于每个人的听力水平程度不一，到底选何种材料最合适，需要自己进行评估或请教英语老师。

3. 结合泛听和精听

   a. 泛听：着重于接触大量听力材料，主要目的是要掌握大意而不必了解每个细节，所以在选材上要广泛，接触不同的语言风格与发音方式，但仍必须适合自己的水平。

   b. 精听：首先熟悉听力材料中的生词，在句子之间或困难处停下来，回放重听，利用可反复播放的听力材料或互动光盘。

4. 区别同音词

   在英语中有不少读音相近、意思却截然不同的词，如：cure（治疗）和 kill（杀死）；food（食物）和 foot（脚）；restaurant（餐厅）和 restroom（厕所）；valentine（情人）和 volunteer（志愿者）；pain（痛苦）、pan（锅）和 pen（笔）等。能分辨相近读音的词是必要的，这又与个人自身的发音有密切关系。

5. 多记惯用语

   英语中许多惯用词组（短语及短句）的含义往往无法从单词字面意义拼凑得出，很难猜测，必须熟记。再者，大家需要了解的是：英语里惯用语的功能与中文里的成语不尽相同，因为中文里的成语多半是为了表现语言能力与素养，用不用都可以，但英语里的惯用语则是英语国家人人时时挂在嘴边的，因此对惯用语若是不熟，就会大大地削弱英语听力能力。

6. 培养根据上下文猜测生词的能力

遇到听不清楚或听不懂的时候，要靠上下文来理解，即上面提过的推论（inferencing），这种能力要靠平时不断的泛听练习加上精听的积累才能逐渐锻炼获得。

7. 多次慢速听力以后，就要开始以英语正常语速不断进行练习

市面上的英语教材都由以英语为母语的人士配音，读得生动有趣、抑扬顿挫，但这些以教学为目的的"朗读"，语速其实放慢了许多，因此当学习者接触到地道的英语新闻或英语访谈时，对正常语速往往来不及反应，所以平常就需要多利用正常语速的听力材料进行练习。

六、分级策略

1. 对于初学者而言，有两种练习可同时进行：

   a. 反复收听日常生活会话，以及跟着录音反复朗诵句子，直到熟悉其连音、省略音、惯用语等。

   b. 反复收听浅显易懂的小故事：旨在听懂大意，加强将前后内容连贯起来的能力。扩大词汇量，而且把学到的文字和声音结合起来。

2. 已具有基本能力的中级学习者，仍需扩充各种题材的背景知识与词汇。这个阶段也有两种听力练习可同时进行：

   a. 反复收听具有一定长度与难度的听力录音：先听后读，或读了之后再听，都可以熟悉英语的语调以及增强头脑对于英文词汇的反应力。

   b. 英语电影或 DVD：英语国家制作的电影内容生活化，可从 DVD 的英文字幕中学习到日常生活所需词汇以及自然的语音语调。

3. 已具有相当水平的高级学习者，追求接近以英语为母语的人的听力水平。这个阶段也有两种听力练习可同时进行：

   a. 看 National Geographic、Discovery 等电视频道，这些电视频道多半是播放有关生物、科技、艺术、历史、音乐等专业领域的节目。

   b.《CNN 名人专访》这种英语学习素材涵盖了各种知识，最重要的一点是使用的是地道的英语访谈材料，再加上英文字幕与中文翻译，提供了全方位学习的英语环境，另外还提供慢速朗读功能，帮助学习者渐入佳境。

七、知己知彼、百战百胜

1. 学习了单词、短语的基本定义以后，更需要了解情境含义。

   市面上英文教材的内容，绝大多数为编写而成，并非真实情境的记录，就像我们的小学课本，与真实的小说、散文、报章杂志的语句，都有着相当大的差别，所以当学习者接触到地道的英语新闻或亲身到英语国家访问时，对于惯用语或特殊用法不会解读，甚至对于课堂上所学的与真实情境含义的差异毫无认知，因而会受到极大震撼与冲击。在这两者中间，目前的市场上很少能找到作为桥梁的工具，而《CNN 名人专访》正是这样一本难得的书籍。

2. 不用掌握每一个词，也不用因无法掌握每个单词而感到气馁。

   听的时候，不用试图掌握每一个词。不断地暂停，极可能挫伤学习兴趣。若是有一句话没听清楚，就让它过去，然后试着从后面的句子来了解整体大意。听完一个段落、在心中做个小结，估计一下大约听懂多少，并且试着判断为何能够了解或不能够了解该段的大意。只要持续地练习，实力就会慢慢增强。

3. 长期累积理解力和语感。

   加强英语听力没有捷径，只有通过有规律且持续的收听，才能累积理解力和语感。每天抽时间观看电视节目、阅读相关刊物，实在不是件容易的事，但必须利用这种方法，才会真正见到成效。

八、最佳起跑线：《Step by Step 听懂 CNN 名人专访》

以上所谈的种种增强英语听力的方法，靠的是正确的方法及毅力。这本《Step by Step 听懂 CNN 名人专访》以地道材料为基础，配合先进的学习工具，可以说是已经做到了一般英语学习用书以及听力教材所做不到的。因此，大家要是希望在创新的英语学习环境中提高听力水平，就从这里开始吧！

前　言

　　英语早已跃升为全球最主要的沟通语言。您一定遇到过这样的情形：谈话的对象来自不同的地方、持不同的口音，即使都使用英语，有些人的发音也与我们最熟悉的美语发音有所不同，以致于无法完全听懂对方的意思。因此，我们想到了搜集 CNN 采访世界名人的专访材料，除了可以了解他们成功的故事、奋斗的过程之外，还可以运用这些多元的素材来练习听力。

　　本书是继《Step by Step 听懂 CNN》后所推出的另一本同系列书籍，主要收录了 CNN 名人专访的材料，内容涉及政治、企业、运动、时尚、音乐、娱乐等不同的领域，提供读者多元化的背景材料及不同口音的听力素材。而在内容编排上，分为【基础训练篇】及【实战应用篇】两个部分，【基础训练篇】节选了 15 篇 CNN 专访，逐句说明受访者所应用的发音规则，您可以依照我们所建议的步骤进行练习，通过反复收听、检验，熟悉英语的音调、节奏，以及揣摩英语中常见的连音、同化音、省略音、弱化等各种发音技巧。

　　【实战应用篇】分为 Part I、Part II 两部分，共收录 24 篇完整的 CNN 专访。Part I 与 Part II 的差别在于前者的受访者均以北美口音为主，而 Part II 中的受访者则来自其他地区、带有不同的口音，不论是哪一种，其实都是训练听力很好的素材。此外，受访者的讲话速度有快有慢，有些人说话时颇具个人特色，这些都有可能是影响能否听懂的因素，但也是最贴近真实的语言情境，只要循序渐进，反复听读，加以时日必能掌握听懂英语访谈的技巧。另外，您也可利用书上所列出的关键词汇、发音提示等作为听力辅助工具，并试着练习书中所附的听力测验题目，来检验自己的学习效果，而各单元中所附的 Notes & Vocabulary 则能提升您的词汇量。

　　黄希敏老师为读者提供了许多提升英语听力能力的方法，在序文中除了解释听力无法提升的原因外，还提供了一些可以学习、运用的方法，相信这些可以有效地帮助读者在听力上获得提高。另外，【附录】中提供了简单的英音、澳大利亚口音与美音之间差异的说明，目的是希望能让读者对不同口音有全面的了解，最重要的还希望读者能多多练习不同领域的听力材料，自然而然听懂持不同口音说话者的口语表达。

　　本书采用中英对照形式，方便读者迅速掌握每篇访谈的内容。另外，主播、特派记者或受访者在新闻播报或访谈中可能会有口误的情况发生，我们的更正方式为在错误单词上加删除线，并在方括号中补注正确的用法，例如：it's very hard to describe ~~that's~~ [whether it's] an ambition or just a dream . . .。另外在新闻播报或访谈中，若省略的词汇会影响到对内容的理解，我们会在原文后方加入方括号标示出省略掉的内容，例如：finally I find [my] identity。

本书中的单词拼写及音标以韦氏词典第 11 版（Merriam-Webster's 11th Collegiate Dictionary）为准。以下为书中词性的缩写说明：

adj.	adjective	形容词
adv.	adverb	副词
conj.	conjunction	连词
n.	noun	名词
phr.	phrase	短语
prep.	preposition	介词
v.	verb	动词

两个单词以上的名词短语，经韦氏词典收录并列为名词词条，标示为 n.，未收录词条则标为 n. phr.。由动词和介词或副词所组成的短语动词（如：hang back），在本书中标示为 v.，而其他作动词用的短语（如：take shape）则标为 v. phr.。

希望《Step by Step 听懂 CNN 名人专访》这本书提供给您更进一步提高英语听力的技巧，引领您逐步听懂地道的英语访谈，只要迈出第一步，您的英语听力能力必能不断提高，使您轻松融入全球化的地球村。

如何使用光盘

● 系统需求建议

- 处理器 Pentium 4 以上（或同等 AMD、Celeron 处理器）
- WINDOWS XP、VISTA、Win7 以上简体中文版
- 512 MB 内存
- 16 倍光驱
- 全彩显卡（16K 色以上）
- 声卡、扬声器、麦克风
- 硬盘需求空间 200 MB
- Microsoft Media Player 9.0

● 光盘安装程序

步骤一：进入中文操作系统。

步骤二：将光盘放进光驱。

步骤三：本产品带有 Auto Run 运行功能，如果您的电脑支持 Auto Run 光盘自动播放功能，则将自动出现【CNN 互动英语系列——Step by Step 听懂 CNN 名人专访】的安装画面。

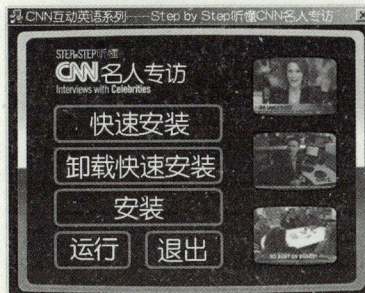

◆ 如果您的电脑已安装过本系列图书的互动光盘，您可以直接点击"快速安装"图标，进行快速安装；否则，请点击"安装"图标，进行安装。

◆ 如果您的电脑无法支持 Auto Run 光盘自动播放功能，请打开 Windows"我的电脑"，点击光驱，并运行光盘根目录下的 autorun.exe 程序。

◆ 如果运行 autorun.exe 仍无法安装本光盘，请进入本光盘的 setup 文件夹，并运行 setup.exe 程序，即可进行安装。

◆ 若要删除【Step by Step 听懂 CNN 名人专访】，请点击"开始"，选择"设量"，选择"控制面板"，选择"添加／删除程序"，并在菜单中点击"Step by Step 听懂 CNN 名人专访"，并运行"添加／删除"程序即可。

◆ 当语音识别系统或录音功能无法使用时，请检查声卡驱动程序是否正常，并确认硬盘空间是否足够，且 Windows 录音程序可以使用。

● 操作说明

点击 Play，即进入本光盘的教学课程。按说明顺序如下：

＊ 主画面 ＊

说明：

1. 主画面共有 7 个图标，分别为：基础训练、实战应用 I、实战应用 II、索引、说明、网站及退出。本书共配有两张互动光盘，第一张内含基础训练、实战应用 I；第二张内含实战应用 II。

2. 点击任一类别（基础训练、实战应用 I 或实战应用 II），将在屏幕中列出所有单元，点击后可进入该主题的听力测验界面。

✳ 听力测验界面说明 ✳

1. 本光盘依难易程度共分为基础训练、实战应用 I、实战应用 II 三个阶段，测验的题型分别为——基础训练：是非题；实战应用 I、II：是非题、选择题、填空题。

2. 当您第一次进入某一单元，您必须依序（是非题 → 选择题 → 填空题）做完该单元所有题目之后才能开启其他学习功能。

3. 当您觉得内容太难，无法理解大部分的意思时，您可以先点击左方的"生词提示"图标，我们列出了该文章中较难的单词及专有名词，可以帮助您听懂原文的意思。

4. 请点击右下方的 Play 图标播放影片并作答，完成该题后，点击 Next 图标进行下一题，完成该测验题型后，请在左下方点击接下来的测验题型进行测验，在您完成所有的测验后，请点击"影片学习"进入影片学习界面。

5. 当您再次进入该影片时，就可以依自己的需求，点击左上方的题型图标选择进行测验或立刻进入课程学习界面。

✳ 题型说明如下 ✳

(1) 是非题：

(2) 选择题：

(3) 填空题：

✳ 影片学习 ✳

说明：

当您做完该课程的所有测验后，点击左方的"影片学习"图标，即进入本界面。

工具列说明：

1. 界面右侧由上至下依序为：播放、暂停、播下一句、播上一句、反复播放本句、全屏幕播放。

2. 在此您可以自行设定"反复朗读"的播放次数，在图标上点击鼠标右键即可设定播放的次数及间隔的秒数；想恢复为原本播放的模式，只要将次数调回 0 即可。

3. 界面左侧由上至下依序为：目录、单词解释、文字学习、回主画面、退出。

4. 界面下方的英文及中文字幕，通过点击字幕前的图标，可选择出现或隐藏字幕，以进行听力练习。

5. 字幕下方有一影片播放控制栏，可确定影片播放起始点。

✳ 文字学习 ✳

说明：

1. 在影片学习中，点击"文字学习"图示，即进入本界面。

2. 在界面的右上方会有一个影片窗口，在声音播放的同时，您可以在此窗口看到该段声音的影片。

工具列说明：

全文朗读

点击"全文朗读"图标，电脑会自动朗读本段新闻的内容。

角色扮演

点击"角色扮演"图标，则会在图标左侧出现人名。此时，您可选择所要扮演的角色，程序将关闭该角色的声音，由您和电脑进行对话练习，当您的发音不正确时，则会出现一个对话框，您可以选择"再读一次"、"略过"、或"读给我听"来完成或跳过该句对话；也可以调整语音识别的灵敏度。若您的发音正确，则对话会一直进行下去。

快慢朗读

当您觉得对话速度太快时，可以点击"快慢朗读"图标，再点击"全文朗读"图标或任意句子，朗读速度将变慢，使您听得更清楚。慢速朗读时，为了让您更容易学习，我们将一句话断成几小段。按左键：则朗读您选取的小段落，按右键：则整句朗读。若您觉得速度太慢，想恢复一般速度，只要再次点击"快慢朗读"图标，即可恢复成一般速度。

↻ 反复朗读

点击"反复朗读"图示后，再点击任一句，即反复播放该句。在此您可以自行设定"反复朗读"的播放次数，在图标上点击鼠标右键即可设定播放的次数及间隔的秒数；若您想恢复为原本播放的模式，只要将次数调回 0 即可。

CN 中文翻译

点击"中文翻译"图标后，界面下方将出现中文翻译框，您可在中文翻译框内看到原文的中文翻译。若您点击中文翻译框中的某句中文，则会朗读相对应的英文句子；同样，点击内文中的任意句子，也会朗读该句英文，并显示出其中文翻译。

录音

1. 点击"录音"图示后，开启录音功能控制栏。

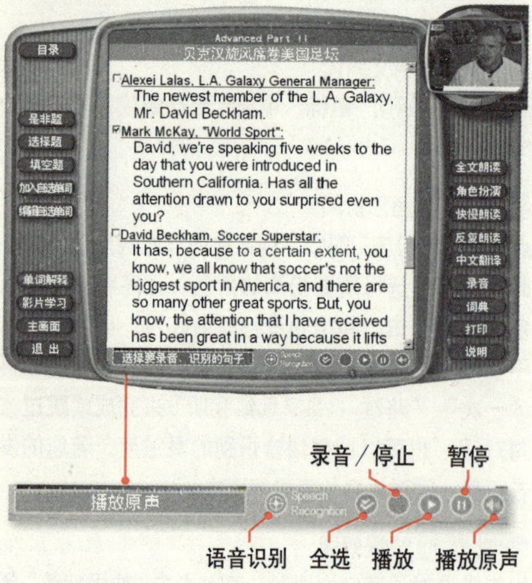

录音／停止　暂停

语音识别　全选　播放　播放原声

播放原声

2. 按键功能由左至右为：全选、录音／停止、播放、暂停以及播放影片声音。按最左方的"全选"图示，会出现全部句子录音；若您只想选择某段内容，只要在该段前方的方框

（□）点击一下即可。若您选取最右方的"播放影片原声"图标，则在您进行录音或播放录音前，都会将播放该段影片原声。

3. 录音步骤如下：
   (1) 选出要进行录音的句子，并选择是否要录音前播放原声。
   (2) 点击"录音"键。
   (3) 请在电脑"播放原声"后，对着麦克风读出您所选取的句子。
   (4) 当您完成该句录音后，请按键盘上的"空格"键（space bar），结束录音。
   (5) 点击"播放"键，即可听到您所录的声音。

4. 点击左边的"Speech Recognition"图标，将启动语音识别功能，请依照以下步骤进行语音识别：
   (1) 先选择要练习发音的句子，并选择是否要在语音识别前播放原声。
   (2) 点击"Speech Recognition"图标。
   (3) 当画面出现"请录音"时，您必须对麦克风读出您选取的句子，如果您的发音正确，则将继续进行下一句；如果发音不正确，则会出现一个对话框，您可选择"再读一次"、"略过"或"读给我听"来完成或跳过该句对话；也可在此调整语音识别的灵敏度。

5. 当您要在中途结束录音或语音识别，请在任意处点击一下即可结束该功能。

词典

当您点击"查阅词典"图标后，在画面下方将出现词典框，此时任意点击原文中的单词，词典框内会出现该单词的音标及中文翻译，并读出该词发音。

▣ 打印

当您点击"打印"图标后，在画面下方将出现打印控制键。您可选择"全部打印"或"部分打印"；打印内容可选择是否包括中文翻译。此外，本光盘还提供储存功能，您可以选择全部储存或部分储存；并选择是否储存中文翻译。

？ 说明

当您点击"说明"图标，将会进入辅助说明页。您可借此了解本光盘内容的各项操作说明及用法。

to a certain extent 学习重点

当您在点击文中蓝色字体的学习重点，画面下方会出现说明框，并提供发音；若在开启"中文翻译"功能时点击，则会朗读您点击的句子。

David Beckham, Soccer Superstar: 段落朗读

当您点击课文中的人名，程序将自动朗读此人说的话。若您是处于"慢速朗读"模式，则播放该段话时，声音及反白文字会以小段方式出现。

□X

✓

.□. 测验题型

进入文字学习画面后，若您想再做一次测验，可以点击任意测验题型，进入该测验界面。

A↓

A≡ 加入及编辑自选单词

点击加入自选单词后，可以点击您要记录的单词。

在此，您可以进行单词学习也可以删除或打印任一单词。

单词解释

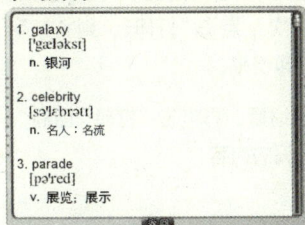

列出本单元的重点单词（词性、音标、中文解释），点击该单词，会给出发音。

＊ 索引 ＊

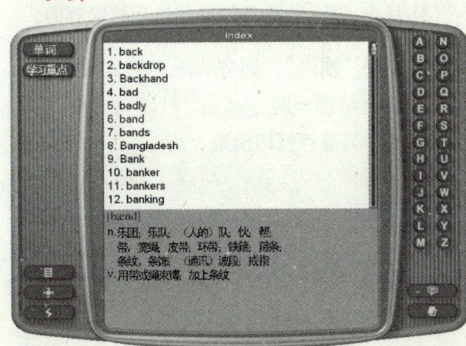

说明：

1. 在主画面点击"索引"图示，进入索引界面，内含单词检索及学习重点索引。

2. 单词检索：

   (1) 在此将所有的单词依字母分类，点击单词会出现该单词的音标、中文翻译及发音。

   (2) 连续点击单词两次或点击"显示例句"图标，即会显现该单词的例句。

   (3) 连续点击例句两次或点击"连接课文"图标，即跳至该例句的"文字学习"界面。

   (4) 点击"自选单词"图标，您可以在此看到您在学习加入的自选单词。

(5) 点击"朗读"，则会将所选字母的单词从头到尾读一次；点击"打印"，则将该字母的单词打印出来。

(6) 点击任一单词后，再点击"打印"图标，可打印该单词的内容。

3. 学习重点：

(1) 在此列出本光盘所有单元的学习重点。光标点击任一学习重点，会自动朗读。

(2) 连续点击两次或点击"连接课文"图标，即跳至该学习重点的"文字学习"界面。

(3) 点击"返回"图标则回到单词检索界面。

(4) 点击"朗读"，则会将所有的词语补充从头到尾读一遍；点击"打印"，则将所有的学习重点打印出来。

✳ 说明 ✳

1. 在主画面点击"说明"图标，在此提供"操作说明"及"语音识别设定说明"。

2. 您可借此了解本光盘内容的各项操作说明、用法及语音识别设定等说明。

✳ 原文朗读 MP3 ✳

光盘中含有原文朗读及慢速朗读 MP3 的内容，您可以放在 MP3 播放器听，也可以将光盘置于电脑中，从"我的电脑"点击您的光驱，再从中选择光盘文件里 MP3 的文件夹，使用播放软件将文件开启收听 MP3 内容。

请注意！

在 Vista 系统中，如果安装互动光盘时遇到以下问题：

1. 出现【安装字体错误】信息。

2. 出现【无法安装语音识别】信息。

请依照下列步骤再操作一次：

1. 删除该程序。

2. 进入控制面板。

3. 点击"用户账户"选项。

4. 点击"开启或关闭用户账户控制"。

5. 将"使用（用户账户控制）UAC 来帮助保护您的电脑"选项取消勾选。

6. 再次运行安装程序。

目　录

基础训练篇

【基础训练篇】建议使用方法：

Step 1　播放 DVD-ROM 或 MP3 原声

Step 2　浏览听力解析

Step 3　再听一遍原声

Step 4　听一遍慢速朗读

Step 5　阅读原文、重要词汇及中文译文

Step 6　反复多听几遍

Gore TV

Academy Award–Winning Former Veep[1] Conquers[2] Cable[3]

戈尔转战有线电视网

听力解析

符号说明：

连音 ⌒

省略音 。

喉塞音 •

弱化音 灰色部分

补充说明：

1. and 是个功能词，口语中常会以简化的发音方式带过，比较特别的是，and 有好几种简化的发音方式，包括：[æn]、[ənd]、[nd]、[ən] 和 [n]。你可以仔细听听这两段报道中 and 的发音。

2. is that 中 [s] 与 [ð] 发音部位接近，因此两个音常会合在一起发成 [ɪˈzæt]。

Jim Boulden, CNN Correspondent

So many other media are launching[4] on the Internet and doing this through the Internet.

Yet you're going back to traditional media and putting it on cable, putting it on satellite.[5] Why is that?

Al Gore, Former U.S. Vice President

Most have cannibalized television content to send it out on the Internet in short little clips[6] and actually the vast majority[7] of the audience is still getting most of their information from satellite and cable television channels.

名人小档案

阿尔·戈尔 （1948－）为美国第 42 任副总统，后来致力于环境保护的工作与气候变化的研究，由他参与制作和演出的纪录片《难以忽视的真相》描述了全球变暖对人类的影响。2007 年，与联合国政府间气候变化专家小组（IPCC）共同获得诺贝尔和平奖。

CNN 特派记者　吉姆·伯登

现在网络上出现了许多新兴媒体，全都通过网络在做这样的事。

可是你却选择回归传统媒体，在有线电视和卫星电视上播放。为什么呢？

美国前副总统　阿尔·戈尔

很多人恣意利用电视节目内容，将其剪成短小片段后放到网络上，但其实绝大部分观众的主要信息仍来自于卫星电视和有线电视频道。

Notes & Vocabulary

cannibalize 将……拆解再利用

cannibalize [ˈkænəbəˌlaɪz] 是指动物“同类相食”，有“生吞活剥”的意思，比喻将物品“拆解再利用”。文中是说许多人任意截取电视节目内容，放到网络上播放。

· The repair shop cannibalized several wrecks for spare parts.
维修站把几辆撞毁的车辆拆卸，取出零件作为备用品。

与 cannibalize 相关的衍生词包括：

· cannibal n. 食人族；自相残食的动物
　　　　 adj. 食人的；自相残杀的；凶残的
· cannibalism n. 同类相食；残忍的行为
· cannibalization n. 为配修而拆用旧设备的部件

1. veep [vip] n. (口) 副总统（从 vice president 的缩写 v. p. 而来）
2. conquer [ˈkɑŋkə] v. 征服；赢得胜利
3. cable [ˈkebəl] n. 有线电视；电缆
4. launch [lɔntʃ] v. 发起；开始
5. satellite [ˈsætəˌlaɪt] n. 人造卫星
6. clip [klɪp] n. (电视) 剪辑的片段
7. majority [məˈdʒɔrətɪ] n. 大多数

Lee Kuan Yew

CNN Exclusive Interview with Singapore's Elder Statesman[1]

李光耀谈现代领袖风范

听力解析 💡

符号说明：

连音　⌣

省略音　。

喉塞音　•

弱化音　灰色部分

补充说明：

1. 因为带有口音，popularity 中的 [r] 发得有点像 [l] 的读音。

2. p、t、k 接在 s 之后时，发音会浊化，变成类似 b、d、g 的读音，所以 squander 的发音类似于 [ˈsgwɑndə]。

Maria Ressa, CNN Correspondent

If you were to conduct[2] a class for future leaders, what lessons would you emphasize?

Lee Kuan Yew, Singapore Senior Minister

Well, I would say first, don't try and seek popularity.

Popularity is an evanescent,[3] fickle[4] thing.

Gain respect. That's not easy to achieve, and if you gain it and you don't misbehave[5] or squander[6] it, it will last.

[In] the modern society, they take polls—straw polls—and they govern[7] according to what's the polls show—which way the wind is blowing.

I think that's a disaster.[8] That's not leadership.

名人小档案

李光耀（1923－ ）曾 8 次连任新加坡总理（1959－1990），任期中带领新加坡独立并积极推动经济建设及国家发展，使新加坡跻身先进国家行列。现任内阁资政，在政坛上的地位举足轻重。对新加坡贡献良多，至今仍广受新加坡人民尊敬。

CNN 特派记者 玛莉亚·雷莎

如果您要为未来的领袖们开一门课，您会把重点放在哪些方面？

新加坡资政 李光耀

首先我会说，别想追求支持率。

支持率稍纵即逝、变化无常。

要赢得尊重，这点并不容易做到。如果你得到尊重，并且不滥用或胡作非为，便能一直拥有。

在现代社会中，有民意调查，根据不科学的粗略民意调查的结果来治国，就是随风转舵。

我认为这是种灾难，并不是领导风范。

Notes & Vocabulary

straw poll 非正式民意调查

从前人们常以稻草（straw）被风吹向哪一边来判断风向，后来 straw poll 就从判断风向演变为一种了解民意的方法，它是指在盖洛普（Gallop）抽样方法出现前，普遍使用的一种较为不科学的、简略的"非正式民意调查"。

- The straw-poll results indicated that many people oppose the new law.
  非正式民意调查的结果显示有许多人反对这项新法令。

....

1. statesman [ˈstetsmən] *n.* 政治家；政治人物
2. conduct [kənˈdʌkt] *v.* 指导；指挥
3. evanescent [ˌɛvəˈnɛsn̩t] *adj.* 昙花一现的；会凋落的
4. fickle [ˈfɪkəl] *adj.* 易变的；无常的
5. misbehave [ˌmɪsbɪˈhev] *v.* 行为不当
6. squander [ˈskwɑndə] *v.* 浪费掉
7. govern [ˈgʌvən] *v.* 治理；管理
8. disaster [dɪˈzæstə] *n.* 灾难

Four More Years

Bush Celebrates Mandate[1] and Joins Kerry in Call for Unity[2]

荣耀与失落的一刻——美国大选结果揭晓

听力解析

符号说明：

连音 ⌣

省略音 。

喉塞音 •

弱化音 灰色部分

补充说明：

1. w 除了最常听到的 [ˈdʌbəlju] 外，也可念成 [ˈdʌbəju]、[ˈdʌbju]、[ˈdʌbjə] 和 [ˈdʌbji] 等几种省略部分音节的发音方式。

2. need your 两词会产生同化现象，从而读成 [ˈnidʒʊr]。

Christie Lu Stout, CNN Anchor

U.S. president George W. Bush is celebrating his reelection[3] triumph.[4]

In a short victory address, Mr. Bush reached out to Kerry supporters.

George W. Bush, U.S. President

To make this nation stronger and better, I will need your support and I will work to earn it.

I will do all I can do to deserve your trust.

A new term[5] is a new opportunity to reach out to the whole nation.

We have one country, one constitution[6] and one future that binds us.

And when we come together and work together, there is no limit to the greatness of America.

名人小档案

小布什（1946-）来自显赫的政治世家，父亲老布什为美国第 41 任总统。小布什曾任得克萨斯州州长，在 2000 年以较多的选票击败戈尔成为第 43 任总统，并于 2004 年竞选连任，以微弱优势打败对手克里（John Kerry）获胜。

CNN 主播　克里斯蒂·卢·斯托特

美国总统乔治·布什正在庆祝连任成功。

布什在一篇简短的获胜演说中，向克里的支持者示好。

美国总统　乔治·布什

为了建设更强大，更美好的国家，我将需要诸位的支持，并将努力争取。

我会竭尽全力获取大家的信任。

新的任期是一个与全国人民培养感情的新契机。

我们共同拥有一个国家、一部宪法和一个与每个人命运紧密相连的未来。

只要我们团结一致，齐心协力，美国的伟大将无远弗届。

Notes & Vocabulary

reach out to sb　与某人沟通争取认同

reach out 原意为"伸出"，reach out to sb 除可引申指"向某人伸出援手"外，在美语中常引申为"与……联络感情"、"与……沟通争取认同"。文中，布什在选举获胜后向克里的支持者宣讲，争取支持（Bush reached out to Kerry supporters），希望大家不要因选举恩怨而造成国家的分裂，并希望在未来的 4 年能与全国人民培养感情（reach out to the whole nation），期盼大家能团结一致，共创美好未来。

• Republicans reached out to conservative Christian voters.
共和党向保守的基督教选民争取支持。

1. mandate [ˈmænˌdet] *n.* （选民的）授权、委任
2. unity [ˈjunəti] *n.* 团结；一致
3. reelection [ˌriəˈlɛkʃən] *n.* 连任；竞选连任；改选
4. triumph [ˈtraɪəmf] *n.* 胜利、成功（的喜悦）
5. term [tɜm] *n.* 任期；学期；条款
6. constitution [ˌkɑnstəˈtuʃən] *n.* 宪法

Buffet

Billionaire Flies in the Face of the Industry Slump[1]

亿万富翁不同寻常的飞机生意

听力解析 💡

符号说明：

连音 ⌣
省略音 。
喉塞音 •
弱化音 灰色部分

补充说明：

1. 主播 Richard Quest 是英国人，所以是英式发音，由于英式英语没有卷舌音，所以 r 常常不会读出来，或者简化为非重读的元音 [ə]，因此 whether 读成 [ˈhwɛðə]、future 读成 [ˈfjutʃə]。

2. 5,500 airports 读成 fifty-five hundred airports，d 和 a 之间产生连音现象。

Richard Quest, CNN Anchor

I sat down with Warren Buffett asked him not only about his expansion[2] plans in Europe, but what was the driving force[3] behind the company and whether he was confident about the economic future.

Warren Buffett, Investing Wizard

Well, what drives it is the fact that it makes so much sense from both the standpoint[4] of economics and the standpoint of ease of use.

If you own a quarter or an eighth of a plane with NetJets, in effect,[5] you've got more service available than if you own an entire plane because you can choose from any one of 11 models. It's there in every airport.

There's 5,500 airports in the United States and you, in effect, your plane is there at anytime you wish.

名人小档案

巴菲特（1930-）为美国投资大师，也是全球首位靠股票投资获取超过 10 亿美元的人。巴菲特因其商业头脑和投资智慧而被称为"股神"。此外，他也是位慷慨的慈善家，曾宣布其过世后要将 99% 的财产捐给慈善事业。

CNN 主播 理查德·奎斯特

我与沃伦·巴菲特促膝而谈，除了问到有关欧洲的扩展计划，也问到公司背后的驱动力是什么，以及他对未来的经济是否有信心。

投资奇才 沃伦·巴菲特

公司的驱动力其实很容易理解，不管是从经济的角度看，还是从简单实用的视角来看。

如果你拥有 NetJets 公司（注）某架飞机的 1/4 或 1/8，事实上，你获得的服务比拥有整架飞机还多，因为你可以在每个机场，从 11 款机型中任意挑选一架乘坐。

全美有 5 500 个机场，而事实上，你的飞机是随传随到的。

注：NetJets 公司在 1998 年由巴菲特经营的伯克希尔·哈撒韦公司（Berkshire Hathaway）所收购，主要是为富豪名流、商务旅客提供包机服务，目前是全球最顶尖、飞机最多的飞机租赁服务公司。

Notes & Vocabulary

fly in the face of . . .
在……面前耀武扬威；公然违抗

标题中的 fly in the face of 具有双重意思，这个短语原来是指"公然违抗；悍然拒绝"的意思，在此用来形容巴菲特在航空业不景气时，竟然还能逆向行事并获得增长，同时暗含了文中的主题"飞"机。

· Tom's argument flies in the face of logic.
  汤姆的论点有背逻辑。

....

1. slump [slʌmp] *n.* 衰落；不景气

2. expansion [ɪk`spænʃən] *n.* 扩张；扩展

3. driving force *n. phr.* 驱动力

4. standpoint [`stænd͵pɔɪnt] *n.* 观点；立场

5. in effect *phr.* 事实上；实际上

Pedaling[1] into the Future

In *The Boardroom* with Bicycle Parts Maker Yoshizo Shimano

他让自行车跑得更快——CNN 专访 SHIMANO 集团会长岛野喜三

听力解析

符号说明：

连音 ⌣

省略音 。

喉塞音 •

弱化音 灰色部分

补充说明：

在 downside that which 中，受访者多说了一个关系代词，故将 which 删除。此外，downside 的词尾多了一个短元音，因此听起来像是 [ˈdaʊnˌsaɪdə]，这种误读现象较多，如 could be good 的 be 之后、time of building up 的 of 之后，都有类似的情况。

Andrew Stevens, The Boardroom

What are the downsides[2] to the American style of management and the downsides of the Japanese style?

Yoshizo Shimano, CEO of Shimano Inc.

[The] American style ~~that~~ could be good for the quick change, you know, but maybe taking less time ~~of~~ [for] building up the consensus.[3]

So [the] understanding level of the people is a little bit shallower.[4]

So, that's the downside that ~~which~~ I feel.

And that Japanese style ~~taking~~ [is to take] a little longer time ~~making~~ [to make] a decision.

That's a downside. But a good side is the understanding level of the management ~~people~~.

名人小档案

岛野喜三是全球知名的自行车零件商 Shimano（禧玛诺）集团会长，除了自行车零件外，还经营渔具、高尔夫球具、滑雪板等各种户外活动用品，其经营管理方式结合了美日两种风格。

"董事会"节目主持人 安德鲁 · 史蒂文斯
美式及日式的管理风格各有何缺点？

禧玛诺集团会长 岛野喜三
美式管理风格有利于快速做出转变，但是花在达成共识过程的时间可能比较少。

所以大家理解的程度也会比较粗浅一些。

这是我所认为的缺点。

而日式作风则是做出决策的时间比较长。

这是缺点，但好处在于管理层对决策的理解会好一些。

Notes & Vocabulary

pedal into the future 骑车驶向未来

pedal 作动词是指"踩踏板；骑自行车"，本文因为是专访自行车变速器巨擘 Shimano 集团的会长，因此特意用了 pedal 这个动词，指骑车驶向光明的未来。

....

1. **pedal** [ˈpɛdl] *v.* 踩踏板；骑自行车
2. **downside** [ˈdaunˌsaɪd] *n.* 不利方面；缺点
3. **consensus** [kənˈsɛnsəs] *n.* 意见一致
4. **shallow** [ˈʃælo] *adj.* 粗浅的；肤浅的

Slam Dunk Business

Q&A with Brett Yormark—The NBA's Youngest CEO

NBA 最年轻的 CEO 畅谈球队经营之道

听力解析 💡

符号说明：

连音　⌣

省略音　。

喉塞音　•

弱化音　灰色部分

补充说明：

1. you 受到前面 sports 中的发音 [ts] 的影响，[j] 的发音听起来像是 [tʃ]。

2. 说话速度很快时，有时会弱化部分音节，如：competitive 中的 ti、personally 中的最后一个音节 ly。

Maggie Lake, CNN Correspondent

You have become known as something of a turnaround[1] person on the business side of sports, you did a lot with NASCAR,[2] you're doing a lot with the Nets.

What is it that you think is key to getting the sponsors, getting the fans on board[3] behind a franchise?

Brett Yormark, CEO of Nets Sports & Entertainment

Very seldom do you find a team out there today in any professional sport, I think, where the front office,[4] if it's dysfunctional,[5] they're competitive on the court.

They go hand in hand.

So for me personally, it's coming in, doing the right thing, getting people to think a little differently, getting them to know that they could be very special in what they do, if we could set a path and a direction, and I've been able to do that.

名人小档案

布莱特·约马克（1967-）曾任篮网运动娱乐公司（Nets Sports & Entertainment）总裁，现任新泽西篮网队（New Jersey Nets）CEO。他凭着对篮球的热情及自身的勤奋和雄心，在 39 岁那年成为 NBA 最年轻的 CEO。

CNN 特派记者 玛姬·雷克

你在体育运动商业界已经成为能起死回生的代表人物。你为北美房车赛做了许多贡献，也为篮网做了许多贡献。

你认为球队争取赞助商以及号召球迷的关键是什么？

篮网运动娱乐公司 CEO 布莱特·约马克

在今天的职业运动赛场上，一支球队的营销服务团队要是不能很好地发挥作用，这支队伍在场上的表现也不可能太好。

这两者是互相依存的。

所以，对我个人来说，就是介入其中，做正确的事情，稍微改变大家的思考方式，让他们知道，只要我们能够设定路线与目标，他们就可以做出极佳的表现。我就是做到了这一点。

Notes & Vocabulary

slam dunk 非常成功

slam dunk 原为篮球术语，指的是"灌篮"；引申为"非常成功"之意。

• Peter's negotiation with the distributor was a slam dunk. He got some good concessions from them.
  彼得与批发商的协商十分成功，从他们那里争取了不小的优惠。

franchise 连锁企业；系列产品；职业球队

在商业中，franchise 本指一家公司授予某人销售其产品的"特许经营权"，后引申指"连锁经营模式"及"连锁企业"。从一个品牌衍生出的系列产品，也可泛称为 franchise，如 film franchise（系列电影）中的 Star Wars / 007 franchise 或 literary franchise（文学系列作品）中的 Harry Potter franchise。而职业运动队（professional sports team），也可称为 franchise。

1. turnaround [ˈtɜnəˌraʊnd] *n.* 回转；逆转；改变

2. NASCAR [ˈnæskɑr] *n.* 美国赛车协会；北美房车赛（= National Association for Stock Car Auto Racing）

3. on board *phr.* 支持……

4. front office 营销、市场、客服人员

5. dysfunctional [dɪsˈfʌnʃənl] *adj.* 不正常的

On the Fast Track

In *The Boardroom* with Formula One[1] CEO Bernie Ecclestone

不只是赛车——F1 赛车的经营之道

听力解析

符号说明：

连音 ⌣

省略音 ₒ

喉塞音 •

弱化音 灰色部分

补充说明：

1. 口语中，because可读成'coz。

2. what you 连音发成 [ˈwɑtʃə]。

3. 结尾说话者讲得很快，两个 as 的 [æ] 音都省略，相连的 [s] 音也都起来发，听起来像是 [ɪtˈsɪmpəlˈzæt]。

Todd Benjamin, The Boardroom

And what do you think makes a good entrepreneur,[2] because obviously you've been very successful?

Bernie Ecclestone, Formula One CEO

I suppose you need to be a little bit courageous[3] and like most very success[ful], well not that I'm very successful, but very successful business people have been lucky, including me.

Todd Benjamin, The Boardroom

What advice would you give to anybody who wants to go into business?

Bernie Ecclestone, Formula One CEO

Well know what you want to do and what you're trying to achieve and be prepared to take [a] few risk[s] and work hard.

And it's as simple as that.

名人小档案

伯尼·埃克莱斯顿（1930–）为 FOM 公司行政管理总裁兼 CEO，媒体称其为"F1 之王"（F1 Supremo）。曾取得 500 C. C. F3 大赛的比赛资格，但在一次比赛时身受重伤，因此决定结束职业赛车手的生涯转而致力于汽车相关产业。

"董事会"托德·本杰明

你认为一个好的企业家需要具备哪些条件？你显然非常成功。

一级方程式 CEO 伯尼·埃克莱斯顿

我认为你必须有一些勇气，而且要和绝大多数非常成功的人一样……我并不是说我非常成功，而是非常成功的企业家都很幸运，包括我在内。

"董事会"托德·本杰明

你会给想要经商的人哪些建议？

一级方程式 CEO 伯尼·埃克莱斯顿

知道自己想要做什么，想要有哪些成就，做好冒险的准备，然后努力打拼。

就是这么简单。

Notes & Vocabulary

go into business 从商

go into 在这里的解释为"从事或进入某行业类别"，所以 go into business 就是"从商"意思。从事其他行业的说法有：go into politics（从政）、go into films（从事影视工作）、go into medicine（从事医药工作）、go into the army（从军）、go into publishing（从事出版工作）等。

- After arriving in the U.S., Alex's father went into business as a butcher.
  亚历克斯的父亲到了美国之后成了肉店老板。

go into 其他常见的解释还有：

a. 讨论
  - The professor went into a long discussion of Middle East politics.
    那位教授就中东的政治问题发表长篇大论。

b. 处于某状态
  - The child went into a scream fit when his toy was taken away.
    那个小孩的玩具被拿走时，他开始放声尖叫。

....

1. **Formula One** [ˈfɔrmjələ] 一级方程式赛车（简称 F1）

2. **entrepreneur** [ˌɑntrəprəˈnɜ] *n.* 企业家；企业创办人

3. **courageous** [kəˈredʒəs] *adj.* 英勇的；勇敢的

Prince of Fashion

Iconic[1] Designer Karl Lagerfeld Brings the House[2] of Chanel to London

香奈儿首席设计师卡尔·拉格斐谈时尚的核心要素

听力解析 💡

符号说明：

连音 ⌣

省略音 。

喉塞音 •

弱化音 灰色部分

补充说明：

1. ￡4 billion a year 读作 four billion pounds a year，其中 pounds a 形成连音，读成 [ˈpaʊndzə]。

2. Karl Lagerfeld 是德国人，在某些读音上有较重的口音，如：think 发成 [sɪŋk]、that 发成 [zæt]、the 发成 [zə] 等。

Nicholas Glass, CNN Correspondent

Karl took over at Chanel in 1983, 12 years after Coco's death.

He reinvented[3] it, made the brand worth allegedly[4] ￡4 billion a year.

Karl is thereby[5] more valuable than most film stars and, as it happens, almost as recognizable.[6]

Karl Lagerfeld, Fashion Designer

I don't think that I would be still interested in fashion the way I'm interested if I had not this nonstop contact and dialog with the world of photography, magazine advertising.

It never stopped[s], and I think that's very, very important, because a designer after collection can become isolated.[7] Huh?

I'm never isolated because I'm involved in so many things.

名人小档案

卡尔·拉格斐（1933–）是当今最具影响力的设计师之一，曾与不少知名品牌合作，如 Chloé、Fendi 和 Chanel。他于 1984 年创立自己的品牌。喜欢艺术和文艺的拉格斐，本身也是一位非常出色的摄影师，他还拥有一家名为 EDITIONS 7L 的出版社。

CNN 特派记者 尼古拉斯·格拉斯

卡尔在 1983 年接手香奈儿，距离香奈儿女士去世已有 12 年之久。

他为香奈儿打造了全新的形象，为这个品牌创造了据说每年高达 40 亿英镑的价值。

因此，卡尔比大多数的电影明星的身价都还要高，而且知名度也不让大明星。

时尚设计师 卡尔·拉格斐

我如果没有一直和摄影及杂志广告不断接触与对话，一定不会对时装这么感兴趣。

这种接触与对话从来没有中断过，我认为这点非常非常重要，因为设计师设计了一系列作品之后就可能与外界脱节。

我从来不会与外界脱节，因为我参与的事物非常多。

Notes & Vocabulary

worth allegedly £4 billion a year
据传每年价值 4 亿英镑

worth 意思是"值得的"，之后可接名词和动名词，许多情况下 worth 可用 worthwhile、worthy 替换，不过之后接价钱时，只能用 worth。

• The book is worth reading.
= It is worthwhile to read the book.
= It is worthwhile reading the book.
= The book is worthy of being read.
= The book is worthy to be read.
这本书值得一读。

1. iconic [aɪˋkɑnɪk] *adj.* 具代表性的
2. house [haʊs] *n.* 公司（尤指出版社、服装公司等）
3. reinvent [ˌriɪnˋvɛnt] *v.* 再次发明；重新打造
4. allegedly [əˋlɛdʒdlɪ] *adv.* 据说；据称
5. thereby [ðɛrˋbaɪ] *adv.* 因此
6. recognizable [ˌrɛkəgˋnaɪzəbəl] *adj.* 可识别的；可认可的
7. isolated [ˋaɪsəˌletəd] *adj.* 孤立的；隔离的

From Bath Beads[1] to the Boardroom
CNN Exclusive Interview with Body Shop Founder Anita Roddick
美体小铺创始人安妮塔·罗迪克谈女性商业竞争哲学

听力解析

符号说明：

连音 ⌣

省略音 。

喉塞音 •

弱化音 灰色部分

补充说明：

1. 英音有个特色，就是 r 常常不会读出来，或简化为非重读的元音 [ə]，你可仔细分辨这段访谈节录中 r 的发音。

2. comes this 中由于 [s] 与 [ð] 发音部位接近，再加上 this 为功能词，通常可以不用读得很清楚，因此这两个词听起来就变成 [ˈkʌmzɪs]。

Todd Benjamin, The Boardroom

I visited Anita at her home in the English countryside and asked her what makes a great entrepreneur.

Anita Roddick, Body Shop Founder

Obsession,[2] bordering[3] on the pathological.[4]

Obsessed with an idea and then pushing it to see how far it can go, but you've got to start with an idea.

That becomes—it takes over your life.

Think of it in the present tense, there's no obstacles.[5]

You're pathologically optimistic[6] and with that comes this amazing sense of wanting to be free.

名人小档案

安妮塔·罗迪克（1942–2007）于 1976 年在英国创立美体小铺（The Body Shop），以天然原料制造各式美容产品，并强调绝不为产品进行动物实验。加上该品牌强调环保概念，因此安妮塔享有"绿色女王"的美誉。

"董事会"托德·本杰明

我到安妮塔在英国乡间的住所拜访，向她请教杰出的企业家需要具备哪些条件。

美体小铺创始人 安妮塔·罗迪克

执著，近乎病态的执著。

执著追求一个想法，然后把这个想法拓展到极限。不过，你首先必须要有想法。

这个想法会成为——会从此占据你整个人生。

随时都不忘这个想法，任何障碍都阻止不了你。

你的乐观超乎寻常，而且伴随着一种极度想要自由的渴望。

Notes & Vocabulary

take over 占据；占领

take over 除了"占据；占领"的意思外，还有"接管"的意思，通常是指接管财产、领地或责任等。

- Gambling has taken over Blake's life.
  赌博已经占据了布雷克的生活。
- After Larry transferred to a new department, Linda took over his role as manager.
  拉里转到新部门后，琳达便接管担任经理一职。

....

1. bath bead [bæθ] [bid] *n. phr.* 沐浴球

2. obsession [əbˈsɛʃən] *n.* 执迷（obsess with 指"对……着迷"）

3. border [ˈbɔrdə] *v.* 近似；趋向于（border on sth 是指某项行为、特质或感受非常接近于某物）

4. pathological [ˌpæθəˈladʒɪkəl] *adj.* 病态的；病理上的

5. obstacle [ˈabstɪkəl] *n.* 障碍；阻碍

6. optimistic [ˌaptəˈmɪstɪk] *adj.* 乐观的

Anna Sui

Exclusive Interview with Fashion Designer

逐梦的时尚魔法师——安娜·苏

听力解析 💡

符号说明：

连音 ⌣

省略音 ◦

喉塞音 •

弱化音 灰色部分

补充说明：

just stay 这两个词听起来是 [ˋdʒʌste]，因为在词尾的 t 通常会弱化得听不见，再加上 just 和 stay 中 [s] 的发音相同，故根据便于发音原则，t 的音就被省略了。

Lorraine Hahn, TalkAsia

Anna, you know there are a lot of Asian designers that are coming out now—gaining more and more recognition[1] worldwide.[2]

What advice would you give to them?

Anna Sui, Fashion Designer

Well, nothing happens overnight,[3] and it's really important to really understand the business that you're in and the craft[4] that you're working with.

And just stay with it and you'll find your time.

Everyone has to find their time.

It, you don't have control over that.

You have to be in the right place at the right time

名人小档案

安娜·苏（1955–）为知名设计师，拥有个人品牌 Anna Sui。安娜·苏的作品洋溢着浓厚的复古气息，华丽的刺绣、花边、烫钻、绣珠等均流露出独特的奢华气质，有时尚界的魔法师之称。她作品中流露出的东方韵味更是让许多时尚女性倾心不已。

"亚洲名人聊天室" 韩玉花

安娜，现在有很多亚洲设计师崭露头角，在全世界得到愈来愈多的赞赏。

你会给他们什么样的建议呢？

时尚设计师 安娜·苏

没有什么事是在一夜之间发生的，要深入了解自己所从事的这个行业以及所运用事的技艺，是非常重要的。

坚持到底，你就会找到适当的时机，

每个人都需要找到自己的时机，

你无法控制，

但你必须把握住恰当的时机和地点。

Notes & Vocabulary

in the right place at the right time
天时地利

这个短语为固定用语，通常用来表示处在最好的时机并善于把握机会，意思与中文的天时地利相同。

• You have to be in the right place at the right time to achieve success easily.
你需要占得天时地利才容易成功。

1. recognition [ˌrɛkəɡˈnɪʃən] n. 认同；赏识
2. worldwide [ˈwɜːldˈwaɪd] adv. 全世界地；世界各地
3. overnight [ˌovəˈnaɪt] adv. 一夜之间
4. craft [kræft] n. 手艺；技艺

Keeping Her Eye on the Ball
TalkAsia Exclusive Interview with Tennis Superstar Venus Williams
她改写了网坛历史——CNN 专访黑人球后大威廉姆斯

听力解析 💡

符号说明：

连音 ⌣
省略音 ₒ
喉塞音 •
弱化音 灰色部分

补充说明：

want to 在口语中常会出现读音省略的现象，因此听起来会变成 [`wɑnə]。

Anjali Rao, TalkAsia

You're still one of the few black faces in an overwhelmingly[1] white game.

Is there racism[2] in tennis?

Venus Williams, Tennis Star

I think I've been fortunate to be at the top of the game and in the media for years, and a lot of times people want to be your friend when you're in the top.

You know, there have been times when I've been injured and I never got a phone call.

So that's the way it is, but as far as if there's racism in the world, for sure, all over the world.

As far as if I've beat the odds, for sure.

Will I continue? Yes, and other than that, that's just how I see it.

I don't focus on what I'm up against. I focus on my goals and I try to ignore[3] the rest.

名人小档案

维纳斯·威廉姆斯（1980-）（又称大威廉姆斯，其妹为小威姆斯）14 岁便在网球界小有名气。1997 年在美国公开赛打进决赛崭露头角。大威廉姆斯以其强劲的击球力度著名，至 2007 年为止已各拿下 6 个女单、女双大满贯，曾为世界排名第一的球后。

"亚洲名人聊天室" 安姿丽

你是网球这项白人占多数的运动中，少数的黑人之一。

网球运动有种族歧视吗？

网球明星 维纳斯·威廉姆斯

我想我算幸运的了，有好几年能登上职业网坛之巅，能成为媒体焦点，当你高高在上的时候，大家都想要跟你做朋友。

过去，有几次我受伤，连一个问候的电话都没接到。

事实就是如此，至于世界上有没有种族歧视，当然有，全世界都有。

至于我是否克服了这样的障碍，当然。

我会继续吗？会的，除此之外，这就是我的看法了。

我不会把注意力放在不利的事情上，而是放在目标上，其余的事物我会尽量不放在心上。

Notes & Vocabulary

beat the odds 克服困难

odds 是指"输赢的几率"，beat the odds 字面意思是击败投注的赔率，引申为"克服灾难、困难"。

- The paraplegic veteran beat the odds and ran in a marathon.
  那位半身不遂的退役军人克服了困难，参加了马拉松比赛。

be up against 对抗

against 是"反对；抵抗"，up against 则有"面临强势的对手或情势与之对抗"的意思。

- The project is up against resistance from environmental groups.
  这项计划面临着环保组织强烈的抵制。

1. overwhelmingly [ˌovəˈwɛlmɪŋlɪ] *adv.* 压倒性地
2. racism [ˈreˌsɪzəm] *n.* 种族歧视
3. ignore [ɪgˈnɔr] *v.* 忽略

Life Coach

Self-Help Guru[1] Robin Sharma's Recipe[2] for Success

励志大师罗宾·夏玛教你活出成功人生

听力解析 💡

符号说明:

连音 ⌣

省略音 ₒ

喉塞音 •

弱化音 灰色部分

补充说明:

有些功能词在口语中常会将元音读成非重音的元音 [ə] 或省略一些读音,比如说 you know 这个语气词中的代名词 you 就常省略元音变成 [jr],或变成 ya [jə]。

Colleen McEdwards, CNN Correspondent
Do you ever get tired of striving?[3]

Robin Sharma, Life Coach
Yes.

I think, you know, in the East they say "the arrow that is too tightly strung is easily broken," and I'm a huge believer in balance.

If you improve one percent each day, after 30 days, that's at least a 30 percent improvement.

And if we just start off with the little things and build habits, well, the days slip[4] into weeks, the weeks slip into months.

Before you know it, six months have gone by and you've installed [instilled] three or four new habits.

Well those habits create momentum,[5] and they actually create a feeling of personal power.

名人小档案

罗宾·夏玛（1965－）为知名励志演说家兼畅销书作者。其著作《和尚卖了法拉利》（*The Monk Who Sold His Ferrari*）译成约 50 种语言，全球卖出数百万本。夏玛曾到欧洲、以色列及印度等世界各地旅行，将其信念传遍全世界。

CNN 特派记者 柯琳·麦德华兹

你会不会对不断的奋斗感到厌倦？

人生顾问 罗宾·夏玛

会。

东方有一句谚语说："强弓易折。"我坚信平衡的观念。

如果你每天改进1%，30天之后就至少改进了30%。

我们如果从小事着手，慢慢养成习惯，从几天延续成几周，几周延续成几个月。

不知不觉间，6 个月就过去了，而你已经养成了三四个新习惯。

这些习惯会产生动力，让你觉得拥有属于自己的力量。

Notes & Vocabulary

the arrow that is too tightly strung is easily broken 强弓易折

在这里罗宾·夏玛误把 bow（弓）说成了 arrow（箭）。原本的谚语是说如果弓弦绑得太紧，拉弓时可能会使弓折断。他引用此言，提醒大家在为人生积极奋斗的同时，要适时地放松。

1. guru [ˈɡʊru] *n.* 印度教的心灵导师；导师
2. recipe [ˈrɛsəˌpi] *n.* 诀窍；方法；食谱
3. strive [straɪv] *n.* 努力奋斗（striving 为动名词）
4. slip [slɪp] *v.* （时间）不知不觉过去；悄悄溜走
5. momentum [moˈmɛntəm] *n.* 动力；势头

A Miracle[1] of Song
Larry King Live Exclusive Interview with Céline Dion
天籁传奇——美声天后席琳·迪翁接受拉里·金专访

听力解析 💡

符号说明：

连音	⌣
省略音	ₒ
喉塞音	•
弱化音	灰色部分

补充说明：

1. pinch yourself 中的 ch 与 y 因连音的关系，听起来像是 [ˈpɪntʃʊrˌsɛlf]。

2. going on 在口语中，going 中的鼻音 [ŋ] 常会简化为 [n]。

Larry King, Host

Poor her. Who'd a thunk it? Do you pinch[2] yourself?

Céline Dion, Singer

To be honest, I don't even think that I'm pinching myself.

Let's put it that way. I don't live with it.

I am conscious[3] of what's going on around me. I am not blind.

I have eyes around my head, around my heart, especially, I think.

I see and I feel what's going on for the last twenty years in show business.

名人小档案

席琳·迪翁（1968-）为英语和法语歌坛天后。生长在贫苦家庭的她 13 岁便推出首支法语畅销单曲，曾在各种国际歌唱比赛中夺得大奖，也曾演唱过许多电影主题曲，如《泰坦尼克号》中的 *My Heart Will Go On*。近些年除了推出新专辑以外，还在赌城拉斯维加斯长期演出，场场爆满，成就非凡。

主持人 拉里·金

她真惹人怜。谁会想到呢？你会不会捏捏自己，看看一切是否是一场梦？

歌手 席琳·迪翁

老实说，这个问题我想都没想过。

这么说吧，我没把这个问题放在心上。

我能察觉出周遭发生的事，我不是瞎子，

我有雪亮的眼睛、敏感的心。

我清楚看到、感受到过去 20 年来演艺圈里的点点滴滴。

Notes & Vocabulary

who'd a thunk it? 谁会想得到呢？

读者乍看这句话，可能会以为单词拼错了，但其实这是十分口语化的用法，相当于 who would have thought it?（谁会想得到呢？），其中 a 是 have 的省略发音，而 thunk 则是 think 的过去分词的玩笑说法。

A: You won the lottery?
　你的彩票中奖了？
B: Yep. Who'd a thunk it?
　没错。谁会想得到呢？

1. miracle [ˈmɪrɪkəl] *n.* 奇迹；不可思议的人或事物

2. pinch [pɪntʃ] *v.* 捏；掐；拧

3. conscious [ˈkɑnʃəs] *adj.* 意识到的；有所觉察的

Larry King Live Exclusive Interview with Film Legend Marlon Brando

拉理·金和马龙·白兰度的珍贵访谈纪录

Larry King, Host

Why Tahiti?

Marlon Brando, Acting Legend

Tahiti. One thing that has been very problematic[1] about being an actor and getting some measure[2] of celebrity[3] is the fact that you lose your identity.[4]

And everybody calls you instantly Mr. Brando, instead of "Hey you!"

I went to Tahiti where they don't give a damn who you are.

The Tahitians are marvelously[5] free.

First of all, it's a classless[6] society, and if you put on airs,[7] they just tease[8] the life out of you

名人小档案

马龙·白兰度 (1924–2004) 为银幕上的风流才子，被公认为演技教父。他曾为了表演下半身瘫痪者到医院中躺了 1 个月揣摩角色。经典作品包括《欲望号街车》(*A Street Car Named Desire*) 及《教父》(*The Godfather*)。

主持人 拉里·金

为什么选择大溪地？（编者按：白兰度定居之地）

演艺传奇 马龙·白兰度

大溪地。身为一名演员和某种意义上的名人，一直有件事很令人困扰，就是失去了自己。

大家马上就称呼你白兰度先生，而不是"喂，那个谁！"

我去大溪地是因为他们根本不在乎你是谁。

大溪地人是如此不可思议地自由自在。

更重要的是，那是个没有阶级差异的社会，如果你摆出一副不可一世的模样，他们会嘲笑你，笑得要命。

Notes & Vocabulary

tease the life out of sb
把某人笑得要命

这个短语表示极为嘲笑某人，也常搭配 scare、frighten 等动词，表示"把某人吓得半死"。

- When the monster appeared in the movie, it scared the life out of Helen.
  当怪兽在电影中出现时，海伦吓得半死。

1. problematic [ˌprɑbləˋmætɪk] *adj.* 难处理的；成问题的
2. measure [ˋmɛʒɚ] *n.* 定额；定量
3. celebrity [səˋlɛbrətɪ] *n.* 名人
4. identity [aɪˋdɛntətɪ] *n.* 认同
5. marvelously [ˋmɑrvləslɪ] *adv.* 令人惊奇地
6. classless [ˋklæsləs] *adj.* 无阶级差别的
7. put on airs *v. phr.* 装腔作势；摆架子
8. tease [tiz] *v.* 取笑；戏弄

Christopher Reeve
The Last Battle for the Man of Steel
永远的超人——克里斯托夫·里夫

听力解析

符号说明：

连音 ⌣

省略音 。

喉塞音 •

弱化音 灰色部分

补充说明：

insurance 词尾的 [s] 音中带了点 [t] 的味道，那是因为从 [n] 发到 [s] 时，舌位会顺势经过发 [t] 的音的位置，使整个发音过程更顺畅些，但是否发出带 [t] 的音因人而异，并非必须的。

Jason Carol, CNN Correspondent

Reeve got well enough to act, and even direct.

But his new role as activist[1] is where he made his mark

He lobbied[2] Congress[3] in support of stem-cell[4] research and better insurance[5] and never gave up hope on walking again.

Christopher Reeve, Actor and Stem-cell Activist

If we keep giving our scientists the funding[6] they need to do the research, very soon I will take my family by the hand.

And I will stand here in front of this star on the Hollywood Walk of Fame.[7]

名人小档案

克里斯托夫·里夫（1952–2004）因主演《超人》一炮而红。1995 年，里夫在马术比赛中坠马导致颈部以下瘫痪，但他并未放弃生活，反而致力于为伤残人士争取福利，并积极声援干细胞研究以期造福身体残障人士。

CNN 特派记者 杰森·卡罗尔

里夫复原的情况良好，能够演出，甚至执导。

但让他名留史册的是他积极推动干细胞研究的这个新角色。

他游说国会支持干细胞研究以及提供更完善的保险，同时他从未放弃能再度行走的希望。

演员兼干细胞研究推动者 克里斯托夫·里夫

如果我们持续为科学家们提供进行这项研究所需的资金，很快地我就可以和我的家人手牵手。

而我也可以站在好莱坞星光大道的这颗星星前。

Notes & Vocabulary

make one's mark
某人在……方面表现卓著

make one's mark 字面意思是"在……留下印记"，也就是指"在……表现出色；对……有影响力"，常用来表示某人在某方面的表现卓著，常与介词 on 连用，也可写成 make a name for oneself。

- Steve was determined to make his mark on the world after graduation.
  史蒂夫立志要在毕业后闯出一片天地。

1. activist [ˈæktɪvɪst] n. 活跃分子；积极分子

2. lobby [ˈlɑbɪ] v. 游说；对……施压

3. congress [ˈkɑŋɡrəs] n. 国会；国会议员（大写特指美国国会及议员）

4. stem-cell [ˈstɛmˌsɛl] adj. 干细胞的

5. insurance [ɪnˈʃʊrəns] n. 保险

6. funding [ˈfʌndɪŋ] n. 资金

7. fame [fem] n. 声誉；声望；名气

NOTES

实战应用篇
Part I

Media Master
In *The Boardroom* with Barry Diller
从收发员到董事长——好莱坞传媒大师的成功历程

Step 1 请浏览下方提示的关键问题后，仔细听录音。

1. What does Diller say about his leadership style?
2. How does Diller use the people around him?
3. What is unusual about his background?
4. What does he look for in new talent?

Step 2 如果你还听不太懂的话，请浏览下方的关键词汇后再听一次。

conglomerate 企业集团	bromidic 陈腐的
scrub 用力洗刷	eke out 竭力维持；弥补……不足
instill 灌输	protégé 门生；被保护者
titan 重要人物	alchemy 促进事物的能力

Step 3 试着回答下列听力测验题目。

True or False 是非题

_____ 1. Barry Diller has worked in companies involved in television, movies and the Internet.

_____ 2. Diller thinks someone could become successful today the way he did.

_____ 3. Diller started working at Paramount after graduating college.

_____ 4. Many people who worked for Diller have also become successful.

_____ 5. Diller teaches his protégés not to take risks.

名人小档案

巴里·迪勒 (1942-) 曾任美国广播公司 (ABC) 副总裁、派拉蒙 (Paramount) 电影公司董事会主席兼 CEO、20 世纪福克斯公司 (20th Century-FOX) 主席兼 CEO。现任全球最大的电子商务网站集团之一的 IAC/InterActiveCorp 集团主席兼 CEO 及 Expedia 董事长。

Multiple Choice　选择题

_____ 1. Why was Diller chosen to be chairman of Paramount?
　　　a. He had good qualifications.
　　　b. He knew about motion pictures.
　　　c. He was the previous chairman's protégé.
　　　d. The owner chose him.

_____ 2. What does Diller say is the key to his management style?
　　　a. His musical talent.
　　　b. Having passionate people around him.
　　　c. Working hard and being passionate.
　　　d. Having everything scrubbed every day.

_____ 3. What are the "Diller Killers"?
　　　a. Diller's competitors.
　　　b. The companies Diller runs.
　　　c. The people Diller trained.
　　　d. The people he finds that become movies stars.

Step 4 试着用较慢的速度，再仔细听一遍，并检查答案是否正确。

Step 5 核对答案、检验成果，并详读原文，若仍有不懂的地方，可反复多听几次。

（答案请见 p.228）

Maggie Lake, The Boardroom

From the mail room[1] to the boardroom,[2]
he became the master of all media. Barry
Diller's career is the stuff of legend. He got his big
break[3] at ABC in the 1960s, where he is credited
with[4] inventing the made-for-TV movie, as well as
the miniseries.[5] He was also in some form or another
behind some of the biggest films and television shows
of all time. In the late 1980s, he decided to take on the
big boys of U.S. broadcasting, creating FOX Network.
Now he's the chairman of travel planning Web site
Expedia as well as InterActiveCorp, a conglomerate[6]
covering both off-line and online media. Barry Diller
spoke to *The Boardroom* at his office about his humble
beginnings and his starring role in global media.

Now, you've said you're not a visionary.[7] How would
you describe your leadership style, your management
style?

Barry Diller, Media Mogul[8]

I think it's best perceived[9] on the receiving end. I mean
the only thing I could say about it is that, I probably—
all these things sound so bromidic[10]—I probably try the
best I can to scrub[11] things to get to the truth, whatever
the truth is or whatever my ear picks up.[12]

Maggie Lake, The Boardroom

Whatever makes sense[13] to you.

Barry Diller, Media Mogul

If my ear is open and I'm listening good, then as much
as I can eke out from the people around me—who are
really doing the work—as much as I can eke out their
passion, hear their true note, then I can hear something.

"董事会"玛姬·雷克

从邮件收发室到董事会议室，他还成为掌控所有媒体的霸主。巴里·迪勒一生的事业有如传奇故事。20世纪60年代，他在ABC电视台得到一个崭露头角的大好机会，电视电影以及电视连续短剧的创始要归功于他。一些史上最著名的电影与电视节目背后也都有他的参与。20世纪80年代晚期，他决定向美国广播电视界的霸主挑战，创立了福克斯电视网。现在，他是旅游网站Expedia及电子商务集团InterActiveCorp的董事长。IAC是企业集团，旗下囊括传统媒体与网络媒体。巴里·迪勒在他的办公室与"董事会"节目谈他白手起家的过程，以及他在全球传媒界扮演的重要角色。

你说过你不是梦想家，那么你会怎么描述自己的领导风格，或者管理风格？

媒体巨子 巴里·迪勒

我想，从受到管理的那一方的角度来想最清楚。我是说，我在这方面只能够说——这听起来很老套——我可能就是尽力去层层探究真相，各式各样的真相，我耳朵所听到的一切。

"董事会"玛姬·雷克

只要是你觉得有意义的事情。

媒体巨子 巴里·迪勒

如果我打开耳朵仔细倾听，那我就能从身旁的人那里尽可能地获取信息——因为他们才是真正做事的人——就像我尽力维持他们的热情一样，倾听他们真正的心声，我就能够听到一些东西。

Notes & Vocabulary

take on 对付；承担

take on 其他常见的意思还包括"承担；聘用"。

- The activists took on the paper manufacturer over the pollution created by its factory.
  社会运动人士因该造纸厂制造出污染而与其对抗。
- As Andrew got promoted, he had to take on more responsibilities.
  因为安德鲁升了职，所以他得承担更多责任。
- The trading firm took Peter on right out of college.
  彼得一毕业就得到那家贸易公司聘用。

eke out 补足；竭力维持

eke [ik] 原有"延长；增加"的意思，eke out 则是指尽量延长某物的使用寿命，或尽管不容易，但仍努力维持下去。

- Megan ekes out a living as an artist.
  梅根靠当艺术家勉强糊口。

....

1. mail room [mel] [rum] *n. phr.* 邮件收发室
2. boardroom [ˈbɔrd͵rum] *n.* 董事会议室
3. big break *n. phr.* 大好机会
4. be credited with 被认为对某事有功
5. miniseries [ˈmɪnɪ͵sɪriz] *n.* 电视连续短剧
6. conglomerate [kənˈɡlɑmrət] *n.* 企业集团
7. visionary [ˈvɪʒə͵nɛrɪ] *n.* 有远见卓识者
8. mogul [ˈmoɡʌl] *n.* 大人物；巨擘
9. perceive [pəˈsiv] *v.* 觉察；感知
10. bromidic [broˈmɪdɪk] *adj.* 陈腐的
11. scrub [skrʌb] *v.* 用力洗刷
12. pick up 获得；获知
13. make sense *v. phr.* 有道理；有意义

Maggie Lake, The Boardroom

I read somewhere, correct me if I'm wrong, that you quit[14] college [and] started out[15] at the mail room at William Morris. Do you think you could do that today and get to where you are?

Barry Diller, Media Mogul

I became chairman of Paramount when I was 32 with essentially[16] no experience in theatrical[17] motion pictures.[18] I wonder if today any of these companies, which now, in the movie business, whether or not they would reach down and out somewhere and pick this unqualified[19] person because somebody, a crazy person in this case, who owned Paramount, had this idea this person might be good at this.

Maggie Lake, The Boardroom

Diller instilled[20] that willingness[21] to take risk in his protégés, the so-called "Diller Killers," ["Killer Dillers"] who went on to become media titans[22] in their own right.

So you find talent[23] that you find willing to take a risk?

Barry Diller, Media Mogul

Well I think there is, somewhere, someone in their late teens or their early 20s who's got whatever alchemy[24] that creates value—the ability to cause things to happen. It is always a question of just mining[25] for it.

"董事会"玛姬·雷克

我若说错了请纠正我,不过我记得在哪读到过说你从大学辍学后,进入威廉莫里斯经纪公司从收发员开始做起。你觉得如果你今天还这么做,会有机会达到目前这种地位吗?

媒体巨子 巴里·迪勒

我 32 岁当上派拉蒙公司董事长的时候,对于电影可以说根本没有经验。我很难想象在今天的电影界会有任何一家公司,四处寻访然后挑个不符合资格的人,就因为某个狂人,在我的例子里是派拉蒙的老板,突发奇想觉得这个人可能会干得不错。

"董事会"玛姬·雷克

迪勒把这种愿意冒险的想法灌输在他的弟子身上,即所谓的"杀手迪勒帮"(注)都是靠自己的本事成为媒体巨擘。

所以,你找到让你愿意冒险的人才了?

媒体巨子 巴里·迪勒

我认为总会在某个地方有 20 岁上下的年轻人,身上带着创造价值的神奇力量——那是成就大事的能力。问题一直就只是有没有人去发掘而已。

注:美国娱乐圈以 Killer Dillers 称呼迪勒及他带出来的后辈,意指他们是一些强悍的厉害人物。巴里·迪勒的弟子大多都是他在派拉蒙担任总裁时的属下,后来都成了圈内赫赫有名的大人物,其中包括 Michael Eisner (迪士尼公司主席兼 CEO)、Jeffrey Katzenberg (前迪士尼动画部门负责人、梦工厂动画公司 CEO) 等。

Notes & Vocabulary

protégé 门徒;门生

这个词为法语词,发音为 [ˌprotəˈʒe],阴性写作 protégée,指受到有权势者照顾和提携的人,类似中文的"徒弟"、"弟子"、"接班人"等。同义词有 apprentice [əˈprɛntəs]、disciple [dɪˈsaɪpəl]、prentice [ˈprɛntəs]、pupil [ˈpjupəl]。

in one's own right 凭自身的条件

这个短语的意思是"靠自己本来的能力或资格",例如本身的能力、身份等,而非依靠他人的关系、特权或运气。

• David is a talented writer in his own right.
  大卫本身就是个有才华的作家。

14. **quit** [kwɪt] *v.* 放弃;中途辍学

15. **start out** 出发;着手进行

16. **essentially** [ɪˈsɛnʃəlɪ] *adv.* 实质上地

17. **theatrical** [θiˈætrɪkəl] *adj.* 戏剧的

18. **motion picture** [ˈmoʃən] [ˈpɪktʃə] 电影

19. **unqualified** [ʌnˈkwɑləˌfaɪd] *adj.* 不合格的;不够资格的

20. **instill** [ɪnˈstɪl] *v.* (慢慢) 灌输

21. **willingness** [ˈwɪlɪŋnəs] *n.* 意愿

22. **titan** [ˈtaɪtn̩] *n.* 巨人;重要人物

23. **talent** [ˈtælənt] *n.* 有才能的人

24. **alchemy** [ˈælkəmɪ] *n.* 炼金术;促进事物的能力

25. **mine** [maɪn] *v.* 挖掘;发掘

Restoring the House of Mouse

Inside *The Boardroom* with Disney CEO Robert Iger

重振米老鼠之家——专访迪士尼新任 CEO 罗伯特·艾格

Step 1 ◎ 请浏览下方提示的关键问题后，仔细听录音。

1. What was the situation at Disney like when Iger took over?
2. What did Iger feel were the important things for Disney to focus on?
3. How does he feel about his time at Disney?
4. What does Iger think is the best way to deal with people he works with?

Step 2 🎧 如果你还听不太懂的话，请浏览下方的关键词汇后再听一次。

bottom line 盈亏表结算线	charismatic 极富魅力的
deputy 副手	skirmish 小冲突
embroil 卷入纠纷	complacent 自满的
rest on one's laurels 满足于已有的成就	consensus 共识

Step 3 💡 试着回答下列听力测验题目。

True or False 是非题

_____ 1. Iger was brought to Disney from ABC to become CEO.

_____ 2. When Iger became CEO, he still had a lot to learn about Disney.

_____ 3. The company exceeded Iger's expectations so far.

_____ 4. With Disney back on track, Iger feels he has done all he needs to.

_____ 5. Iger says it is very important to say what he thinks to people he works with.

名人小档案

罗伯特·艾格（1951–）于 2000 年担任迪士尼董事长一职，并于 2005 年接任 CEO，一上任就积极消除迪士尼与其他公司的嫌隙，彼此建立友好关系。带领迪士尼于 2006 年以 74 亿美元并购皮克斯公司（Pixar）。

Multiple Choice 选择题

_____ 1. What does Iger say that the company had to focus on to move forward?
   a. The skirmishes they had had.
   b. Exercise and keeping healthy.
   c. Things that create value.
   d. Embroiling what was behind.

_____ 2. What did Iger say that he learned from Michael Eisner?
   a. How to fight in the boardroom.
   b. How to treat Disney with glory.
   c. How to be charismatic.
   d. What Disney still could do.

_____ 3. How does Iger deal with the egos of people he works with?
   a. Be clear and don't try to trick them.
   b. Talking about fashion with them.
   c. Compromise and consensus.
   d. Look into their eyes and listen.

Step 4 试着用较慢的速度，再仔细听一遍，并检查答案是否正确。

Step 5 核对答案、检验成果，并详读原文，若仍有不懂的地方，可反复多听几次。

（答案请见 p.228）

Andrew Stevens, The Boardroom

It was one of the toughest jobs in corporate America: Restoring[1] the corporate image of The Walt Disney Company. The House of Mouse was in the headlines more for its boardroom battles than its bottom line.[2] Last year, after 21 years at the helm,[3] the charismatic[4] Michael Eisner was forced out by angry shareholders.[5] And coming into the hot seat as CEO was his long-time deputy,[6] Bob Iger. Disney is now back on track, its major problems in the past. I began by asking Iger his strategy for restoring Disney's corporate image to its former glory.

Robert Iger, CEO of Walt Disney Company

Well, I had great training. I had worked at Disney since they bought the company that I had worked for, ABC, in the mid-90s. I also had the benefit of working for Michael Eisner, who taught me a tremendous[7] amount about the company—about its both its past and its present and what the potential of the company could be. And so at the time that I got the job, I was pretty focused on what I wanted to accomplish and when. So one thing that was very important was putting some of the skirmishes[8] that we had been embroiled[9] in behind us. I did not feel it was healthy for the company to have that distraction,[10] nor was it healthy for me. Focusing the company on what really would drive the most value going forward.

Andrew Stevens, The Boardroom

Obviously easier said than done, I mean did it go according to plan?

"董事会"安德鲁·史蒂文斯

美国企业界最艰困的一件工作，就是重建迪士尼公司的企业形象。米老鼠之家登上新闻版面不是因为盈亏状况，而是因为董事之争。去年，极富个人魅力的艾斯纳在执掌迪士尼 21 年之后，却遭到愤怒的股东逼迫下台。接下这个尴尬位置的继任者就是他长期以来的副手罗伯特·艾格。迪士尼现在已经重回正轨，重大的问题都已过去。在访谈一开始，我首先请问艾格打算用什么样的策略，让迪士尼的企业形象恢复先前的辉煌。

迪士尼公司 CEO 罗伯特·艾格

我受过很好的培训。我本来在 ABC 工作，他们在 90 年代中期买下迪士尼之后，我就开始在迪士尼工作了。我也有幸担任艾斯纳的属下，他教了我很多关于这家公司的事情——包括迪士尼的过去和现在，还有公司未来的潜力。因此，我得到这份工作之后，就全神贯注于我想要达成的目标和时间。所以，很重要的一点就是我们必须把先前的某些不愉快抛在脑后。我认为内部争执对公司的发展不利，对我个人也不利。公司必须全力追求真正能够带来价值的东西。

"董事会" 安德鲁·史蒂文斯

说起来容易，做起来难。我是说，一切都确实按照计划进行的吗？

Notes & Vocabulary

back on track 重回正轨

track 是 "轨道" 的意思，be/get back on track 则指 "重回正轨" 的意思。文中出现另一个意思相近的短语 pull ... back into shape，shape 本身是 "形状" 的意思，当事物失去了形状也就是说失去了原有的水平，所以 pull ...back into shape 便是指把 "事情再度拉回正轨、重整旗鼓" 的意思。

· Judith got her career back on track.
朱迪思在工作上重整旗鼓。

· Tracy pulled her team back into shape.
特蕾西使她的队伍恢复了原来的水准。

....

1. restore [rɪˋstɔr] *v.* 恢复；修整

2. bottom line 盈亏表结算线；底线

3. helm [hɛlm] *n.* 领导地位

4. charismatic [ˏkærəzˋmætɪk] *adj.* 极富魅力的

5. shareholder [ˋʃɛrˏholdə] *n.* 股东

6. deputy [ˋdɛpjətɪ] *n.* 副手

7. tremendous [trɪˋmɛndəs] *adj.* 极大的；极多的

8. skirmish [ˋskɜmɪʃ] *n.* 小冲突

9. embroil [ɪmˋbrɔɪl] *v.* 卷入纠纷

10. distraction [dɪˋstrækʃən] *n.* 不愉快的事

Robert Iger, CEO of Walt Disney Company

Well, I actually feel looking back on what has been a pretty interesting number of months in this job, that as a team we accomplished more than I expected to in this period of time. Now that doesn't mean that it's time to become complacent[11] or to rest on our laurels because there's always a lot more that needs to be done, but I'd say slightly ahead of plan.

Andrew Stevens, The Boardroom

When you were pulling the Disney house back into shape, you obviously had to deal with some very big egos[12]—Michael Eisner, Steve Jobs. How did you manage[13] that? How did you manage those sort[s] of personalities? Is it compromise[14] and consensus?[15]

Robert Iger, CEO of Walt Disney Company

Well for me it's never about egos. It's about dealing with people in a very open, straightforward[16] fashion. I think it's incredibly important to be open, accessible,[17] treat people fairly, look them in the eye and tell them what's on your mind.

迪士尼公司 CEO　罗伯特·艾格

回顾起来，我觉得过去这几个月其实非常有趣，我们整个团队在这段时间内所完成的事情比我想象的还多。不是说我们可以为自己取得的成果感到自满，因为永远都会有许多需要做的事情。不过，可以说我们稍稍超过了原定计划。

"董事会" 安德鲁·史蒂文斯

你在把迪士尼拉回正轨的过程中，显然必须面对某些自我意识非常强的人——例如艾斯纳和乔布斯。你怎么处理这方面的问题？你怎么应对这些大人物？是通过寻求妥协和共识吗？

迪士尼公司 CEO　罗伯特·艾格

对我来说，问题向来不在于自我意识，而是在于怎么以真诚坦率的方式和别人互动。我认为最重要的是要开诚布公、平易近人、并且公平待人，直截了当地把自己的想法告诉他们。

Notes & Vocabulary

rest on one's laurels 满足于已有的成就

laurel [ˈlɔrəl] 原指"桂冠"，引申为"胜利；成就"的意思。rest on 在这里则是"安于、满足于"。

· Eric rested on his laurels after college.
埃里克大学毕业后就不想再进修了。

rest 作动词用时，意思是"休息、放松"，和不同介词连用有不同的意思：

a. rest on/against 倚、靠
　·The man rested against the brick wall.
　　那个男人倚靠在砖墙上。

b. rest with 由……负责
　·The company's success ultimately rests with management.
　　公司的成功最终还是取决于管理方式。

look them in the eye
直截了当、诚实以对

look sb in the eye/face 即是字面衍生的意思，表示说话时注视着某人、毫不相瞒、诚实以对的意思。

· George looked the man right in the eye and said he was wrong.
乔治看着这个男人，诚实地告诉他自己错了。

· Kevin was so ashamed he couldn't look his wife in the eye.
凯文感到十分羞愧而不敢直视他太太。

- -

11. **complacent** [kəmˈplesn̩t] *adj.* 自满的

12. **big ego** 大人物

13. **manage** [ˈmænɪdʒ] *v.* 处理；应付

14. **compromise** [ˈkɑmprəˌmaɪz] *n.* 妥协

15. **consensus** [kənˈsɛnsəs] *n.* 共识

16. **straightforward** [ˌstretˈfɔrwəd] *adj.* 明确的；直接的

17. **accessible** [ækˈsɛsəbəl] *adj.* 易被理解的

Master Manager
Q&A with Former General Electric CEO Jack Welch
通用前 CEO 杰克·韦尔奇的制胜秘诀

Step 1 请浏览下方提示的关键问题后，仔细听录音。

1. What qualities do Welch say are important in a leader?
2. Where does Welch get his competitiveness from?
3. What are the things that his mother taught him?
4. How did Welch learn how to lose gracefully?

Step 2 如果你还听不太懂的话，请浏览下方的关键词汇后再听一次。

superlative 最高级；赞美词	galvanize 刺激；引起
inherent 内在的；与生俱来的	storm 暴怒；袭击
punk 浑蛋；笨蛋	humiliate 羞辱

Step 3 试着回答下列听力测验题目。

True or False 是非题

_____ 1. Being comfortable as the smartest person in the room is important to Welch.

_____ 2. Jack Welch feels his mother had a very large influence in his life.

_____ 3. Jack Welch was the oldest of several children.

_____ 4. His mother humiliated him because he threw his hockey stick during the game.

_____ 5. Welch thinks humiliating people gives them a great learning lesson.

名人小档案

杰克·韦尔奇（1935-）在通用公司工作了 41 年。他带领通用公司 20 年，打造了"通用传奇"，使通用身价攀升至 4 千亿美元，并跻身全球最有价值的企业之列。韦尔奇本人也赢得"世纪经理人"、"美国企业的标杆人物"等美誉。

Multiple Choice 选择题

_____ 1. Where does Welch say leader get their ability to stimulate their employees?

    a. It can't be taught.

    b. Playing competitive sports.

    c. Having many victories.

    d. Serving in the army and having troops.

_____ 2. What quality does Welch not say his mother taught him?

    a. How to be competitive.

    b. How to tell the difference between things.

    c. How to find the best and the brightest.

    d. How to lose and keep fighting.

_____ 3. What advice does Welch give to people who want to stay on top?

    a. Read more books.

    b. Build a great team and keep it.

    c. Be satisfied with what you have.

    d. Keep looking for better people.

Step 4 试着用较慢的速度，再仔细听一遍，并检查答案是否正确。

Step 5 核对答案、检验成果，并详读原文，若仍有不懂的地方，可反复多听几次。

（答案请见 p.228）

Todd Benjamin, CNN Financial Editor

When it comes to Jack Welch, superlatives usually follow. While running General Electric, the value of the shares[1] increased by $400 billion, making it the world's most valuable corporation. *Fortune* magazine called him "Manager of the Century", and *BusinessWeek*, an "icon[2] of American business". I recently caught up with him here in London.

Why do you think you were so good at business?

Jack Welch, Former CEO of General Electric

I think I knew how to galvanize[3] people. I think I knew how to find good people. I was comfortable[4] hiring people smarter than I was. I was never the smartest person in the room. And I searched for the best and brightest all the time.

Todd Benjamin, CNN Financial Editor

But why is it you think that some leaders have that quality to galvanize and others don't?

Jack Welch, Former CEO of General Electric

Well, I think that a lot of it is inherent[5]—do you have an inner[6] feeling that makes you want to have your troops,[7] if you will, or your employees, if you will, or whatever, be as victorious[8] in every way as you are?

Todd Benjamin, CNN Financial Editor

Now, you played competitive sports as a kid. Do you think this is where this competitiveness[9] came from or do you think it came from someplace else?

CNN 金融主编 托德·本杰明

一谈到杰克·韦尔奇，通常会出现各种溢美之词。在他经营期间，通用公司的股票增值 4 千亿美元，成为世界上价值最高的公司。《财富》杂志称他为"世纪经理人"，《商业周刊》称他为"美国企业的标杆人物"。我最近和他在伦敦进行了一次访谈。

你认为，你为什么如此善于企业经营？

通用公司前 CEO 杰克·韦尔奇

我想是因为我懂得该怎样激励员工，还有该怎么找寻人才。我不怕雇用比我聪明的人。我向来都不是团队里最聪明的人，因此我随时都在找寻最聪明最杰出的人才。

CNN 金融主编 托德·本杰明

可是为什么不是所有领导人都具备激励他人的特质呢？

通用公司前 CEO 杰克·韦尔奇

我认为这种特质大半是与生俱来的——你心里是否有一种感受，令你想让自己的团队，或者说自己的员工在各方面都像你一样成功？

CNN 金融主编 托德·本杰明

你从小就参加竞赛性的体育活动。你认为你的好胜心是来自运动场上吗？还是有其他的原因？

Notes & Vocabulary

superlative 溢美之词

superlative [su`pɜlətɪv] 这个词原意为"夸大的、最好的"，后来开始当作名词使用，指语法中的"最高级"或"最高级的形式"，引申出"盛赞之词"或"溢美之词"这层意义。

- Discussions of China are full of superlatives, like oldest civilization, largest population, and fastest growing economy.

  有关中国的形容都是"最"字开头的，像是文化"最"悠久、人口"最"多及经济发展"最"迅速。

1. share [ʃɛr] n. 股份；股票
2. icon [`aɪ͵kɑn] n. 偶像；图像
3. galvanize [`gælvə͵naɪz] v. 刺激；引起
4. comfortable [`kʌmftəbəl] adj. 放心的；不担心的
5. inherent [ɪn`hɪrənt] adj. 内在的；与生俱来的
6. inner [`ɪnə] adj. 内心的；内部的
7. troop [trup] n. 部队；一群人
8. victorious [vɪk`torɪəs] adj. 胜利的；战胜的
9. competitiveness [kəm`pɛtətɪvnəs] n. 竞争力

Jack Welch, Former CEO of General Electric

I think it came from that, my mother. I was an only child. She was always pushing me.

Todd Benjamin, CNN Financial Editor

This is the thing that struck me doing the research for this interview. Everything I read, what comes across more than anything else, was what a powerful influence your mother was in your life.

Jack Welch, Former CEO of General Electric

Incredibly so. I mean [the] ability to … she taught me the ability to hug and kick, to differentiate[10] a whole series of things. She had characteristics that always said you can do better. "Come on, Jack, you can do better. What are you doing?"

Todd Benjamin, CNN Financial Editor

And there is even an example, of course, in a hockey game. You lost the game; you threw your hockey stick across the ice; you came storming[11] into that locker room and what did she tell you?

Jack Welch, Former CEO of General Electric

[She] grabs me by the shirt and says, "You punk.[12] If you don't know how to lose, you shouldn't play the game." And in front of all my friends, [she] humiliated[13] me. But it was a great learning lesson. I mean, people say to me "You hate to lose, don't you?" I say I hate to lose, but I know how to do it. Get up off the floor and go at the next one.

通用公司前 CEO　杰克·韦尔奇

我想是来自比赛活动和我的母亲。我是独生子，所以她总是不断督促我。

CNN 金融主编　托德·本杰明

我在准备这次访谈的过程中也发现了这一点。在我阅读的所有资料当中，最常出现的一点，就是你母亲在你一生中具有重大的影响力。

通用公司前 CEO　杰克·韦尔奇

确实如此，她对我的影响之大，实在令人难以置信。我是说，她教我学会"恩威并济"，还教我区别各种不同事物。她有种特质，会不断要求你做出更好的表现。"加油，杰克，你还可以做得更好，你在干什么呢？"

CNN 金融主编　托德·本杰明

还有一个例子，就是当初的一场曲棍球比赛。你输球之后，把球棒甩在比赛场上，然后带着一肚子火回到更衣室。那时候她跟你说了什么？

通用公司前 CEO　杰克·韦尔奇

她一把抓住我的上衣对我说："浑小子，你如果输不起，一开始就不该参赛。"她就这样在我所有的朋友面前羞辱我，可是她为我上了宝贵的一课。别人常对我说："你不喜欢失败，对不对？"我说没错，可是我知道该怎么面对失败。爬起来，再追求下一次的成功。

Notes & Vocabulary

come across　形成某种印象

本文中出现的 come across 指"让别人产生某种印象"，常见的用法是 sb come across as sth。

- Tom's plan came across as poorly thought out.
  汤姆的计划让人觉得欠缺周详的考虑。

come across 其他常见的意思有"遇见某人；偶然发现某事物"、"（一个人的观念、想法）真正传达给对方，并使对方理解"。

- Barbara came across a deer while hiking.
  芭芭拉爬山时碰巧看到了一只鹿。

- His point came across loud and clear to the audience.
  他将论点清楚而明确地传达给在场观众。

....

10. differentiate [ˌdɪfəˈrɛnʃiˌet] v. 区分

11. storm [stɔrm] v. 暴怒；横冲直撞；袭击

12. punk [pʌŋk] n. 浑蛋；笨蛋

13. humiliate [hjuˈmɪliˌet] v. 羞辱；使丢脸

Todd Benjamin, CNN Financial Editor

And if you had to give advice to a CEO, in terms of staying on top, what would it be?

Jack Welch, Former CEO of General Electric

Keep learning. Drive[14] for learning. Drive for better people. Don't be satisfied with—quote—"your team". Keep making it better and keep learning.

CNN 金融主编 托德·本杰明

如果有一位 CEO 问你该如何保持领导地位，你会给他什么建议？

通用公司前 CEO 杰克·韦尔奇

不断学习。全力学习，全力寻找更优秀的人。不要满足于所谓"自己的团队"。不断让自己的团队更加精进，不断学习。

Notes & Vocabulary

in terms of 就……方面来说

term 这个词可以解释为"看待某事的一种方式"，也就是"视角"、"观点"之意。in terms of 是英语中出现频率相当高的介词短语，意指"在……方面"或"从……的角度来说"。

- Indonesia has improved in terms of press freedom over the past year.
  在新闻自由度方面，印尼在过去一年有所进步。

14. **drive** [draɪv] *v.* 努力进行

A Philosophy[1] of Giving[2]
An Interview with CNN Founder Ted Turner on Philanthropy[3]
CNN 创办人泰德·特纳的慈善哲学

Step 1 请浏览下方提示的关键问题后，仔细听录音。

1. What does Turner think philanthropy is?
2. Why does Turner think more people are giving to charity?
3. What does Turner think is the best way to help people?
4. What responsibility does Turner think corporations have to be philanthropic?

Step 2 如果你还听不太懂的话，请浏览下方的关键词汇后再听一次。

philanthropy 慈善事业；慈善行为	eradicate 根除；消灭
polio 小儿麻痹症	catastrophic 灾难的
signpost 标示牌	grant 许可；授予
reservation 保留；犹豫	alternative 替代选择

Step 3 试着回答下列听力测验题目。

True or False 是非题

_____ 1. Turner believes philanthropy is people with less helping people with more.

_____ 2. He believes that philanthropy is making people kinder and smarter.

_____ 3. Turner believes that just giving money to people doesn't help.

_____ 4. Turner says he is making investments because he will get his money back.

_____ 5. Turner believes there is no alternative to being philanthropic.

名人小档案

泰德·特纳（1938-）是媒体大亨兼慈善家。1980 年创立
"有线电视新闻网"（Cable News Network, CNN），创办
24 小时新闻频道。1997 年捐献 10 亿美元给联合国，也为
其他许多促进世界和平及环境保护的计划提供资助。

Multiple Choice 选择题

_____ 1. What does Turner think is the reason people are thinking
　　　more about philanthropy?

　　a. He has become a leader.

　　b. They've seen the recent catastrophes.

　　c. People are becoming smarter and better.

　　d. Humanity sees itself as a whole.

_____ 2. What does Turner think people who receive charity should
　　　be taught?

　　a. How to fish.

　　b. How to invest the money.

　　c. About the future of humanity.

　　d. Skills they can use to make money.

_____ 3. According to Turner, what responsibilities do corporations
　　　have in terms of philanthropy?

　　a. They should invest in the future of humanity.

　　b. They have no responsibility in terms of philanthropy.

　　c. Their philanthropy should be corporate based.

　　d. They must give money to the board of directors.

Step 4 试着用较慢的速度，再仔细听一遍，并检查答案是否正确。

Step 5 核对答案、检验成果，并详读原文，若仍有不懂的地方，可反复多听几次。

（答案请见 p.228）

Christie Lu Stout, Global Office

CNN founder Ted Turner made his billions from the media industry, but now he's left the corporate[4] world behind to invest his time, energy and personal wealth to help others. Now one of his foundation's aims is to eradicate[5] polio[6] in developing countries. And he tells Rusty Dornin why you don't have to be a billionaire to do your bit

Rusty Dornin, CNN Correspondent

If you, Ted Turner, had to say what you thought "philanthropy" meant, what would that be?

Ted Turner, CNN Founder

I would say that it would probably be the sharing of those that are very fortunate[7] with those that are less fortunate.

Rusty Dornin, CNN Correspondent

Do you think also recent events, catastrophic[8] events caused people to perhaps think more in this direction?

Ted Turner, CNN Founder

I'd like to think, because I'm an optimist,[9] that we are making progress—that humanity[10] as a whole is making progress and gifts, and generosity[11] like this are just another indication[12] and signpost[13] that we are making progress that we're becoming kinder, gentler, more intelligent, better-educated human beings.

"环球办公室"克里斯蒂·卢·斯托特

CNN 创办人泰德·特纳在媒体产业创造了数十亿美元的财富，但他现在已经离开企业界，转而将他的时间、精力以及个人财富用来帮助他人。他的基金会所追求的其中一个目标，就是在发展中国家根除小儿麻痹。他向拉斯缇·多南表示，不需要是亿万富翁，一般人也一样可以尽一己之力。

CNN 特派记者 拉斯缇·多南

泰德·特纳，如果请你说明你认为"慈善"的意义是什么，你会怎么说？

CNN 创办人 泰德·特纳

我认为意思大概就是非常幸运的人，把他们拥有的东西分享给没那么幸运的人。

CNN 特派记者 拉斯缇·多南

你认为近期的事件，一些灾难性的事件，是否也促进人们更加朝这个方面思考？

CNN 创办人 泰德·特纳

我是个乐观的人，所以我会这么认为，我们不断在进步——人类整体而言不断在进步，像这样的赠予与慷慨付出的行为恰恰只是我们正在进步的另一种表现，显示我们人类越来越仁爱、越来越和善、越来越有智慧、越来越有教养。

Notes & Vocabulary

do one's bit 尽一己之力；做自己可以做到的工作

bit 是"小块；小片"的意思。虽然每个人只是社会中的一个小分子，但是若每个小分子都能尽一己之力 (do one's bit)，就会对社会有巨大贡献。其他类似的说法还有：do one's part、do one's share、play one's part。

- This project was a group effort; everyone did their bit to make it a success.
  这个项目是整个小组的辛劳付出，每个人都出了一份力才能使它完成。

- If you do your part in cleaning up the park, others will be happy to help.
  如果你尽力打扫公园，其他人也会乐意协助。

....

1. philosophy [fə`lɑsəfɪ] *n.* 哲学；人生观

2. giving [`gɪvɪŋ] *n.* 给予；馈赠

3. philanthropy [fɪ`lænθrəpɪ] *n.* 慈善事业；慈善行为

4. corporate [`kɔrprət] *adj.* 法人的；企业的；公司的

5. eradicate [ɪ`rædə‚ket] *v.* 根除；消灭

6. polio [`poli‚o] *n.* 小儿麻痹症

7. fortunate [`fɔrtʃnət] *adj.* 幸运的

8. catastrophic [‚kætə`strɑfɪk] *adj.* 灾难的；惨重的

9. optimist [`ɑptəmɪst] *n.* 乐观主义者；乐观者

10. humanity [hju`mænətɪ] *n.* 人性；人道；慈爱

11. generosity [‚dʒɛnə`rɑsɪtɪ] *n.* 慷慨；宽大

12. indication [‚ɪndə`keʃən] *n.* 征兆；迹象

13. signpost [`saɪn‚post] *n.* 标示牌

Rusty Dornin, CNN Correspondent

There are a lot of people out there who are also trying to teach people how to give money away[14] properly. What are the important things that these people need to be taught in terms of when they give the money away?

Ted Turner, CNN Founder

When people say "what's your philosophy of philanthropy?" I say, "I'm trying to make an investment in the future of humanity." Not give money away, but make an investment wherever we possibly can, we try and have our giving teach people how to take care of themselves rather than just making grants[15] to them because, you know, the old saying, "You give a man a fish and you've fed him for one meal; you teach him how to fish and he can feed himself."

Rusty Dornin, CNN Correspondent

What kind of responsibility do just corporations[16] have in terms of philanthropy?

CNN 特派记者 拉斯缇·多南

另外有许多人也都尝试要教别人怎么适当地捐赠财物。这些人捐赠的时候，必须知道哪些重要的事情？

CNN 创办人 泰德·特纳

如果有人问我："你的慈善哲学是什么？"我总是回答："我想要投资人类的未来。"不是捐赠钱财，而是在任何能够投资的地方尽量投资。我们不是单纯地把财物送给他们，而是设法借此教他们好好照顾自己。就是那句俗语："给他鱼吃不如教他钓鱼；授之以鱼不如授之以渔。"

CNN 特派记者 拉斯缇·多南

热心公益的企业在慈善方面负有哪些责任？

Notes & Vocabulary

you give a man a fish . . .
与其给他鱼吃，还不如教他钓鱼

泰德·特纳在此所引用的谚语常见的说法有以下两种：

Give a man a fish and you feed him for a day. Teach him how to fish and you feed him for a lifetime.
授人以鱼只救一时之急；授人以渔则解一生之需。

Give a man a fish, and he will eat for a day. Give him a hook and he will eat for life.
给他一条鱼，他只能今日吃饱，给他鱼钩，他可以一生吃饱。

14. **give away** 赠送；分发

15. **grant** [grænt] *n.* 许可；授予

16. **corporation** [ˌkɔrpəˈreʃən] *n.* 法人；财团法人；股份有限公司

Ted Turner, CNN Founder

I think as far as corporations are concerned, it's really up to the corporations to decide. Whether they want to give and whether their major shareholders want them to have a significant philanthropic[17] program or whether they would prefer to pass the revenues[18] on to the owners of the company. It's really up to the board of directors[19] and the shareholders of a company to decide whether their philanthropy should be corporate based or individually based, with the profits being passed through to then be reinvested[20] in the future of humanity.

Rusty Dornin, CNN Correspondent

Do you have any reservations[21] about philanthropy?

Ted Turner, CNN Founder

We can't give up! If we give up, what's the alternative?[22] I mean we have to keep trying to make things better and that's what I'm dedicating my life to,[23] the rest of it, to try and make things better.

CNN 创办人　泰德·特纳

就企业而言，我认为应该由企业自己决定。他们是否愿意付出，他们的大股东是否希望公司制定意义重大的慈善计划，还是宁可把收益分配给公司股东。只有董事会与股东才能决定，公司究竟是要从事整体的慈善活动，还是由员工个人参与，把利润分配出去，再由大家分别投资于人类的未来。

CNN 特派记者　拉斯·多南

你对慈善事业是否有些疑虑？

CNN 创办人　泰德·特纳

我们不能放弃！我们如果放弃，还有什么其他选择？我是说，我们必须不断努力改善现状，我就是要把我的余生投入在改善现状上面。

Notes & Vocabulary

major shareholder 主要股东

持有一家公司半数以上的现有股份，即是此家公司的"主要股东"，可以主导公司的决策与管理。而一家公司半数以上的股权则称为 majority stake/share（主要股权／绝对多数股权）。

- The major shareholders voted to sack the CEO.
  公司的主要股东投票要解雇 CEO。
- Tom owns a majority stake in a mining company.
  汤姆持有一家矿业公司的主要股权。

17. **philanthropic** [ˌfɪlənˈθrɑpɪk] *adj.* 慈善的；博爱的；仁慈的

18. **revenue** [ˈrɛvəˌnu] *n.* 营业收入

19. **board of directors** *n. phr.* 董事会

20. **reinvest** [ˌriənˈvɛst] *v.* 再投资

21. **reservation** [ˌrɛzəˈveʃən] *n.* 犹豫；保留

22. **alternative** [ɔlˈtɜːnətɪv] *n.* 替代选择

23. **dedicate to** [ˈdɛdɪˌket] *v.* 献给；奉献给

Lou Gerstner:
The Man Who Saved IBM
让大象起舞的男人——IBM 前 CEO 葛斯特纳

Step 1 ◉ 请浏览下方提示的关键问题后，仔细听录音。

1. What was the situation at IBM like when Gerstner took over?
2. What did Gerstner say IBM had looked like from a customer's perspective?
3. What was the plan for IBM before Gerstner took over? Why did he stop it?
4. What changes did Gerstner say IBM needed in terms of compensating employees?

Step 2 🏠 如果你还听不太懂的话，请浏览下方的关键词汇后再听一次。

unassailable 不容置疑的	wuss 软弱无用的人
forte 特长；专长	ax 解雇；削减
fiefdom 控制范围	entrepreneurship 创新精神
complacency 故步自封	malaise 抑郁；心神不定

Step 3 💡 试着回答下列听力测验题目。

True or False 是非题

_____ 1. In the 1960s, IBM was more dominant in the marketplace than today's Microsoft.

_____ 2. Only 60,000 workers were laid off in Gerstner's six years as CEO.

_____ 3. Gerstner felt that people who worked hard should share in the rewards.

_____ 4. IBM's service and consulting departments created most of the growth under Gerstner.

名人小档案

路·葛斯特纳（1942-）曾任麦肯锡公司（McKinsey）顾问、美国运通（American Express）总裁、纳贝斯克（RJR Nabisco）CEO。入主 IBM 后大力改革内部组织，力行企业转型政策，成功扭转乾坤。著有《谁说大象不会跳舞？》（*Who Says Elephants Can't Dance? Inside IBM's Historic Turnaround*）。

_____ 5. After Gerstner took over, IBM became arrogant and complacent.

Multiple Choice 选择题

_____ 1. What about IBM did Gerstner find frustrating as a customer?
   a. He was dependent on them as a supplier.
   b. IBM didn't think about technology.
   c. IBM didn't think about customer needs.
   d. It was losing billions.

_____ 2. Why did Gerstner oppose the breakup of IBM?
   a. People would lose their jobs.
   b. It would have destroyed IBM's strengths.
   c. He didn't recognize the vertical integration.
   d. It would confuse customers.

_____ 3. When Gerstner took over IBM, who was getting stock options?
   a. People who worked hard.
   b. Tens of thousands of workers.
   c. People who had victories.
   d. A small number of people.

Step 4 试着用较慢的速度，再仔细听一遍，并检查答案是否正确。

Step 5 核对答案、检验成果，并详读原文，若仍有不懂的地方，可反复多听几次。

（答案请见 p.228）

Becky Anderson, Global Office

IBM pretty much invented computing back in the 1960s. Big Blue was hailed[1] as one of the world's great companies. Then, spectacularly,[2] it all went wrong. And one man stepped in[3] to save it.

Nineteen sixty-four was the year that IBM went from being good to great. Chairman Thomas Watson, Jr., son of the company's founder, bet the future of IBM on the System 360, investing almost double annual revenue on the project.

It became the classic mainframe[4] computer. Its speed and compatibility[5] revolutionized[6] the way that businesses could process information. IBM was unassailable,[7] as business guru[8] Michael Hammer explains.

Michael Hammer, Business Guru

It's hard for people today who weren't around at the time to understand the market dominance[9] that IBM had in the computer industry. It would make today's Microsoft and Intel look like wusses.[10]

Becky Anderson, Global Office

But by the early 1990s, the situation had changed dramatically. It missed out[11] on the rise of the PC and overlooked[12] the market power of Microsoft's operating system. The company was losing billions and by March 1993, it had just 100 days left before cash ran out.

Enter Lou Gerstner.

"环球办公室" 贝基·安德森

IBM 在 20 世纪 60 年代一举发明了电子计算。蓝色巨人在当年曾被誉为世界上最伟大的企业之一。不过，后来却出了问题，错得一塌糊涂。这时候，有个人出面力挽狂澜。

1964 年是 IBM 从优秀提升到卓越的一年。董事长托马斯·沃森二世是 IBM 创始人之子，他当时把公司的未来押在 360 系统上，为这项计划投注了将近两倍的年收益。

IBM360 系统后来成为经典的大型计算机。这套系统的速度与兼容性彻底改变了企业处理信息的方式。诚如企管大师迈克尔·哈默（注）所说的，当时的 IBM 实在所向无敌。

企管大师 迈克尔·哈默

今天的人如果没有亲眼见证那个时代，实在很难理解当时 IBM 在计算机行业的主宰地位。跟那时候的 IBM 相比而言，今天的微软和英特尔根本就不算什么。

"环球办公室" 贝基·安德森

不过，到了 20 世纪 90 年代初期，形势已彻底改变。IBM 没有赶上个人电脑的潮流，也忽视了微软操作系统的实力。当时 IBM 的损失以数 10 亿计，而到了 1993 年 3 月，整个公司可用的资金更是只剩下不足以维持 100 天。

路·葛斯特纳就在这时登场。

注：曾被《时代》杂志与《商业周刊》评选列为最杰出管理大师之一。

Notes & Vocabulary

Big Blue 蓝色巨人

Big Blue 是 IBM 的别称，关于它的起源有好几种说法。其中一个说法认为源自于六七十年代 IBM 都是用蓝色的电脑主机，而当时也有人以 all blue 来称呼 IBM 的忠实顾客。另一个说法则是认为这个别称仅仅是指 IBM 以蓝色虚线组成的识别商标。不论是哪一种说法，"蓝色"已成为 IBM 的品牌形象之一，使顾客对 IBM 留下深刻的蓝色印象。

1. hail [hel] v. 把……称作；把……誉为
2. spectacularly [spɛk`tækjələlɪ] adv. 壮观地；引人注目地
3. step in 插手；介入
4. mainframe [`men,frem] n. 大型电脑；大型计算机
5. compatibility [kəm,pætə`bɪlətɪ] n. 兼容性
6. revolutionize [,rɛvə`luʃə,naɪz] v. 彻底改革
7. unassailable [,ʌnə`seləbəl] adj. 不容置疑的；攻不破的
8. guru [`gʊru] n. 专家；权威
9. dominance [`dɑmənəns] n. 优势；支配地位
10. wuss [wʊs] n. 软弱无用的人
11. miss out 失败
12. overlook [,ovə`lʊk] v. 忽略；漏掉

Lou Gerstner had a track record of success. He'd run American Express and RJR Nabisco. Biscuits and credit cards rather than IT were his forte.[13] But what he did have was experience as an IBM customer.

How did you view IBM when you were at AmEx?

Lou Gerstner, Former IBM CEO

Well, when I was at American Express, IBM was absolutely essential as a supplier, so I was very dependent on them. But I was so frustrated that I couldn't get them to think in terms of my business needs as opposed to[14] technology.

Becky Anderson, Global Office

Losing sight of[15] the customer, the company was already getting ready to break itself up into up to a dozen independent units. Gerstner axed[16] the plan, recognizing IBM's vertical integration of hardware, software and services was its greatest strength.

Lou Gerstner, Former IBM CEO

What I said to the IBMers is "Look. Right now the plan is to bust the company up[17] and sell it off in pieces." I said, "As a customer, I don't really think that makes a lot of sense, because what I'd really like from IBM is for it to put all the pieces together and give me a solution."

Becky Anderson, Global Office

Costs and staff numbers was slashed,[18] 60,000 were laid off[19] in the first six months. And Gerstner also took on the fiefdoms[20] that have come to characterize[21] the company, forcing IBMers to pull together.

葛斯特纳过去功绩卓著，经营过美国运通和纳贝斯克公司。他经营的强项是饼干和信用卡，不是信息科技，但是他拥有身为 IBM 客户的经验。

你在美国运通公司的时候，对 IBM 有什么看法？

IBM 前 CEO 路·葛斯特纳

我在美国运通的时候，IBM 是我们不可或缺的供应商，因此我非常依赖他们。不过，他们总是以科技为思考重点，不会为我的商务需求着想，这点在当时让我觉得很不满意。

"环球办公室" 贝基·安德森

IBM 因为无法掌握客户需求，当时已经准备把公司分割成十几个独立单位。葛斯特纳极力排斥这项计划，肯定 IBM 在硬件、软件和服务方面的垂直整合是公司最强的优势。

IBM 前 CEO 路·葛斯特纳

我对 IBM 的员工说："你们看，现在的计划是要把公司拆散，逐个卖掉。从客户的角度来看，我觉得这种做法实在没什么道理。我真正想要 IBM 提供的服务，是把所有零碎的部分拼凑起来，给我一个完整的解决方案。"

"环球办公室" 贝基·安德森

成本与员工数量于是大幅削减，刚开始的 6 个月就解雇了 6 万人。此外，葛斯特纳也着手应对 IBM 旗下单位各自为政的问题，以往这几乎已成了 IBM 的特征。他迫使公司各部门通力合作。

Notes & Vocabulary

track record 过去的纪录

这个惯用语中的 track 一词原指体育的 "径赛" 项目（"跑道" 的英文就是 track），而 track record 即为径赛的最佳成绩纪录，后来此语的使用范围扩大，引申表示一个人以往表现的记录。其中 track record of success 这个用法相当常见，即指 "过去的成就"。

- The company has a poor environmental track record.
  那家公司过去在环保方面的表现很差。

13. forte [fɔrt] *n.* 特长；专长

14. as opposed to *phr.* 相对于……；而非……

15. lose sight of *v. phr.* 忽略；忘记

16. ax [æks] *v.* 解雇；削减

17. bust …up [bʌst] 打断；弄破；破坏

18. slash [slæʃ] *v.* 大幅度地削减

19. lay off 解雇

20. fiefdom [ˈfifdəm] *n.* 控制范围；封地；采邑

21. characterize [ˈkærɪktə‚raɪz] *v.* 具有……的特质；将……描述为

Lou Gerstner, Former IBM CEO

We had a miniscule[22] number of people getting stock options. Well, I said, wait a minute. If these people are going to work hard, and they're going to carry us to the victory we want, a lot of people have to share in the rewards. So we had tens of thousands of more people who were given stock options and participated in our success.

Becky Anderson, Global Office

In Gerstner's eight years as Chief Executive, the company grew by 40 percent, with services and consulting leading the growth. Its stock value rose eight fold.[23] Critics charge that later years were marked by a lack of entrepreneurship.[24] But for bringing IBM back from the brink,[25] his claim to a place in the pantheon of great CEOs is a strong one.

Michael Hammer, Business Guru

IBM had all the ingredients for failure: arrogance, complacency,[26] bureaucracy,[27] a sense of malaise[28] in the organization. Personally, I think that Gerstner's turnaround of IBM is the single greatest turnaround in modern business history.

IBM 前 CEO 路·葛斯特纳

我们原本只有极少数人享有股票认购权。我说，等一下，如果我们要这些人努力工作，为我们争取我们所要的胜利，就必须让大家共享成果。于是，我们让好几万人共同享有股票认购权，一起分享我们的成功。

"环球办公室" 贝基·安德森

在葛斯特纳担任 CEO 的 8 年期间，IBM 成长了 40%，其中以服务和咨询方面的业务增长幅度最大。IBM 的股价也增长了 8 倍。尽管批评人士指责他掌权的后几年缺乏创新精神，但是由于他令 IBM 起死回生，所以他还是有很大机会跻身伟大的CEO 之列。

企管大师 迈克尔·哈默

IBM 原本集合了所有失败的元素于一身：傲慢狂妄、自鸣得意、官僚作风，而且组织内部弥漫着不满的气氛。我个人认为，葛斯特纳扭转了 IBM 的命运，堪称是当代企业史上最伟大的壮举。

Notes & Vocabulary

stock option 员工股票认购权

此处的 stock option 指员工股票认购权（employee stock option；ESOP）。公司往往通过认购契约赋予员工在将来一段时间内以约定的价格购买公司股票的权利，若逾期不行使购买公司股票的权利，则该契约失效，此谓员工股票认购权。这类认购权的发行对象仅限于发行公司的员工，为公司与员工之间的契约协定，而不涉及外在第三人。通过此制度，可让员工的利益与股东的利益一致化，对提升员工向心力有正面效果。

- Several employees received stock options as part of their compensation package.
  有几位员工薪资组合中的一部分是员工股票认购权。

pantheon 万神庙；名人堂

词首 pan- 表示"泛、全部"，而词根 theos 相当于 god（神）的意思，pantheon 一词的原意指"敬拜诸神的殿堂"，例如罗马著名的古迹"万神庙"英文名称即为 Pantheon。后来这个词的意义扩大涉及世俗的伟人，例如巴黎的 Pantheon 为"先贤祠"，供奉的是伏尔泰、卢梭等人。演变至今，pantheon 常借指"名人之列"，近似 hall of fame（名人堂）的意味。

- Bill Gates and Donald Trump are among the pantheon of top business leaders.
  比尔·盖茨和唐纳德·特朗普都是赫赫有名的一流企业领袖。

· ·

22. miniscule [ˈmɪnəsˌkjul] *adj.* 极小的

23. fold [fold] *n.* ……倍

24. entrepreneurship [ˌɑntrəprəˈnɜˌʃɪp] *n.* 创新精神

25. brink [brɪŋk] *n.* (峭壁等的) 边缘；关头

26. complacency [kəmˈplesn̩sɪ] *n.* 自满；故步自封

27. bureaucracy [bjuˈrɑkrəsɪ] *n.* 官僚；形式主义

28. malaise [məˈlez] *n.* 抑郁；心神不定；不快

All That Jazz
TalkAsia Exclusive Interview with Diana Krall
CNN 专访爵士天后黛安娜·克瑞儿

Step 1 请浏览下方提示的关键问题后，仔细听录音。

1. Why has Diana started to write her own songs?
2. How does Diana feel about singing songs written by other people?
3. What does Diana think are the best things about playing jazz?
4. How does Diana feel about the future?

Step 2 如果你还听不太懂的话，请浏览下方的关键词汇后再听一次。

soulful 充满感情的；灵魂音乐的	vocalist 歌手
collaborator 合作伙伴	soar 翱翔；上扬
transcribe 誊写	genre （文艺作品的）类型

Step 3 试着回答下列听力测验题目。

True or False 是非题

_____ 1. Singing other people's songs give Diana a feeling of freedom.

_____ 2. Diana feels that singing pop songs is like being a character in a play.

_____ 3. Writing songs is something that comes easily all the time to Diana.

_____ 4. Diana sometimes feels like she's reading the other musicians' mind when they're playing.

_____ 5. Diana feels uncomfortable when she's talking about the future.

名人小档案

黛安娜·克瑞儿 (1964–) 4 岁开始学习钢琴，15 岁便已在爵士酒吧固定演出。1993 年发行首张专辑《独领风骚》(*Stepping Out*)，正式踏入爵士乐坛。曾赢得格莱美奖，2003 年与乐坛才子艾维斯·卡斯提洛结婚，并开始尝试词曲创作。

Multiple Choice　选择题

_____ 1. Why is Diana starting to compose her own songs?
   a. She met Elvis Presley.
   b. She wanted to be like Elvis Costello.
   c. She had never wanted to do it before.
   d. She met the right collaborator.

_____ 2. What Diana does when she writes songs?
   a. She writes something new every day.
   b. She doesn't have one way.
   c. She writes down things she hums.
   d. She tries to improvise all the time.

_____ 3. What does Diana not say draws her to jazz?
   a. It can be fun and funny.
   b. She doesn't know what will happen.
   c. There are no risks when you're playing.
   d. It can touch her emotionally.

Step 4 试着用较慢的速度，再仔细听一遍，并检查答案是否正确。

Step 5 核对答案、检验成果，并详读原文，若仍有不懂的地方，可反复多听几次。

(答案请见 p. 228)

Lorraine Hahn, TalkAsia

Hello, and welcome to *TalkAsia*, I'm Lorraine Hahn. My guest today is Diana Krall, a singer whose soulful[1] voice and musical interpretations[2] have made her one of the best-selling[3] jazz vocalists[4] in history. Born in Nanaimo, British Columbia, Diana was heavily influenced by her father's love of music from the 1920s and '30s. She started music lessons, learning to play the piano, at the age of four and never looked back. Her ten-year professional career has been full of awards, including several Grammys[5] and Junos.[6] And now she's turned songwriter with several original compositions[7] in her latest album, *The Girl in the Other Room*. Diana, thank you very much for speaking with us. Welcome to Hong Kong.

Diana Krall, Jazz Singer

Thank you.

Lorraine Hahn, TalkAsia

You, up until recently, have really been known as an interpreter of songs by other people, and I just mentioned you are now writing a lot of your own compositions. Why are you doing this?

Diana Krall, Jazz Singer

I met the right collaborator.[8]

Lorraine Hahn, TalkAsia

Being?

Diana Krall, Jazz Singer

Elvis Costello.

Lorraine Hahn, TalkAsia

Right. Your husband.

"亚洲名人聊天室"韩玉花

大家好，欢迎收看"亚洲名人聊天室"，我是韩玉花。今天的来宾是黛安娜·克瑞儿，这位歌手以她热情奔放的歌声与音乐诠释，成为史上作品最畅销的爵士歌手之一。黛安娜生于加拿大不列颠哥伦比亚省纳奈莫市，她深受父亲对 20 世纪二三十年代以来音乐推崇的影响。她 4 岁开始上音乐课学钢琴，从此在这个领域发展一路顺利。她过去 10 年来的专业生涯颇受奖项肯定，包括数座格莱美奖与朱诺音乐奖。现在，她转向歌曲创作，在最新的专辑《似曾相恋》里收录了几首她自己的原创歌曲。黛安娜，非常感谢你来参加节目，和我们谈话。欢迎来到香港。

爵士歌手 黛安娜·克瑞儿

谢谢。

"亚洲名人聊天室"韩玉花

直到最近，你一直都以诠释其他人的歌曲而著名，我刚刚也提到你现在开始创作歌曲。你为什么会想要这么做呢？

爵士歌手 黛安娜·克瑞儿

我遇到了有默契的搭档。

"亚洲名人聊天室"韩玉花

是哪一位？

爵士歌手 黛安娜·克瑞儿

艾维斯·卡斯提洛。（注 1）

"亚洲名人聊天室"韩玉花

是的。你先生。

注 1：英国全能型歌手，有"流行乐百科"之称。

Notes & Vocabulary

all that jazz 诸如此类的事

all that jazz 为起源于 20 世纪 30 年代的口语用法，意思等同于 all that sort of things、et cetera，表示"与前面所提到的性质相同的种种事物"。由于 jazz 有"爵士乐"之意，因此碰到与此类音乐相关的主题时，常会以 all that jazz 作为双关语。例如百老汇名剧《芝加哥》（*Chicago*）的开场曲即以此为题，既可指城"夜生活的点点滴滴"、也代表这样的生活"充满了爵士乐"。至于本篇标题选用 all that jazz，也是针对专访对象 Diana Krall 的爵士歌手身份所设计的文字游戏。

- This is not a class of "Advanced Literary Theories", so would you please spare me the talk of post-structuralism, postmodernism and all that jazz?
  这门课可不是"高级文学理论"，所以请别提什么后结构主义、后现代主义那一套好吗？

never look back 一帆风顺

look back 在此应解释为"发展受阻"或"退步"，因此 never look back 常用来强调某人在初尝成功滋味之后，"从此一帆风顺"。

- After her first taste of show business success, Debbie never looked back.
  黛比自从在演艺圈首试成功后，便一帆风顺。

....

1. soulful [ˈsolfəl] *adj.* 充满感情的；灵魂音乐的

2. interpretation [ɪnˌtɜprəˈteʃən] *n.* 诠释；解读（interpret 为动词；interpreter 为"解读者；口译人员"）

3. best-selling [ˈbɛstˈsɛlɪŋ] *adj.* 畅销的

4. vocalist [ˈvokəlɪst] *n.* 歌手

5. Grammy [ˈgræmɪ] *n.* 格莱美奖

6. Juno [ˈdʒuno] *n.* 朱诺奖（加拿大年度音乐大奖）

7. composition [ˌkɑmpəˈzɪʃən] *n.* 作曲；作文

8. collaborator [kəˈlæbəˌretə] *n.* 合作伙伴；搭档

Diana Krall, Jazz Singer

Mmm. My husband.

Lorraine Hahn, TalkAsia

Was it something that you always wanted to do but never really got a chance to do, or …

Diana Krall, Jazz Singer

Yes, because I think that I look at interpreting the music of the great American songwriters—George and Ira Gershwin, Cole Porter, Sammy Cahn, Jimmy Van Heusen—you know, like a character interpreting a great play. So, you have to believe in what you're singing about, but then you have the freedom to soar[9] and play.

Lorraine Hahn, TalkAsia

When you write, what is it? What is the process that goes through your mind? Is it just something that you wake up one day, and, you say, you hum[10] a tune, or, you know, or is it something you've … a story you've seen. What's the process?

Diana Krall, Jazz Singer

The process is varied.[11] It's the creative process, so some days it comes easily to you, and it's improvised and you turn on the tape recorder, and you can transcribe[12] what you improvised, and you [then] you work with that as a basis.

Lorraine Hahn, TalkAsia

Diana, why jazz? Why not pop? Why not R&B?[13] Why not, I don't know, some other kind of genre?[14]

爵士歌手 黛安娜·克瑞儿

嗯，我先生。

"亚洲名人聊天室" 韩玉花

这是你一直想做，但是没机会做的事，还是……

爵士歌手 黛安娜·克瑞儿

是的，因为我认为诠释美国伟大作曲家的音乐——包括格什温兄弟、柯尔·波特、萨米·卡恩以及吉米·胡森（注2）——就像是演员诠释一部伟大的剧作。因此，你必须相信你所演唱的歌曲，这样你才能够自由挥洒。

"亚洲名人聊天室" 韩玉花

你创作的时候是什么样子？你脑海中会经历什么样的过程？你是不是一早醒来，嘴里就哼着曲调，还是你先前看过的什么东西，例如你看过的故事。是什么样的一个过程？

爵士歌手 黛安娜·克瑞儿

不一定。这是一种创造的过程，所以有时候灵感会自然涌现，而成为即兴创作。这时候只要把录音机打开，就可以把即兴创作的成果誊写下来，然后再拿来当成创作的基础。

"亚洲名人聊天室" 韩玉花

黛安娜，为什么选择爵士乐？为什么不是流行歌曲？为什么不是节奏布鲁斯？为什么不是……该怎么说……总之就是其他类型的音乐？

注2：George and Ira Gershwin、Cole Porter、Sammy Cahn and Jimmy Van Heusen 均为美国著名词曲创作者。

Notes & Vocabulary

improvise 即兴演出；临时完成的

improvise 一词源自拉丁文，本意为 unforeseen（未预见的），在现代英语中则作动词使用，表示"在毫无事前准备下所做的（事）"。它可用来形容人在突发状况下，"临时做成"的事物，例如：I had to improvise a meal since my parents dropped by unexpectedly at lunchtime.（由于我爸妈在午餐时间突然来访，我不得不临时煮饭招待二老。）但若用在表演者身上，则是指"即兴演出"或"临场自由发挥"之意。

- At the song's climax, the trumpeter improvised a solo. 在这首曲子的高潮，小喇叭乐手即兴来了段独奏。

9. soar [sɔr] v. 翱翔；上扬

10. hum [hʌm] v. 哼（曲调）

11. varied [ˋvɛrɪd] adj. 差异极大的

12. transcribe [trænˋskraɪb] v. 誊写

13. R&B 节奏布鲁斯（为 rhythm & blues 的缩写）

14. genre [ˋʒɑnrə] n. （文艺作品的）类型；文类

Diana Krall, Jazz Singer

It's fun, and it's exciting, and there's lots of humor, and also it can be very moving as well. And we're all telepathic when we are improvising. You never know what's going to happen. You have to take those risks in jazz music. That's why I love it so much, because, when you are ... when it's right there, it's like, oh my God. And, it's a great experience to be playing this music.

Lorraine Hahn, TalkAsia

If I turn the clock back, rather, clock forward, where do you see yourself ...

Diana Krall, Jazz Singer

Don't turn it too far forward.

Lorraine Hahn, TalkAsia

All right, ten years How about ten years?

Diana Krall, Jazz Singer

I don't live in the future. I try to live in the moment. I try not to think about that because it freaks me out.[15] And I just hope that I'm healthy, and happy, and still inspired,[16] and that I can still play music if I want to ... and ...

Lorraine Hahn, TalkAsia

Very, very true. Diane, thank you so much.

Diana Krall, Jazz Singer

Thank you.

Lorraine Hahn, TalkAsia

And that is *TalkAsia* this week. I'm Lorraine Hahn. Let's talk again, next week.

爵士歌手 黛安娜·克瑞儿

爵士乐很有趣，令人兴奋，既可以充满幽默感，又可以非常动人。而且，我们即兴演奏的时候都有心电感应。你永远不会知道接下来会发生什么。在爵士乐里面充满了未知。这就是为什么我这么热爱爵士乐，因为在演奏的时候，就像是：天啊。弹奏这种音乐是一种很棒的体验。

"亚洲名人聊天室" 韩玉花

如果把时间向后推，或者应该说把时间调快，你认为自己会在哪里……

爵士歌手 黛安娜·克瑞儿

不要调得太多。

"亚洲名人聊天室" 韩玉花

好吧，10 年。10 年如何？

爵士歌手 黛安娜·克瑞儿

我不活在未来。我尽量活在当下。我尽量不想未来，因为未来总是让我觉得很可怕。我只希望我到时候会健康快乐，依然灵感充沛，而且如果我愿意的话，也还是能够弹奏音乐……

"亚洲名人聊天室" 韩玉花

说得真是太好了。黛安娜，非常感谢你。

爵士歌手 黛安娜·克瑞儿

谢谢你。

"亚洲名人聊天室" 韩玉花

以上就是本周的"亚洲名人聊天室"。我是韩玉花。下周我们再一起来聊天。

Notes & Vocabulary

telepathic 心电感应的

名词为 telepathy，其中 -pathy 为表示"感觉"的词根，例如 sympathy（怜悯心）、empathy（同情心）等。而 tele- 这个词首表示"远距离的"，如 telegram（电报）、telephone（电话）。因此 tele- 与 -pathy 这两部分合起来便表示"在远端就可以感觉得到"的意思，即中文所说的"心电感应"。

15. freak (sb) out [frik] [aut] 将……吓坏

16. inspired [ɪnˋspaɪrd] *adj.* 有灵感的

Business Re-Imagined
Management Guru Tom Peters Breaks the Global Enterprise Mold
重新想象——管理大师汤姆·彼得斯谈现代企业竞争力

Step 1 🔘 请浏览下方提示的关键问题后，仔细录音。

1. What changing circumstances in the world does Peters say has affected business?
2. Why does Peters say that change is necessary for business?
3. What does Peters think the crazy circumstances represent for businessmen?
4. What advice does Peters give to executives in this new business environment?

Step 2 🎧 如果你还听不太懂的话，请浏览下方的关键词汇后再听一次。

renewal 更新；重建；修补	radical 激进的；极端的
revolutionary 革命性的；大变革的	yield 产生（效果、收益等）
extrapolate 推断	shed 摆脱；去除

Step 3 💡 试着回答下列听力测验题目。

True or False 是非题

_____ 1. Peters says that companies talk about change more than they actually change.

_____ 2. Because the world has changed, Peters thinks businesses have to make significant changes.

_____ 3. Companies looking to change, Peters says, should look at drama and movies.

_____ 4. Peters says that only big companies have to change their strategies.

名人小档案

汤姆·彼得斯（1942-）是一位深具个人魅力、充满热情与爆发力的管理思想家，常在各管理大师排行榜中位列前五名。与 Robert Waterman 合著的《追求卓越》(*In Search of Excellence*) 被评选为 20 世纪最具影响力的 3 本管理书籍之一。

_____ 5. Peters feels that it is only necessary to focus on what is possible.

Multiple Choice 选择题

_____ 1. What does Peters not mention as contributing to the changing circumstances?

　　a. Changes in information technology.

　　b. Changes in the environment.

　　c. Changes in health and medicine.

　　d. The growth of China and India.

_____ 2. Why does Peters draw a distinction between "better" and "different"?

　　a. Improving what you're doing makes money.

　　b. The projects he's working on are radical.

　　c. Companies have to re-imagine themselves.

　　d. It yields dollars and cents.

_____ 3. What is Peter's final piece of advice for business leaders?

　　a. They should do what's cool.

　　b. They have to constantly change.

　　c. They have to do what makes money.

　　d. They have to extrapolate.

Step 4 试着用较慢的速度，再仔细听一遍，并检查答案是否正确。

Step 5 核对答案、检验成果，并详读原文，若仍有不懂的地方，可反复多听几次。

（答案请见 p.228）

CNN Anchor

For more than 20 years, companies have turned to[1] Tom Peters for his unique insight. In our new series, *Forward Thinking*, he recently sat down with CNN and explained why corporate success depends not just on renewal[2] but on re-imagining.

Tom Peters, Management Guru

The number one trouble with enterprises small or large is too much talk, too little do.

One lesson is that the circumstances[3] are altered[4] so much that only dramatic[5] solutions will work. Between the technology changes, life sciences, information technology changes, we have dramatic changes in the global landscape[6]—the three billion Indians, Chinese and so on. The way of doing enterprise in the world, because of external conditions, has got to change dramatically. Are the half-dozen projects that you're working on, are they on a scale of one to ten pretty radical[7] and pretty revolutionary?[8]

CNN 主播

20 多年来，企业纷纷找到汤姆·彼得斯以听取他独到的见解。在我们新推出的"前瞻思考"系列中，汤姆·彼得斯接受了本台专访，并说明了企业要想成功为何不能只靠革新，还得要靠重新想象。

管理大师 汤姆·彼得斯

任何企业无论大小面对的第一大问题就是光说不练。

教训之一是形势已经明显改变，唯有靠极端的解决办法才能奏效。随着科技的演变、生命科学和信息科技的变革，全球风貌也起了极大的变化。印度人和中国人加起来共有 30 亿人。由于外在环境的关系，如今要在世界上经营企业，就必须做出彻底的改变。贵公司正在进行中的 6 项计划，若用 1 分到 10 分的量表来评分的话，是否属于极端而具有革命性的计划？

Notes & Vocabulary

break the mold 打破窠臼；独一无二

此语可指"打破旧有的固定模式，破除常规，开创出新的方式或做法"或"独特；独一无二"。

- They broke the mold when they expanded their tiny startup into developing markets.
  他们打破了原有的模式，将创立时期的小企业扩展成为发展中的市场。
- They broke the mold when they made Elvis. There's never been a star to match him.
  猫王在全世界独一无二，恐怕从来没有另一位歌星能与其相比。

too much talk, too little do/action
光说不练；只说不做

意思相同的说法有 all talk, no action、talks a good game、all show and no go、all hat and no cattle、all bun and no beef 等。

on a scale of one to ten
由 **1** 到 **10** 的分数来评价

以 1 为最低，10 为满分的量表来计分，以表示程度的高低。可在打分数、作比较时使用。若以 100 分为满分则可说 on a scale of one to one hundred。

....

1. turn to 求助于；向……询问

2. renewal [rɪˋnuəl] n. 更新；重建；修补

3. circumstance [ˋsɜkm͵stæns] n. 事实；情况

4. alter [ˋɔltə] v. 改变；使变样

5. dramatic [drəˋmætɪk] adj. 戏剧性的；激烈的

6. landscape [ˋlænd͵skep] n. 景象

7. radical [ˋrædɪkəl] adj. 激进的；极端的

8. revolutionary [͵rɛvəˋluʃə͵nɛrɪ] adj.
   革命性的；变革性的；大变革的；完全创新的

And I drew a distinction between the word "better" and the word "different". Improving what we're doing today would certainly can yield[9] dollars and cents, or preparing ourselves for a completely different competitive environment.

You are not going to get from here to there running a 20-person or 20,000-person company just by extrapolating[10] from where you have been before. Somebody said to me, "Is this possible?" And I responded to him, "I don't know whether it's possible; I do know it's necessary."

I think this craziness in the world is a fabulous[11] opportunity. And the old structures which we're shedding[12] weren't a lot of fun.

The one piece of advice would be this re-imagined, constant renewal and, you know, look to do truly exciting stuff.

Is that cool, or what?

我认为"更好"和"不同"两者之间是有所区别的。改进我们目前的做事方式，肯定能赚更多钱，或是我们可以改造自己，准备迎接一个完全不同的竞争环境。

无论你经营的是一家 20 人的企业还是 2 万人的企业，你都不可能靠持续延用既有经验而达成目标。有人跟我说，"这有可能做到吗？"，我回答他："能不能做到我不知道，但我明白这么做绝对必要。"

我认为当今世界的疯狂形势，其实是绝佳的机会。而我们正摒弃的陈旧结构也并不值得留恋。

我的忠告是：要能重新想象，并经常更新，开始做一些真正令人兴奋的事吧！

这样够酷吧，不是吗？

Notes & Vocabulary

draw a distinction between A and B
在 A 与 B 间做出区分

将 A 与 B 划分开来，强调两者之间有所不同。也可以说 draw a comparison/line between A and B。

- The article draws a distinction between moderates and religious extremists.
  这篇文章区分出温和主义者和宗教激进分子间的差异。
- The law draws a line between peaceful demonstrations and civil unrest.
  此项法律界定出和平示威与暴乱行为两者之间的不同。

9. yield [jild] *v.* 产生（效果、收益等）

10. extrapolate [ɪkˋstræpəˌlet] *v.* 推断；根据已知推测

11. fabulous [ˋfæbjələs] *adj.* 难以置信的；非常棒的

12. shed [ʃɛd] *v.* 摆脱；去除

A Matter of Faith

Larry King Interviews *Purpose Driven Life* Author Rick Warren

拉里·金专访《标杆人生》作者里克·沃恩牧师

Step 1 请浏览下方提示的关键问题后，仔细听录音。

1. Why does Warren think his book has sold so many copies?
2. What does Warren say is more important than brilliance? Why?
3. What did Warren do when writing the book?
4. What does Warren say about having doubts?

Step 2 如果你还听不太懂的话，请浏览下方的关键词汇后再听一次。

pastor 牧师	surrender 投降
alleged 被指控的	verse （《圣经》的）节
brilliance 聪明	calamity 灾难

Step 3 试着回答下列听力测验题目。

True or False 是非题

_____ 1. Warren was surprised that the book has sold as well as it has.

_____ 2. Warren thinks there are many things in his book that no one has said before.

_____ 3. According to Warren, it doesn't matter how smart you are if you can't express things clearly.

_____ 4. Warren says he has great faith in the Bible, and he never doubts his faith.

_____ 5. Warren believes doubt can be a good thing, because it makes you question things.

名人小档案

里克·沃恩（1954-）为美国加州马鞍峰教会的创立牧师，所著的基督教心灵成长书籍《标杆人生》（*The Purpose Driven Life*）在美一经问世立即缔造销售佳绩，更曾创下在美国各大畅销书排行榜同时夺冠的惊人纪录，而此书也让里克成为全美最具影响力的牧师之一。

Multiple Choice 选择题

_____ 1. What does Warren say is the reason that his book has sold so many copies?

    a. It has many Bible verses in it.

    b. It helped resolve a hostage situation.

    c. People buy copies for their friends.

    d. It contains thousands of stories.

_____ 2. Which is not true about *The Purpose Driven Life*?

    a. It took seven months to write.

    b. Einstein helped write it.

    c. It tells old stories in new ways.

    d. The book is based on Christian beliefs.

_____ 3. What does Warren say about what most people do when it comes to belief?

    a. Doubt their doubts.

    b. Believe their beliefs.

    c. Doubt their beliefs.

    d. Believe their doubts.

Step 4 试着用较慢的速度，再仔细听一遍，并检查答案是否正确。

Step 5 核对答案、检验成果，并详读原文，若仍有不懂的地方，可反复多听几次。

（答案请见 p.228）

Larry King, CNN Host

Tonight, Atlanta hostage[1] hero Ashley Smith and *Purpose-Driven Life* author Pastor[2] Rick Warren. She read his book to the accused[3] courthouse[4] killer during a long night of terror.[5] The next morning he surrendered.[6] What role did the book play in that dramatic encounter between a troubled single man [mother] and an alleged[7] killer? Ashley Smith, Rick Warren together for the hour. We'll take your calls next on *Larry King Live*.

You sold 25 million books. How many more have sold since this?

Rick Warren, Author of "The Purpose Driven Life"

Oh, I don't know. You know, it's just a—somebody told me the other day that the book's kind of like Dr. Spock's baby book. It's just, it's a perennial. And it just keeps selling. It's in 56 languages now.

Larry King, CNN Host

So, you don't now have figures[8] since this occurred?

Rick Warren, Author of "The Purpose Driven Life"

I'm sure it's a lot.

Larry King, CNN Host

Let's go to calls. To Ft. Lauderdale, Florida. Hello.

Caller

Here is my question. Pastor Rick, did you anticipate[9] your book doing this?

CNN 主持人　拉里·金

今晚我们请到的是亚特兰大人质事件的英雄阿什莉·史密斯与《标杆人生》的作者里克牧师。在一个令人心惊胆战的漫漫长夜，阿什莉读里克牧师的书给一位因谋杀罪被告上法庭的人听，隔天早上他就自首了。在这场杀手与单亲妈妈戏剧性的相逢过程中，这本书究竟扮演了什么样的角色？在今天的"拉里·金直播现场"，阿什莉·史密斯与里克牧师要与我们共度 1 个小时，接下来我们会接听您的来电。

你的书卖了 2 500 万本，在这件事之后又卖了多少？

《标杆人生》作者　里克牧师

我不清楚。先前有人和我说这本书的销量有点像斯波克博士（注）的婴儿书一像，长居排行榜，销路一直很好。如今它已有 56 种语言的版本。

CNN 主持人　拉里·金

所以你并没有这件事之后的销售数据了？

《标杆人生》作者　里克牧师

我相信一定很可观。

CNN 主持人　拉里·金

我们来接听观众的电话。这一个来自佛罗里达州的劳德代尔堡，您好！

观众

我的问题是：里克牧师，你可曾预料到你的书会有这样的影响力？

注：Dr. Spock（1903–1998）是美国最著名的婴儿书作者。他在 1946 年出版的 *Baby and Child Care*，在美国长销数十年而不衰，也改变了美国人对幼儿养育的观念。

Notes & Vocabulary

perennial 畅销且长销的商品

perennial [pə`rɛniəl] 作形容词时具有"长期的、永久的"之意，若修饰植物时可解释为"多年生的；四季不断的"。作为名词时，则可指在排行榜上长年占据的事物（如歌曲、书籍、唱片等商品）。

以下为读者介绍几种相关说法：

- seasonal favorite 季节性热门商品
- sleeper 低开高走；爆出冷门
- a flash in the pan 昙花一现（通常暗示产品质量不佳）

....

1. hostage [`hɑstɪdʒ] *n.* 人质
2. pastor [`pæstə] *n.* 牧师
3. accused [ə`kjuzd] *n.* 被告
4. courthouse [`kɔrt͵haʊs] *n.* 法院
5. terror [`tɛrɚ] *n.* 惊骇；恐怖
6. surrender [sə`rɛndə] *v.* 投降
7. alleged [ə`lɛdʒd] *adj.* 遭指控的
8. figure [`fɪgjɚ] *n.* 数字
9. anticipate [æn`tɪsə͵pet] *v.* 预期

Rick Warren, Author of "The Purpose Driven Life"

You know, I don't really …

Larry King, CNN Host

Good question.

Rick Warren, Author of "The Purpose Driven Life"

I don't really think that my book has anything magical in it. It does have about 1,500 *Bible* verses[10] in it. And I have great faith in what the *Bible* says. And I have seen literally[11] tens of thousands of lives changed. This is a book that people give to their friends. They read it and then they go out and buy ten other copies.
That's the only way a book could sell as many copies as it has. So, I'm surprised that it sold so many. I'm not surprised about the changed lives. I've literally heard thousands of stories.

Larry King, CNN Host

If you are quoting *Bible* verses, what do you do different? What are you doing in this book that other books haven't done?

Rick Warren, Author of "The Purpose Driven Life"

You know, Larry, it's simple. Einstein once said, you can be brilliant, but if you can't express it in simple ways, your brilliance[12] isn't worth much. And actually I spent 12 hours a day for seven months writing that book. Pulled myself away. And if there was a 15-word sentence I'd try to make it in seven. I really just tried to make—there's not a single new thought in *The Purpose Driven Life* that hasn't been said over the last 2,000 years. Not one. I just happened to say it in a fresh way.

《标杆人生》作者 里克牧师

我并不……

CNN 主持人 拉里・金

问得好。

《标杆人生》作者 里克牧师

我并不觉得我的书本身有什么魔力，但书中的确有 1 500 多条《圣经》的经文，而我对《圣经》上的话有极大的信心。我的确曾见证过数万人的生命改变。这是一本人们会买来送给朋友的书。他们读完之后又会再去买 10 本送人。一定是因为这样，一本书才有可能卖这么好。所以说我会因为它卖得这么好而感到惊讶，但对于它能改变人的生命，我并不意外。类似的例子我确实听过好几千个。

CNN 主持人 拉里・金

如果你只是引述《圣经》经文，那你的做法有何特别之处？你这本书做到了哪些其他书没做到的事？

《标杆人生》作者 里克牧师

拉里，这说来很简单。爱因斯坦曾说过："或许你才智过人，但你若不能将自己的才智用简单浅显的方式表达，那么你再聪明也没什么用。"我在 7 个月的时间里，每天整整花了 12 小时写这本书。然后反过来重新看它的内容。如果一句话用了 15 个字，我就会试着用 7 个字来表达它。《标杆人生》全书没有一个观念是过去 2 000 年来从未有人讨论过的。连一个都没有。我只不过是用新的方式去表达它而已。

Notes & Vocabulary

pull away 脱离

pull away 指人的时候，意思是"抽离、脱离（某一状况或局面）"，另外可以指车子"向前移动"。

- After days of hard work, Rita finally pulled herself away from the project.
  辛苦多日后，丽塔终于能够脱离那个项目了。

- Justin got to the bus stop just in time to see the bus pull away.
  贾斯汀赶到公车站，刚好看到公车开走。

10. verse [vɜs] *n.* （《圣经》的）节；诗句；诗节

11. literally [ˈlɪtərəlɪ] *adv.* 事实上（强调用）

12. brilliance [ˈbrɪljəns] *n.* 聪明；才智过人

Larry King, CNN Host

Do you ever doubt your faith?

Rick Warren, Author of "The Purpose Driven Life"

Of course.

Larry King, CNN Host

Daily?

Rick Warren, Author of "The Purpose Driven Life"

No. But...

Larry King, CNN Host

When you see calamity?[13]

Rick Warren, Author of "The Purpose Driven Life"

Doubts **are meant to** be doubted. Beliefs are meant to be believed, doubts are meant to be doubted. What people do is they get it backwards. You should doubt your doubts and believe your beliefs. What people do is they believe their doubts. That's dumb.[14] So doubt is an OK thing. If it keeps you searching, if it keeps you moving, it's an OK thing.

Larry King, CNN Host

Thank you both very much.

Ashley Smith

Thank you.

Rick Warren, Author of "The Purpose Driven Life"

Thank you.

CNN 主持人 拉里·金
你可曾怀疑过自己的信仰？

《标杆人生》作者 里克牧师
当然。

CNN 主持人 拉里·金
每天都怀疑吗？

《标杆人生》作者 里克牧师
没有，但是……

CNN 主持人 拉里·金
当你目睹灾难发生的时候吗？

《标杆人生》作者 里克牧师
当怀疑的事就应怀疑。当相信的事就该相信，当怀疑的事就该怀疑。一般人的问题是把两者弄反了。你应该怀疑你所怀疑的、信你所信的。但人们却往往信其所疑，这是很笨的。有所怀疑并没什么不对，如果它促使你不断追寻、不停前进的话，它并没什么不对。

CNN 主持人 拉里·金
谢谢两位。

阿什莉·史密斯
谢谢。

《标杆人生》作者 里克牧师
谢谢。

Notes & Vocabulary

be meant to 注定

mean 当动词时，最常见的意思是"意指；表示……的意思"，文中则是指"指定；注定要……"，常用被动语态，用法为 be meant to V. / be meant for N.。当你的爱人跟你说 we are meant to be together 或 we are meant for each other 便是指"我们注定要在一起"或"我们是天生一对"。

· The costume was meant to look stylish, but really look sloppy and crude.
这服饰本来是要看上去很时尚的，事实上看起来却土里土气的。

· This sort of movie isn't meant for children.
这种电影不适合儿童。

13. **calamity** [kə`læmətɪ] *n.* 灾难
14. **dumb** [dʌm] *adj.* 愚蠢的

In His Blood

Harold McGraw Heads[1] Family Media Empire[2]

百年出版企业的经营之道——CNN 专访麦格劳·希尔 CEO

Step 1 🔘 请浏览下方提示的关键问题后，仔细听录音。

1. According to McGraw, what does a company need to be able to do to be relevant?
2. What does McGraw think is the most important thing in his workers?
3. What does McGraw look for when choosing supervisors?
4. What lessons did McGraw learn from studying acting?

Step 2 🔘 如果你还听不太懂的话，请浏览下方的关键词汇后再听一次。

pedigree 名门；出身	high-profile 备受瞩目的
preside 管辖；指挥	patriarchal 父系的
entitlement 应得的权利	nurture 养育

Step 3 💡 试着回答下列听力测验题目。

True or False 是非题

_____ 1. When McGraw took over the company, it had only been run by his family.

_____ 2. McGraw thinks that, in business, when people are comfortable it's a nice situation.

_____ 3. McGraw feels that helping the environment should be his whole job.

_____ 4. McGraw said that attitude can be learned, but skills can't be replaced.

_____ 5. Employees at McGraw-Hill were all happy with the changes McGraw made.

名人小档案

哈罗德·麦格劳三世（1948-）为麦格劳·希尔公司现任总裁兼 CEO。 麦格劳·希尔国际出版公司于 1888 年成立，在教育、出版、传播、财经与商业等领域享有盛名。*BusinessWeek*《商业周刊》和 *Aviation Week*《航空周刊》等均为该公司出版的杂志。

Multiple Choice 选择题

_____ 1. What did McGraw think his company needed to be relevant in the market?
  a. The ability to change.
  b. A certain entitlement.
  c. Jobs for life.
  d. A new type of umbrella.

_____ 2. What does McGraw say are important qualities in his key employees?
  a. They are willing to travel.
  b. They have the right skills.
  c. They exercise and stay healthy.
  d. They have passion about things.

_____ 3. What does McGraw not say is an important thing in business?
  a. The ability to change.
  b. Developing talent.
  c. Being passionate.
  d. Being entitled.

Step 4 试着用较慢的速度，再仔细听一遍，并检查答案是否正确。

Step 5 核对答案、检验成果，并详读原文，若仍有不懂的地方，可反复多听几次。

（答案请见 p.228）

Todd Benjamin, *The Boardroom*

They say business is in the blood, and what a pedigree.[3] Founded in 1888, The McGraw-Hill Companies are made up of high-profile[4] brands like *BusinessWeek* and Standard & Poor's.

It's a leader in educational publishing and owns television stations. Presiding[5] over it all: Harold McGraw III.

One of the challenges you had coming in was that back in 1993 when you were made president, you had a company that was very patriarchal.[6] It had been a family-run business. It was a type of culture that was jobs for life, and you had to change that culture. How did you do that?

Harold McGraw III, McGraw-Hill

It is never a nice situation when people are very comfortable and think that, you know, there's a certain umbrella[7] and there's a certain entitlement.[8] If you're going to be relevant[9] in the market place, and that is very very important. If you really are serious about the impacts you're going to make, then you've got to be able to make the changes, and internally,[10] you know, that's what we did.

"董事会"托德·本杰明

有人说经商是一种天赋，是某种家族渊源。成立于 1888 年的麦格劳·希尔公司是由包括《商业周刊》和标准普尔这类高知名度的品牌所组成的公司。该公司是教育出版界的领导者，还拥有电视台。执掌这一切的人则是哈罗德·麦格劳三世。

您在接掌公司时所面临的挑战之一是，当您在 1993 年被任命为公司总裁时，贵公司是个非常家族化的企业。它在过去一直是个家族企业，是那种奉行终身雇用企业文化的公司，而您必须去改变这样的文化。您是如何做到的？

麦格劳·希尔公司 哈罗德·麦格劳三世

当人们觉得很自在，认为有某种保障存在，并理所应当得到某些东西的时候，这绝非是一种好的状态。如果你要在市场上发挥影响力，而这点又非常非常重要，如果你真的很在乎自己能发挥怎样的影响力，那么你就必须做出改变，而这就是我们在公司内部做的事。

Notes & Vocabulary

in one's blood　与生俱来；家传的

blood 是 "血；血液；血脉"，in one's blood 字面意思是 "在某人血液之中"，引申为 "某人与生俱来的能力" 或是 "某人家传得来的"。

- Sports are in Jenny's blood.
  运动的天赋对珍妮来说是与生俱来的。

the challenges you had coming in
一开始出现的难题或挑战

这句话中的 coming in 等于 from the beginning。

coming 的惯用句型有：

a. have it coming 应得的报应
- Most people thought the businessman had it coming when he was convicted of fraud.
  当那个企业家因诈欺被定罪时，大部分的人都认为他是罪有应得。

b. see it coming 预测某事来临
- When Julia was fired, she never saw it coming.
  朱莉娅一点也没有预计到她会被开除。

1. head [hɛd] v. 率领；站在……的前头

2. empire [ˈɛmˌpaɪr] n. 帝国；大企业

3. pedigree [ˈpɛdəˌgri] n. 名门；出身

4. high-profile [ˈhaɪˈproˌfaɪl] adj. 备受瞩目的；高姿态的

5. preside [prɪˈzaɪd] v. 管辖；指挥

6. patriarchal [ˌpetriˈɑrkəl] adj. 父系的；族长制的

7. umbrella [ʌmˈbrɛlə] n. 保护伞；庇护

8. entitlement [ɪnˈtaɪtlmənt] n. 应得的权利

9. relevant [ˈrɛləvənt] adj. 有关的；切题的

10. internally [ɪnˈtɜnəlɪ] adv. 内部地；内在地

Talent is the most important thing that you've got—how you nurture[11] it, how you develop your talent, how you career path your talent, how you look at challenges and all of those kind of things is really important. People matter,[12] and therefore, you know, your whole job really needs to be focused on the environment in which people work and the people that are actually doing the work.

Todd Benjamin, The Boardroom

And when you look for certain qualities in your key lieutenants,[13] what are you looking for?

Harold McGraw III, McGraw-Hill

The first thing that I look for in any individual[14] is passion. You know: hey, you got energy? Are you alive and well? You know, do you get excited about things? Do you, you know, is life worth it and all those kind of things? And if you are, hey, we can go a lot of places with that. Skill sets you can learn; attitude you can't.

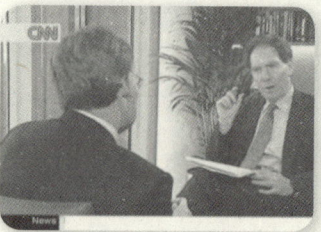

天赋是你能拥有的最重要的一件事，你要如何去培育它，如何开发你的天赋，如何为你的天赋规划出职业生涯，你如何看待挑战，这一切都很重要。重要的是人，因此你必须把工作重点放在人们的工作环境上，以及实际在从事那些工作的人身上。

"董事会" 托德·本杰明

您在看待您的重要高层员工时会特别注意哪些特质？

麦格劳·希尔公司 哈罗德·麦格劳三世

我在看一个人的时候最先想看到的是热情。你知道的，你有没有精神？你还活力四射吗？你会对事情感到兴奋吗？你的生命是否活得有价值这一类的事。如果你是这样的一个人，我们就能成就很多事。你可以学会做事的技巧，但态度是学不来的。

Notes & Vocabulary

career path 职业轨迹

career path 原为名词，指"职业轨迹"，文中改变词性作动词用，是特例的用法。

· At age 50, Bonnie began a new career path as a writer.
邦尼在 50 岁时转换新的职业轨迹成了作家。

· ·

11. **nurture** [ˈnɜtʃə] *v.* 养育；供给养分

12. **matter** [ˈmætə] *v.* 有关系；要紧

13. **lieutenant** [luˈtɛnənt] *n.* 副官员；助理官员

14. **individual** [ˌɪndəˈvɪdʒwəl] *n.* 个人；个体

Todd Benjamin, The Boardroom

So, did you always know that you would end up[15] in business?

Harold McGraw III, McGraw-Hill

I think so, yeah. You know, back at one point there was no question that I wanted to be an actor, and I wanted to, you know, think about the theater and all of that. I really love it. And I had a great professor and, you know, [he would] sit me down and say, "Do you know how competitive it is, you know, to achieve all of these goals and everything? You know, you should really think, also, of the business world. It needs a lot of actors."

"董事会" 托德·本杰明

所以你一直都知道你最终会从商？

麦格劳·希尔公司 哈罗德·麦格劳三世

我想是的。你知道吗，我曾经一度很确定自己想当一名演员，一心想着剧院这一类的事。我真的很爱演戏。过去我有一位很棒的教授郑重地跟我说："你知道戏剧这个行业的竞争有多激烈、达到这些目标有多难吗？你应该好好想想从商这件事，商业界一样需要许多演员。"

Notes & Vocabulary

back at one point　曾经一度

point 是 "点；特定的时刻" 的意思。

• Back at one point, Jeff never imagined himself married with children.
曾经一度，杰夫从未想象过自己会结婚生子。

其他与 point 连用的短语：

a. the point of no return　无法回头的地步
• When the defector requested political asylum, he had passed the point of no return.
当叛逃者寻求政治庇护时，就无法回头了。

b. at the point of sth　某事即将发生的时刻
• Lily was at the point of quitting her job.
莉莉当时几乎快要提出辞呈了。

sit sb down　郑重告诉某人

sit sb down 可直接照字面解释为 "要某人坐下"，目的是要当事人专注聆听某件重要的事情，所以也表示 "郑重告诉某人" 的意思。

• The boss sat Mike down and told him that he better improve the quality of his work.
老板郑重地告诫迈克让他改进工作表现。

....

15. **end up** 结束

Lord of Luxury[1]
Tom Ford Left Gucci to Forge[2] His Own Fashion Empire
找回真正的奢华——CNN 专访时尚名家汤姆·福特

Step 1 请浏览下方提示的关键问题后，仔细听录音。

1. What does Ford say he learned from working at Gucci?
2. What is the "Tom and Dom Show"?
3. What does Ford want his new line of menswear to be like?
4. What does Ford say has happened to luxury brands in recent years?

Step 2 如果你还听不太懂的话，请浏览下方的关键词汇后再听一次。

forge 打造；锻炼	resurrect 使复活
drape 使（布、衣服等）呈褶皱状	atelier 艺术家或设计师的工作室
prelude 前奏；序幕	duo 二人组
dry 乏味的；无趣的	cross 混合物

Step 3 试着回答下列听力测验题目。

True or False 是非题

_____ 1. Ford says that he can make clothes with his own hands very well.

_____ 2. When Ford left Gucci, it was almost in bankruptcy.

_____ 3. At his new store, Ford is working with Savile Row tailors.

_____ 4. Ford thinks that real luxury brands don't really exist now.

_____ 5. Ford thinks that true luxury isn't something that is available to everyone.

名人小档案

汤姆·福特（1962–）曾任古琦（Gucci）设计总监，其一系列的新款设计使几乎面临破产的古琦总价值累积到 43 亿美元。1999 年兼任伊芙圣罗兰（Yves Saint-Laurent , YSL）创意总监。2004 年离开古琦与伊芙圣罗兰，开始创造自己的品牌王国。

Multiple Choice　选择题

_____ 1. How long did Ford work at Gucci?
a. A year.
b. Four years.
c. D decade.
d. Fifteen years.

_____ 2. What did Ford think about getting suits made in Savile Row?
a. It was a great experience.
b. It was not very interesting.
c. He was too old to wear them.
d. It was very trendy.

_____ 3. What happened to luxury brand in the nineties?
a. They became more expensive.
b. They stopped being the best.
c. They became available to everyone.
d. They became less trendy.

Step 4 试着用较慢的速度，再仔细听一遍，并检查答案是否正确。

Step 5 核对答案、检验成果，并详读原文，若仍有不懂的地方，可反复多听几次。

（答案请见 p.228）

Monita Rajpal, Art of Life

Hello, I'm Monita Rajpal. Welcome to this special edition of *Art of Life*, our entire program dedicated to the fashion designer Tom Ford. Here on Madison Avenue, his new store, housing[3] the Tom Ford menswear line, his first fashion offering since leaving Gucci and Yves Saint-Laurent in 2004.

A decade as the Gucci Group's creative director, he became the brand—confident, sensual,[4] desirable[5]—qualities reflected in the clothes he designed. But failed negotiations[6] with the parent company, PPR, meant he had to leave the house he resurrected.[7] Shortly afterwards, his swan song from Yves Saint-Laurent, his days with the Gucci Group officially over.

Tom Ford, Fashion Designer

I grew so much in the 15 years I was at Gucci. Working at Saint-Laurent was also something. I learned an enormous amount about how to construct[8] women's clothes. It was very different from my experience at Gucci. I always knew how to make clothes. I knew how to cut and drape[9] and sew myself—not very well, but I could certainly do it. But I learned a lot from Saint-Laurent and from my four years working with those wonderful ateliers[10] where people really do still make things by hand. And I learned a lot because of the fact that the whole thing fell apart, and I was no longer going to be happy in the company and I decided to leave. So, as I said to you earlier, it really might have been the prelude[11] and prepared me for what will now be my own company—Tom Ford.

"生活艺术" 莫妮塔·拉吉波

大家好，我是莫妮塔·拉吉波。欢迎收看这期"生活艺术"的特别节目。今天是时装设计师汤姆·福特的专辑。在麦迪逊大道上，他新开的门店里摆着汤姆·福特的男装系列，这是他在 2004 年离开古琦与伊芙圣罗兰之后，首次推出的时装作品。

福特担任古琦集团的创意总监长达 10 年之久，早已与这个品牌合而为一。自信、性感、魅力——这些特质都反映在他设计的服装里。不过，由于和总公司巴黎春天集团（注）交涉失败，福特因此不得不离开他一手挽救的品牌。过后不久，他在伊芙圣罗兰推出最后一批精彩作品之后，与古琦集团的合作就正式结束了。

时装设计师 汤姆·福特

我在古琦的 15 年间成长了非常多。在伊芙圣罗兰工作也很有收获。我在女性服饰制作方面学到了很多，和我在古琦的经验非常不同。我向来都懂得该怎么制作服装。我自己就会剪裁、做出缀褶，也会缝纫——不是很精通，可是确实懂得这些技术。不过，我在圣罗兰学了很多，而且和那些真正纯手工制作服装的优秀工作室合作了 4 年，这也让我获益良多。然而，因为这一切开始破碎，我在这个公司不再快乐，所以决定离开，这段过程也同样让我学到了很多事情。所以，就像我先前说的，这段经验确实可能是我人生中的序曲，让我做好准备，以便经营我自有品牌的公司——汤姆·福特。

注：PPR 是一家法国的跨国控股公司（multinational holding company），专门经营奢侈品牌和高档卖场零售业。

Notes & Vocabulary

swan song 最后的作品

swan song 一词来自古老的神话，原指"疣鼻天鹅"（Cygnus olor），即"哑天鹅"（mute swan）。这种天鹅终其一生静默无声，只有在临死前发出令人悲痛的美妙旋律。后来引申为最终戏剧性或是夸张性的表现，或是最后完成的作品。

- Tonight's performance was the aging dancer's swan song.
  今晚这场表演是那位青春渐逝的舞者最后的绚烂的演出。

fall apart 分崩；瓦解

fall apart 原指"瓦解；崩溃"，另有抽象的含意，比喻"关系结束"或"计划失败"等，例如文中表示汤姆·福特与古琦的合作关系已不可收拾。

- Plans for Jan's outdoor wedding fell apart when the weather turned foul.
  为珍的户外婚礼所准备的所有计划因为天气变坏全泡汤了。

- The paper lantern fell apart in the rain.
  纸灯笼在雨中泡烂了。

....

1. luxury [ˈlʌkʒrɪ] n. 奢侈；奢华；奢侈品
2. forge [fɔrdʒ] v. 打造；锻炼
3. house [haʊz] v. 储放；收留
4. sensual [ˈsɛnʃwəl] adj. 性感的；感官的
5. desirable [dɪˈzaɪrəbəl] adj. 富有魅力的；令人愉悦的
6. negotiation [nɪˌgoʃɪˈeʃən] n. 谈判；协商
7. resurrect [ˌrɛzəˈrɛkt] v. 使复活；使复兴
8. construct [kənˈstrʌkt] v. 制造；构成
9. drape [drep] v. 使（布、衣服等）呈褶皱状
10. atelier [ˌætlˈje] n. （法）艺术家或设计师的工作室
11. prelude [ˈprɛljud] n. 前奏；序幕

Monita Rajpal, Art of Life

I do love this.

Tom Ford, Fashion Designer

I love this suit as well.

Monita Rajpal, Art of Life

And with his own company, the return of the dynamic[12] duo,[13] or the "Tom and Dom Show", as it was known in fashion circles. Back in the days of Gucci, Vice Chairman Tom Ford and Chairman Domenico De Sole enjoyed a close working relationship, taking Gucci from near bankruptcy[14] to a $10 billion empire. Their current partnership, the Tom Ford menswear line.

Tom Ford, Fashion Designer

A lot of fashion brands are very trendy.[15] I was a little bit younger when I was first at Gucci, and I think I did quite a few collections that pushed fashion, men's fashion, in a certain direction. But I was a little too old to wear those things. The quality from a lot of our competitors wasn't up to my standard, so then I started having all of my clothes made in London where I live part of the time, on Savile Row, and that was a very dry[16] experience. There was really the need for something that I don't think ever existed for men before, which is a cross[17] between a Savile Row tailor and a fashion company.

Monita Rajpal, Art of Life

So how then would you define a luxury brand in this day and age?

"生活艺术" 莫妮塔·拉吉波

我很喜欢这个。

时装设计师 汤姆·福特

我也很喜欢这件套装。

"生活艺术" 莫妮塔·拉吉波

成立了他自己的公司之后，充满活力的双人搭档也随之重现江湖。这就是时装界众所周知的"汤姆与多姆"。在古琦的那段日子里，副董事长汤姆·福特与董事长多明尼科·德·索尔合作得非常愉快，把古琦从破产边缘重振为百亿美元的时装帝国。他们现在合作的成果，就是汤姆·福特男装系列。

时装设计师 汤姆·福特

现在许多时装品牌都很时髦。我在古琦的时候比较年轻，我想我当时设计的许多系列确实把时装——男性时装——的潮流推往特定方向。不过，我穿那种衣服未免有些老了一点。我们很多竞争者的产品品质都达不到我的标准，所以我就开始在伦敦制作所有的衣服，我有时候会在那儿的萨维尔街住一阵子，那是种非常枯燥的经历。我认为男装确实有必要出现前所未有的东西，也就是萨维尔街的裁缝师与时装公司合作激发出来的产品。

"生活艺术" 莫妮塔·拉吉波

你会怎么定义当今这个时代的奢侈品牌？

Notes & Vocabulary

up to one's/the standard 达到标准

standard 是指"标准；水准"，up to 则是指"一直到某个程度"，这个短语就表示"达到要求、水准"。

- The toy was not up to the standard of current safety regulations.
  这个玩具不符合当前的安全标准。

其他与 standard 连用的短语：

a. meet the/a standard 达到标准
  - Mandy's new boyfriend doesn't meet the tough standard set by her father.
    曼迪的新男友无法达到她父亲设下的严格标准。

b. by one's standards 依照某人标准
  - By Trevor's standards, the new James Bond movie is the best of the series.
    以特雷费的标准来看，新的邦德电影是该系列中最好的。

....

12. dynamic [daɪˋnæmɪk] *adj.* 有活力的；动态的

13. duo [ˋduo] *n.* 二人组

14. bankruptcy [ˋbæŋkˌrʌpsɪ] *n.* 破产

15. trendy [ˋtrɛndɪ] *adj.* 时髦的；流行的

16. dry [draɪ] *adj.* 乏味的；无趣的

17. cross [krɔs] *n.* 混合物

Tom Ford, Fashion Designer

I think that most brands today that are called luxury brands are not really true luxury brands. In the nineties, and I have to say we were partially[18] responsible for this trend at Gucci, we made luxury quite accessible.[19] And the globalization[20] of fashion and of luxury in the nineties—because of the globalization of everything, you know you now find the same luxury brands in every city, the stores look the same, it's all the same, the product is the same. What I'm trying to do now at this stage in my life and at this stage in my business is bring back the notion[21] of true luxury, which is really creating the very best thing you can possibly have.

时装设计师 汤姆·福特

我认为今天大多数称为奢侈品牌的牌子都不算真的奢侈。在 90 年代，我们把奢侈变成大家都可以得到的东西。我必须说，我们对古琦的这种潮流确实要负部分责任。由于时装与奢华在 90 年代的全球化——由于一切事物的全球化，所以你知道你现在到每个城市都找得到同样的奢侈品牌，每家商店看起来都一样，什么都一样，产品也一样。在我的人生与事业的当前阶段，所要做的就是重新找回真正的奢华概念，也就是竭尽全力，真正创造出你可能拥有的最好的东西。

Notes & Vocabulary

at this stage 在此阶段；如今

stage 在这里当作"时期；阶段"的意思，文中 at this stage in my life 表示"在我生命的这个阶段"，in 也可用 of。

• At this stage of her life, Nancy had hoped to be married with children.
南希希望自己活到这个年纪时早已结婚生子了。

其他与 stage 连用的短语有：

a. stage by stage 逐步地；逐渐地
• Stage by stage, the new house took shape.
这栋新房子逐渐地成形了。

b. take center stage 吸引注意；成为焦点
• Mandy loves to take center stage in any project she is working on.
曼迪总是喜欢主导每个企划案。

18. **partially** [ˈpɑrʃəlɪ] *adv.* 部分地

19. **accessible** [ɛkˈsɛsəbəl] *adj.* 可得到的

20. **globalization** [ˌglobələˈzeʃən] *n.* 全球化

21. **notion** [ˈnoʃən] *n.* 概念；想法

The Liberation[1] of Paris

Exclusive *Larry King Live* Interview with the Jailbird[2] Heiress[3]

CNN 专访媒体焦点帕丽斯

Step 1 请浏览下方提示的关键问题后，仔细听录音。

1. Why was Paris sent home from jail?
2. What does Paris say is the biggest misconception people have about her?
3. Why does Paris think people don't see the other side of her?
4. What does Paris think she can do with her position in the spotlight?

Step 2 如果你还听不太懂的话，请浏览下方的关键词汇后再听一次。

jailbird 囚犯	heiress 女继承人
claustrophobia 幽闭恐惧症	infraction 违法
misconception 误解	submit 提交
superficial 肤浅的	multiple sclerosis 多发性硬化症

Step 3 试着回答下列听力测验题目。

True or False 是非题

_____ 1. Paris feels that going out and talking to people is part of her business.

_____ 2. Most people arrested for the same charge as Paris don't stay in jail for their full term.

_____ 3. Most people didn't think that Paris had been treated fairly by the legal system.

_____ 4. Paris thinks she is famous because everyone knows her family.

名人小档案

帕丽斯·希尔顿（1981–）是希尔顿饭店集团大亨的长女，为该集团的继承人之一。曾代言不少知名品牌、推出过唱片及自传、在电影中客串演出，并参与演出电视真人秀。她曾因酒后驾车被捕，及无照驾驶被判入监服刑 23 天，为名人界的话题女王。

_____ 5. Paris has helped with charities before, and raised money for cancer research.

Multiple Choice　选择题

_____ 1. Why was Paris released from jail?
   a. She was having emotional problems.
   b. She served her full term.
   c. She had to give an interview.
   d. She had to go to the hospital.

_____ 2. For which industry has Paris not created products for?
   a. The fashion industry.
   b. The music industry.
   c. The film industry.
   d. The perfume industry.

_____ 3. While in jail, what new things did Paris think about doing with her life?
   a. Write a book.
   b. Raise awareness of serious issues.
   c. Get involved in politics.
   d. Do more interviews.

Step 4 试着用较慢的速度，再仔细听一遍，并检查答案是否正确。

Step 5 核对答案、检验成果，并详读原文，若仍有不懂的地方，可反复多听几次。

（答案请见 p.228）

Larry King, Host

We're happy to welcome Paris Hilton to *Larry King Live*. Good to have her with us. Her parents have been with us. This is her first appearance on this show. Why are you doing this interview?

Paris Hilton, Socialite

I consider you an icon and I really respect you and it's an honor for me to be here today.

Larry King, Host

Well, we're happy to hear that but …

Paris Hilton, Socialite

Thank you.

Larry King, Host

… mainly, though, why do any interview? Why come out and talk?

Paris Hilton, Socialite

I just want to let people know what I went through.

Larry King, Host

The other day, Sheriff[4] Baca—in fact, yesterday— testified[5] before the L.A. City Council[6] when he released you from, he released you because you had an illness that he was very concerned about, and everyone was wondering what that was. What was it?

主持人 拉里·金

我们很高兴地欢迎帕丽斯·希尔顿来到"拉里·金直播现场"。她的父母亲也来上过我们的节目。这是她第一次参加本节目。你为什么要进行这次访谈呢？

社交名人 帕丽斯·希尔顿

我把你当偶像看待，我真的很尊敬你，今天能来这里是我的荣幸。

主持人 拉里·金

这样啊，我们很高兴听你这么说，可是……

社交名人 帕丽斯·希尔顿

谢谢你。

主持人 拉里·金

……可是，为什么要接受访问呢？为何要站出来讲话呢？

社交名人 帕丽斯·希尔顿

我只是想让大家知道我经历的事。

主持人 拉里·金

那天，巴卡长官——其实就是昨天——他因释放你而需要在洛杉矶市议会作证，因为他非常担心你的病情，大家都想知道是什么病。是什么病呢？

Notes & Vocabulary

go through 经历

短语动词 go through 有好几种意思，文中是指"经历"，尤指"某种不愉快或难的情况"。

go through 还有下列几种意思：

a. 指"检验；细查"
  - Tom went through the pictures looking for something to use on his Web site.
    汤姆仔细看察这些照片，找寻可用在网站上的。

b. 指"（议案）通过；（交易）完成"
  - The proposal to turn the old school building into a library went through.
    将旧的学校大楼改造成图书馆的提案通过了。

c. go through with sth 表示"履行某项承诺"。
  - Angie said she would go skydiving with us, but in the end, she couldn't go through with it.
    安吉说她要跟我们去跳伞，但最后，她无法做到。

1. liberation [ˌlɪbəˈreʃən] n. 释放；解放

2. jailbird [ˈdʒel.bɜd] n. 囚犯（尤指"惯犯"）

3. heiress [ˈɛrəs] n. 女继承人

4. sheriff [ˈʃɛrəf] n.（美）司法长官

5. testify [ˈtɛstə.faɪ] v. 作证；证实

6. council [ˈkaʊnsəl] n. 地方议会

Paris Hilton, Socialite

Well, I suffer[ed] from claustrophobia[7] my entire life, and when I first got in that cell,[8] I was having severe panic attacks, anxiety attacks, my claustrophobia was kicking in. I wasn't sleeping. I wasn't eating. It was—the doctors talked to the Sheriff and he could see that it would be better that if I just did it on house arrest.[9]

Plus, I had already served[10] more than—most people on that kind of infraction[11] will only serve 10 percent of their stay, and I had already done more than that. So he just thought it would be better for everyone for me just to be at home.

Larry King, Host

If perception[12] is reality, the perception of you was party girl, right? You're saying that's not true? What part of it was true?

Paris Hilton, Socialite

You know I am a social person. I love to dance. I love to go out. I love music. But a lot of people don't know that I'm a businesswoman and I run several businesses, and I like to go out, as well. I'm social.

Larry King, Host

Which leads to the e-mail question from Celia in Miramar, Florida. "What's the biggest misconception[13] about you?"

社交名人 帕丽斯·希尔顿

我一辈子都有幽闭恐惧症，我刚进牢房的时候，恐慌感和焦虑感袭上心头，我的幽闭恐惧症又犯了。我睡不着，吃不下。医生和警长谈过之后，警长便明白我在家拘禁会比较好。

况且我服刑的时间已经比——大部分触犯那类法律的人只会服 1/10 的刑期，我已经服了超过 10% 的刑期了。所以他觉得让我待在家里，对我和对大家都比较好。

主持人 拉里·金

如果所知即真实，大家对你的认知是个爱交际的女孩，对吧？你说那不是真的？那么哪一部分才是真的呢？

社交名人 帕丽斯·希尔顿

你知道我是个好交际的人。我爱跳舞，我爱玩，我爱音乐。但是很多人不知道我是个生意人，我经营了好几个企业，而我也喜欢外出、喜欢交际。

主持人 拉里·金

现在佛罗里达州米拉玛尔的西莉亚通过电子邮件问了这个问题："你认为大家对你误解最深的地方是什么？"

Notes & Vocabulary

panic/anxiety attacks 恐慌症发作

panic 是"惊恐；惊慌"的意思，panic attack 就是突然间遭受惊恐感觉的冲击，使得患者身心无法承担。"恐慌症发作"主要是由极度的焦虑（anxiety）与恐惧造成的，尤其容易发生在患有各种"恐惧症"（phobia）的病人身上。发作时的症状可能会有：发抖（trembling）、呼吸急促（shortness of breath）、盗汗（sweating）、心悸（heart palpitation）、晕眩（dizziness）、胸闷（chest tightness）、恶心（nausea）等。

kick in 发生效用；产生作用

动词 kick 是"踢"的意思，kick in 解释为"开始发生作用"，常常特指药效或是某种心理状态开始起作用；kick in 另外有"出钱；捐助"的意思。

- Alex's fear of heights kicked in when the helicopter took off.
  亚历克斯的恐高症在直升机起飞时开始发作。
- Mary kicked in for dinner.
  晚餐钱玛丽也出了一份。

----

7. claustrophobia [ˌklɔstrə`fobiə] *n.* 幽闭恐惧症

8. cell [sɛl] *n.* 牢房；囚房

9. arrest [ə`rɛst] *n.* 拘留；逮捕

10. serve [sɜv] *v.* 服刑

11. infraction [ɪn`frækʃən] *n.* 违背；违法

12. perception [pə`sɛpʃən] *n.* 认识；观念；看法

13. misconception [ˌmɪskən`sɛpʃən] *n.* 误解

Paris Hilton, Socialite

Well, a misconception that I always hear is, "Paris doesn't work for a living. She just, you know, gets money from her family." And I completely disagree with that. I've made a name on my own, by myself. I've not taken any money from my family. I work very hard. I run a business. I've had a book on the *New York Times* best sellers[14] list. I'm on my fifth season of a TV show. I've done an album, do movies …

Larry King, Host

OK, how did you like that …

Paris Hilton, Socialite

… clothing line.

Larry King, Host

Is it all their fault or how did you let that happen?

Paris Hilton, Socialite

I think as people just focus on the party part, and my business and what I do is at my office and in my meetings, and that's not really made public, because I'm, you know, in the boardroom talking with everyone who works with me. So people just don't know about it.

Larry King, Host

We have a quick vote on our Web site, cnn.com/LarryKing, asking: Did the legal system treat Paris Hilton fairly? And the last check—and they're still voting—63 percent said yes. They thought you were treated fairly.

社交名人 帕丽斯·希尔顿

我最常听到的对我的误解是："帕丽斯不用工作，她伸手向家里要钱就可以了。"我完全不同意这点。我靠自己的力量闯出了知名度，我没有从我家人那儿拿过一毛钱。我很努力地工作。我经营企业。我曾经出过一本名列《纽约时报》畅销书排行榜的书。我的一档电视节目即将进入第 5 季拍摄。我出过一张唱片，拍过电影……

主持人 拉里·金

好的，你对此的看法是……

社交名人 帕丽斯·希尔顿

……开发专属服饰品牌。

主持人 拉里·金

这一切都是他们的错？或者是你自己让它发生的？

社交名人 帕丽斯·希尔顿

我想大家都只把焦点放在聚会那部分，我的企业和我真正在做的，都在我的办公室里和我参与的会议中，那些都没有对外公开，因为我都是在董事会里，和跟我共事的员工谈话。大家只是不知道这部分罢了。

主持人 拉里·金

我们网站进行了一次即时投票，网址是 cnn.com/LarryKing，题目是：司法制度对帕丽斯·希尔顿的处置公平吗？最新投票结果——大家还在投票—— 63％的人认为公平。他们认为你得到的处置是公平的。

Notes & Vocabulary

make a name (for sb) 成名；出名

name 在这里指的是"名声；名气"，make a name for sb 则解释为"某人因此而成名"。

• Jim made a name for himself in show business.
  吉姆在娱乐界闯出了名号。

....

14. best seller 畅销作品

We also have an I-Ask question, submitted[15] by a self-described fan of Paris. Let's take a look and listen, and then get Paris' answer. Watch.

Paris Hilton Fan

I was just wondering what you're planning to do to help others since you were released from jail. And I was also wondering what message you'd like to send out to other people who might make the decision to drink and drive?

Paris Hilton, Socialite

That's something I was actually thinking a lot about in jail, because I feel like, you know, being in the spotlight,[16] I have a platform[17] where I can raise awareness[18] for so many great causes[19] and just do it so much with this, instead of, you know, superficial[20] things like going out. I want to help raise money for kids and for breast cancer, multiple sclerosis[21] and ...

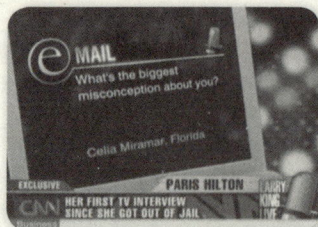

Larry King, Host

You would be get involved in all of it.

Paris Hilton, Socialite

Yes.

Larry King, Host

All right. We're going to see a new Paris Hilton.

Paris Hilton, Socialite

Yes.

我们还有个"由我来问"的问题，是由自称帕丽斯迷所提出的。我们来瞧瞧，然后请帕丽斯回答。请看。

帕丽斯·希尔顿迷

我想知道你出狱之后，要计划怎么做来帮助别人。我也想知道对那些可能会喝酒开车的人，你想传达些什么样的信息？

社交名人 帕丽斯·希尔顿

关于这点我在监狱里真的想了很多，因为我觉得，你知道，在聚光灯下，我有个平台可以唤起众人对许多伟大事业的关注，而不该只是一味地去做出去玩那类肤浅的事。我想要为儿童、乳腺癌和多发性硬化症等筹募资金以及……

主持人 拉里·金

你会去做这么多的事。

社交名人 帕丽斯·希尔顿

对。

主持人 拉里·金

好的，我们即将看到一个全新的帕丽斯·希尔顿。

社交名人 帕丽斯·希尔顿

是的。

Notes & Vocabulary

drink and drive 酒后驾车

drink and drive 是常常表示"酒后驾车"的用法，也可以说 drive drunk，对于酒后驾车的行为，较正式的用法是 driving under the influence，常简称为 DUI，例如"因酒后驾车被逮捕"则可说成 be arrested for DUI。

酒后驾车是非常危险的行为，但若非要喝酒，为了安全，可以在参加聚会的朋友当中指定一位要开车的人（designated driver），这个人必须不能喝酒、保持清醒（remain sober），那么就可以既尽兴又不会因为酒后驾车而违法或发生危险。

15. **submit** [səbˋmɪt] *v.* 提交；呈递
16. **spotlight** [ˋspɑtˌlaɪt] *n.* 聚光灯；焦点
17. **platform** [ˋplætˌfɔrm] *n.* 平台
18. **awareness** [əˋwɛrnəs] *n.* 察觉；意识
19. **cause** [kɔz] *n.* 目标；理想
20. **superficial** [ˌsupəˋfɪʃəl] *adj.* 肤浅的；表面的
21. **multiple sclerosis** [ˋmʌltəpəl] [skləˋrosəs] 多发性硬化症

Building the Starbucks Experienc

A Boardroom Master Class with the Coffee Empire Chairman Howard Schultz

从一杯咖啡到咖啡王国——星巴克总裁霍华德·舒尔茨的咖啡哲学

Step 1 请浏览下方提示的关键问题后，仔细听录音。

1. What has Starbucks done that Schultz says has made it different?
2. What traits does Schultz say a great leader must have?
3. According to Schultz, what do businesses have to do to continue to be relevant?
4. What do business leaders have to do to continue to succeed?

Step 2 如果你还听不太懂的话，请浏览下方的关键词汇后再听一次。

boutique 精品店	purveyor 供应商
quintessential 经典的	experiential 经验的
entitlement 应得的权利	dilute 削弱
vulnerability 弱点	unbridled 无拘束的

Step 3 试着回答下列听力测验题目。

True or False 是非题

_____ 1. Howard Schultz started Starbucks in Seattle in the late '70s.

_____ 2. According to Schultz, Starbucks spends less on advertising than on training.

_____ 3. Schultz says Starbucks succeeded because he had experience running companies.

_____ 4. Schultz thinks it is important to change, even if it means changing the company's main products.

名人小档案

霍华德·舒尔茨（1952–）为星巴克现任董事长。舒尔茨于 1982 年加入星巴克，曾想将意式咖啡引进美国但遭公司反对，他便决定离开，自己开设咖啡馆。后来星巴克经营者将公司卖给他，之后他迅速扩大规模，彻底将意大利咖啡推广到全美国。

_____ 5. Schultz feels that Starbucks is a model of growth through customer satisfaction.

Multiple Choice   选择题

_____ 1. What does Schultz say is the most important element of Starbuck's growth?
   a. Marketing.
   b. Advertising.
   c. Customer satisfaction.
   d. Branching out into other fields.

_____ 2. What does Schultz not say is a trait of great leaders?
   a. They can make personal sacrifices.
   b. They know the rules of business.
   c. They can work with smarter people.
   d. They have enthusiasm for their work.

_____ 3. How do great businesses succeed, according to Schultz?
   a. They focus on art, not science.
   b. They maintain their appeal to the customer.
   c. They make sure their profits are high.
   d. They have good marketing departments.

Step 4 试着用较慢的速度，再仔细听一遍，并检查答案是否正确。

Step 5 核对答案、检验成果，并详读原文，若仍有不懂的地方，可反复多听几次。

（答案请见 p.228）

Andrew Stevens, The Boardroom

One of the most recognizable[1] brands in the world. At last count, 14,000 stores across more than 40 countries, and 10,000 more planned in the next four years. This is where it all started, Pike Place Market in Seattle on the U.S. west coast. Back in the late 1970s, a small boutique[2] purveyor[3] of high-quality coffee beans, today a mass market phenomenon[4] that sells tens of millions of cups of coffee every week, and the man who made it happen—Howard Schultz.

He took over Starbucks in 1987 with a vision of bringing Italian coffee house culture to the U.S. "The Starbucks experience," he called it. In 20 years, he's created not only a worldwide chain, but an operation that's regularly voted one of the worlds most admired companies. Howard Schultz, chairman of the Starbucks coffee company, joins us here in Shanghai at the China Europe International Business School for *The Boardroom Master Class*.

When you look at a market do you radically[5] alter the Starbucks model, or is it much more of a case of one size fits all with a few sort of modifications,[6] minor modifications?

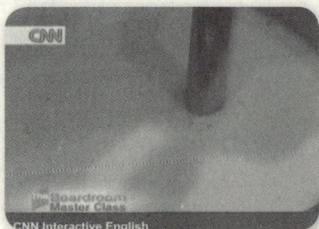

"董事会"安德鲁·史蒂文斯

它是全球最知名的品牌之一。根据最新统计，它在全球 40 多个国家共设有 1.4 万家店面，未来 4 年更计划增设 1 万家分店。这里是它的发源地，美国西海岸西雅图市的派克市场。20 世纪 70 年代末期，它是一家小规模的高品质咖啡豆供应商，如今则成了市场中的一大奇观，每周售出数千万杯咖啡，而成就这一切的人则是霍华德·舒尔茨。

他在 1987 年接掌星巴克，梦想要将意大利的咖啡店文化引进美国，他称之为"星巴克经历"。20 年内，他不止创造了一家全球连锁企业，而且还是一家经常被选为全球最令人羡慕的公司。星巴克咖啡公司的总裁霍华德·舒尔茨，莅临上海中欧国际工商学院，担任"董事会大师课堂"的嘉宾。

您在观察一个市场的时候，会大幅度地改变星巴克模式，还是套用同一个模式，只做微小修改？

Notes & Vocabulary

it is (much) more of a case
实际上的情形是……

case 常作"案件；个案"解释，it is more of a case 是在解释"实际上的情形是……"，后接 of 或 that 来说明详细的情况。case 在这里指的是"事实；实情"。

- It's not so much that Dan is unlucky in love. It is more of a case that he hasn't met the right girl yet.
  丹并不是没有桃花运，他只是还没遇到对的女孩。

one size fits all 以不变应万变

one size fits all 按照字面解释是"同一个尺寸合用于所有的……"，也就是中文"以不变应万变"的意思。这里主持人是问霍华德·舒尔茨是否以同一种模式在世界各地经营星巴克。加上连字符 one-size-fits-all 可作形容词使用。

- We only sell one version of the T-shirt, so one size fits all.
  我们这款 T 恤只有一个尺寸，没有大小区别。
- The security firm offers a one-size-fits-all solution to its clients.
  这家安保公司提供给所有客户一样的服务。

1. recognizable [ˌrɛkəɡˈnaɪzəbəl] *adj.* 可辨识的；知名的

2. boutique [buˈtik] *n.* 精品店

3. purveyor [pəˈveə] *n.* 供应者；供应商

4. phenomenon [fɪˈnɑməˌnɑn] *n.* 现象；奇迹

5. radically [ˈrædɪkəlɪ] *adv.* 完全地；极端地；根本地

6. modification [ˌmɑdəfəˈkeʃən] *n.* 修改；改变

Howard Schultz, Starbucks Chairman

Well, I think when you look at Starbucks as a business case, what we've done and the way we do business is quite different than a classic consumer brand, and let me be specific.[7] Most consumer brands that have emerged[8] in the last 10, 20 years have been built through traditional marketing and traditional advertising. Starbucks is not an advertiser. People think we're a great marketing company, but in fact we spend very little money on marketing, more money on training our people than advertising.

The point I want to make is that we built the brand by the experience. And when you look back on the history of Starbucks, we are the quintessential[9] experiential[10] brand built by what happens inside of our stores.

I'm very fond of encouraging our people to recognize that our success is not an entitlement.[11] It has to be earned. And we have no right to enduring[12] success unless we continue to be relevant[13] and close to the consumer. But there is a real balance here. The world is changing so quickly and the consumer has so many choices, that the important thing is not only staying relevant, but the important thing is preserving and enhancing your core business so that it's not diluted[14] by other things that you do. And this is an art, not a science.

Andrew Stevens, The Boardroom

If anything you learned here today, you'll be able to take this back with you. And that is, what are your golden business rules which don't just apply to Starbucks but apply right across the board?

星巴克总裁 霍华德·舒尔茨

当你从商业的角度来看星巴克，我们过去的做法和经营方式，与一个老字号的消费品牌有很大的不同，请让我说得清楚点。在过去 10 年、20 年间问世的消费品牌，大部分都是通过传统的营销和广告方式建立起知名度。但星巴克是不打广告的。大家认为我们是一家很会做营销的公司，但事实上我们在营销上的花费很少，花在培训员工方面的钱比广告还多。

我想说的重点是，我们是靠体验来建立品牌。你在回顾星巴克的历史时，会发现我们是典型地靠现场体验起家的体验型品牌。

我很喜欢鼓励员工，让他们知道我们的成功不是从天上掉下来的，而是要靠争取。除非我们能保持在消费者心目中的重要性，持续贴近他们，否则我们没有资格经久不衰。这其中真的存在着某种平衡。世界变化如此快速，消费者的选择何其多，因此重要的不只要能够保持现状，而是要维护和提升你的核心业务，使核心业务不会被你其他的行为削弱。这是一门艺术，不是科学。

"董事会"安德鲁·史蒂文斯

如果各位听众今天在这里能学到什么，并且能够把学到的带回去实践。那就是：您有哪些经商的金科玉律，不只可以运用在星巴克上，而是可以运用到别的地方？

Notes & Vocabulary

across the board 通用

across the board 原指赛马中的一种下注法。当赌博者在赌盘中对前 3 名都下了注，就可以用 across the board 来表示，后来衍生指"通用"的意思，加了连字符后 across-the-board 可作形容词用。

- The company released 6,000 employees; the cuts were made across the board.
  那家公司上上下下裁了 6 000 名员工。

- The rising price of oil has resulted in an across-the-board increase in consumer prices.
  油价飞涨使得消费物价全面上涨。

7. specific [spɪˋsɪfɪk] *adj.* 明确的；具体的

8. emerge [ɪˋmɝdʒ] *v.* 出现；浮现

9. quintessential [ˌkwɪntəˋsɛnʃəl] *adj.* 精髓的；经典的

10. experiential [ɪkˌspɪrɪˋɛnʃəl] *adj.* 经验的

11. entitlement [ɪnˋtaɪtlmənt] *n.* 应得的权利

12. enduring [ɪnˋdʊrɪŋ] *adj.* 持久的；耐用的

13. relevant [ˋrɛləvənt] *adj.* 有关的；相应的

14. dilute [daɪˋlut] *v.* 削弱；降低

Howard Schultz, Starbucks Chairman

I think you have to be a hundred percent authentic[15] and true. I think when you're building a business or joining a company, you have to be transparent.[16] You can't have two sets of information for two sets of people. I think you have to... a great leader, at times, has to demonstrate[17] a level of vulnerability,[18] and share with people how you really feel.

In order to achieve success it takes unbridled[19] enthusiasm and passion. You have to find something that you really, really love. And I think you have to be willing to understand that this is hard to do, to build great enduring success. And it takes personal sacrifice.[20] And you have to find people who share your dream, not only to make money.

Great businesses do not succeed because they're focused purely on making a profit. Great businesses succeed at a high level of profitability[21] because they are doing fantastic things for their people, for their customers and their communities. Find that fragile[22] balance and you will build a profitable business. Surround yourself with people who are smarter and more experienced than yourselves and share the success with them.

星巴克总裁 霍华德·舒尔茨

我认为你必须完全讲诚信。不论是创业或加入一家公司，你必须是坦率的。你不能给两批人不同的两套信息。我认为你必须……一个优秀的领导者有时候必须展现脆弱的一面，让别人了解你真正的感受。

为了能够成功，你必须有永无止境的热忱和热情。你必须找到自己真正热爱的东西。我想你必须能够理解，要经营经久不衰的企业是很困难的，这要牺牲小我才能做到。你必须找到志同道合的人，而不只是想赚钱的人。

只专注于获利并不能成就伟大的事业。伟大的事业之所以能成功创造高获利，是因为他们在为自己的员工、顾客和群体做了不起的事。只要在这中间找到那个细致微妙的平衡点，你就能建立起一个赚钱的企业。使自己身边围绕着比你聪明、比你有经验的人，并且和他们一起分享成功。

Notes & Vocabulary

focus on 着重于

focus 在此作动词用，搭配介词 on，表示"把重点放在……"，与 concentrate on 意思相同。另外，focus 也可作名词，意思是"焦点；重点"。

· The teachers concentrated on preparing the students for the test.
老师们把重点放在辅导学生准备考试。

· The focus of the book is on how the developments in Iraq affected the economy.
这本书的重点为伊拉克的发展如何影响经济。

15. authentic [ɔ`θɛntɪk] *adj.* 可信的；真实的

16. transparent [træns`pɛrənt] *adj.* 透明的；光明正大的

17. demonstrate [`dɛmən‚stret] *v.* 展示；表露

18. vulnerability [‚vʌlnrə`bɪlətɪ] *n.* 弱点

19. unbridled [ʌn`braɪdl̩d] *adj.* 无拘无束的；放纵的

20. sacrifice [`sækrə‚faɪs] *n.* 牺牲

21. profitability [‚prɑfətə`bɪlətɪ] *n.* 利益

22. fragile [`frædʒəl] *adj.* 脆弱的；纤细的

A Drive to Compete
CNN Exclusive Interview with Golf Superstar Tiger Woods
CNN 专访高尔夫球之王泰格·伍兹

Step 1 请浏览下方提示的关键问题后，仔细听录音。

1. What does Tiger say his greatest love is?
2. What goal does Tiger say he always has?
3. How does Tiger say that his wife has helped him?
4. How does Tiger say golf has been evolving in recent years?

Step 2 如果你还听不太懂的话，请浏览下方的关键词汇后再听一次。

transcend 超越；优于	prioritize 按优先顺序处理
revolve around 以……为中心	inseparable 不可分割的
distraction 令人分心的事物	illusion 幻想；幻觉

Step 3 试着回答下列听力测验题目。

True or False 是非题

_____ 1. Competition for Tiger is talking with other people and seeing who has more things.

_____ 2. After 18 months of work, Tiger thinks his swing is as fluid as it can be.

_____ 3. Tiger says he likes diving because it's the only place he isn't recognized.

_____ 4. Tiger feels that more people are watching golf because of him.

_____ 5. Tiger says his wife helps him deal with the public.

名人小档案

泰格·伍兹（1975–）3 岁就挥出 9 洞 48 杆的成绩，5 岁就登上《高尔夫球摘要》(*Golf Digest*)。25 岁时拿下名人赛冠军，完成了高尔夫球大满贯（即包揽了四大公开赛的冠军）。职业生涯中拿过无数奖杯，四大公开赛成绩斐然，到目前为止仍为世界排名第一的高尔夫球选手。

Multiple Choice　选择题

_____ 1. What gift does Tiger say he has that few people have?
    a. The ability to play a sport very well.
    b. A job that he loves to do.
    c. Being young and athletic.
    d. His wife.

_____ 2. What does Tiger say has helped his game the most in recent years?
    a. Always working on his stroke.
    b. Refocusing on the Masters.
    c. Getting married.
    d. The lengthening of golf courses.

_____ 3. What does Tiger think the game of golf is evolving away from?
    a. Having young, athletic players.
    b. Having old, out of shape players.
    c. Having longer golf courses.
    d. Players becoming superhuman.

Step 4 试着用较慢的速度，再仔细听一遍，并检查答案是否正确。

Step 5 核对答案、检验成果，并详读原文，若仍有不懂的地方，可反复多听几次。

（答案请见 p.228）

Don Riddell, Living Golf

Tiger Woods is a truly global phenomenon. Over the last decade, he's redefined[1] and transcended[2] his sport, and he's made golf cool. There's barely a corner of the globe where his face and name isn't known, and the Tiger Woods brand continues to grow.

Being Tiger Woods is just a full-time job. Do you ever get a chance to pinch yourself and think, jeez,[3] this is amazing? I mean can you believe what is happening to you sometimes?

Tiger Woods, Golf Player

I don't look at it that way. You know, it is what it is. And I enjoy what I do. I enjoy competing, and that's my love. I love to get out there and mix it up with the boys here and see what I got, see if I can take them down[4] and hopefully they don't take me down, and that's the fun. And that's the fun of competing and I . . . I just enjoy it.

Don Riddell, Living Golf

You are one of the most famous faces on the planet though. I mean, how does that feel? Is there anywhere you can go where you're left alone?

Tiger Woods, Golf Player

Yeah, underwater! That's why I love diving. But, you know, as I said, I don't look at myself that way. I look at myself as a competitor. I love to compete and this is my arena. And it's just gained awareness because, as I said, I made a couple putts.[5] But, I think it's . . . I wake up every day and can't wait to go to work, and that's something that I think is a gift that not too many people have an opportunity to feel that way every day.

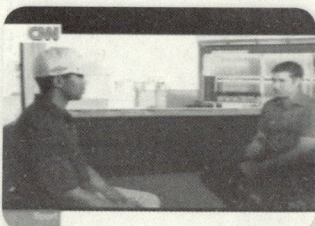

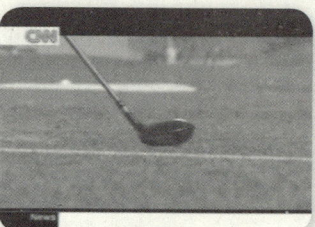

"高球俱乐部" 唐·里德尔

泰格·伍兹是世界上名副其实的一号人物。过去 10 年来，他重新诠释并提升了高尔夫运动，并且让高尔夫成为一项很酷的运动。全世界没有人不认识他，没听过他的名字，泰格·伍兹这个品牌仍在茁壮成长。

作泰格·伍兹根本是一份全职工作。你是否曾经捏自己一下，心想，天啊，这还真是神奇啊？我的意思是，有时你是否不敢相信自己有这样的经历？

高尔夫球员 泰格·伍兹

我不会这么想。是怎么样就是怎么样。我很享受我的工作。我喜欢竞争的感觉，这也是我最爱做的事。我喜欢到球场上和其他男选手一起比赛，看看我的本事如何，看看我能不能打败他们，并且希望他们不会击败我，这就是乐趣所在，而这也是竞争让人觉得有意思的地方，我就是喜欢这样。

"高球俱乐部" 唐·里德尔

但是你是全世界知名度最高的人之一，对此你有何感觉？有没有哪里是你在那里不会被打扰的地方？

高尔夫球员 泰格·伍兹

有啊，水面下。这就是我热爱潜水的原因。但我说过，我不会这样看我自己。我认为自己是个竞争者。我爱竞争，而这是我的竞技场。我说过，是因为我打进了几个球，所以才会受到瞩目。我每天起床后都迫不及待想去工作，我认为这是一种恩赐，每天都有机会拥有这种感受的人并不多。

Notes & Vocabulary

arena 业、界、竞争领域

原意是指"赛场、竞技场"，引申为"领域"。运动在西方人生活中占了很大的一部分，因此运动对语言的影响也相当大，英语中不乏由运动衍生出来的词汇，现在就来介绍由高尔夫球衍生出来的词语：

- bogey 柏忌，高于标准杆一杆
  引申表示"不好的表现、赔钱的生意"
- caddie 球童
  引申表示"助理、跑腿或打杂的人、跑龙套者"
- upswing 往上挥球杆
  引申表示"（股市等）上扬、（经济等）好转"
- on a par with 平标准杆
  引申表示"旗鼓相当、不相上下"
- up to par 平标准杆
  引申表示"合乎标准"
- within a golf drive 两杆间的距离
  引申表示"近在咫尺"
- par for the course 打出标准杆
  引申表示"不足为奇的事"
- back nine 后 9 洞
  引申表示"事情发展或人生的后半段"

---

1. redefine [ˌridɪˈfaɪn] v. 重新定义

2. transcend [trænˈsɛnd] v. 超越；优于

3. jeez [dʒiz] interj. 天啊（Jesus 的简略谐音说法）

4. take sb down 击败

5. putt [pʌt] n. 推杆

Don Riddell, Living Golf

You don't have anything special you would like to achieve or is it just keep going in the way you have?

Tiger Woods, Golf Player

In golf?

Don Riddell, Living Golf

Yeah.

Tiger Woods, Golf Player

Win. Three letters.

Don Riddell, Living Golf

Are you prioritizing[6] the Majors again?

Tiger Woods, Golf Player

Always. My golfing year revolves around[7] those four events.

Don Riddell, Living Golf

You've been making some adjustments to your swing[8] over the last 18 months or so, are they finished now or are you still working on …?

Tiger Woods, Golf Player

You're never finished, ever, and golf is fluid.[9] Golf is always evolving,[10] every day, every shot.

Don Riddell, Living Golf

You see, my wife thinks that one of the reasons that you came good after the 2004 year was the fact that you got married and that helped you out. Is that fair? I mean, how much credit do you give to[11] Mrs. Woods?

"高球俱乐部" 唐·里德尔

你有没有哪些特别想做到的事，还是就想按照原本的目标走下去？

高尔夫球员 泰格·伍兹

你是指高尔夫吗？

"高球俱乐部" 唐·里德尔

对。

高尔夫球员 泰格·伍兹

赢球，就这么简单。

"高球俱乐部" 唐·里德尔

你是否再次把四大公开赛摆在第一位？

高尔夫球员 泰格·伍兹

永远都是，我每年的高尔夫球活动都是以四大赛事为中心。

"高球俱乐部" 唐·里德尔

过去 18 个月左右，你一直在调整你的挥杆，你现在已经调整好了吗？还是还在调整中？

高尔夫球员 泰格·伍兹

永无休止，高尔夫是不断变化的，它一直都在演变，每一天，每一杆。

"高球俱乐部" 唐·里德尔

我太太认为你在 2004 年之后成绩变好的原因之一是因为你结了婚，这对你而言是一种帮助。这样说对吗？你认为伍兹太太的功劳有多大呢？

Notes & Vocabulary

Majors 四大公开赛

伍兹此处讲的 Majors 是指高尔夫球的四大公开赛，又称大满贯 (Grand Slam) 或者是 the major championships，介绍如下：

1. U.S. Open（美国公开赛，1895 年开创），每年 6 月在不同地点举行。

2. (British) Open Championship（英国公开赛，1860 年开赛），每年 7 月在英国不同地点举行，是四大公开赛中唯一不在美国境内举办的比赛。

3. PGA Championship（PGA 锦标赛，1916 年开赛），每年 8 月举行，是每年赛季最后举行的大满贯赛。

4. Masters Tournament（名人赛，1934 年开赛），每年 4 月固定在美国佐治亚州奥古斯塔（Augusta, Georgia）举办，是四大公开赛中唯一固定场地的比赛。绿夹克 Green Jacket 为其特色，由上一届冠军替本届冠军穿上。此项比赛冠军自动获得其他三项大满贯的参赛权。

6. prioritize [praɪˋɔrəˌtaɪz] v. 按优先顺序处理；把事情按优先顺序排好

7. revolve around [rɪˋvɑlv] 以……为中心

8. swing [swɪŋ] n. 挥杆

9. fluid [ˋfluəd] adj. 不固定的；易变的

10. evolve [ɪˋvɑlv] v. 发展；进化

11. give credit to sb v.phr. 归功于某人

Tiger Woods, Golf Player

Oh, without a doubt! Ever since she's moved in, 2002, we've been a great team, an inseparable[12] team and I think a lot of the success I've had certainly is due to her, because there are so many different things and distractions[13] that go on in my life and things that I have to deal with, things that the public probably doesn't know and doesn't see … she's got to help me with all that and she's certainly brought balance to my life and I'm very lucky to have that.

Don Riddell, Living Golf

The lengthening of golf courses, which seems to be happening everywhere now, that sounds to me like it just plays into your hands

Tiger Woods, Golf Player

Well, that's where the game's evolving. It's not about the short hitter anymore, it's about guys who are big and athletic.[14] And wait until you get kids who are athletic playing the game, who aren't fat and out of shape,[15] and the only sport they could play is golf. Wait until you get guys who … they could play any sport. They're gifted, and they decide to play golf. That's what's coming in the future, so the game has changed. It's evolving, and the golf courses have to adapt.

Don Riddell, Living Golf

Now, earlier this week, your manager Mark Steinberg said that Tiger Woods is not a superhuman.

高尔夫球员　泰格·伍兹

她的功劳毋庸置疑。自从 2002 年她搬进我家之后，我们就成了最佳拍档，我们俩密不可分，我认为我的成功有很大一部分肯定要归功于她，因为我的生活中有很多杂七杂八和让人分心的事要面对，这些可能都是一些大家不知道也看不到的事，她必须帮我处理那些事，而且她使我的生活得以平衡，这让我觉得自己很幸运。

"高球俱乐部" 唐·里德尔

高尔夫球场的球道距离加长，现在似乎每个球场都在这么做，我觉得这好像对你比较有利。

高尔夫球员　泰格·伍兹

这就是高尔夫这项运动演进的结果。现在的高尔夫运动已经不适合击球距离短的球员了，而是身高力大，运动神经发达的人的天下。到时候你就会看到一些有运动细胞、身材好的年轻人开始打高尔夫球，他们不是肥胖臃肿到身材变形，也不是只能打高尔夫球而已。到时候你会看到一些能从事任何运动的人。他们决定将运动天赋用在高尔夫球上。这些都是未来会发生的事，所以高尔夫球运动的面貌已经改变了。它不断在演进，所以高尔夫球场也必须随之改变。

"高球俱乐部" 唐·里德尔

这个星期早些时候，您的经纪人马克·斯坦伯格说泰格·伍兹不是超人。

Notes & Vocabulary

play into sb's hands
做对某人有利的事

play into sb's hands 或 play into the hands of sb 是指做对某人（尤指对手）有利的事，或是做使对手占便宜却使自己吃亏的事。

· David's image of being an outsider played into the hands of his political opponents.
大卫置身事外的形象反倒让政治对手占了便宜。

. . . .

12. **inseparable** [ɪnˋsɛprəbəl] *adj.* 不可分割的；分不开的

13. **distraction** [dɪˋstrækʃən] *n.* 令人分心的事物

14. **athletic** [æθˋlɛtɪk] *adj.* 体格健壮的

15. **out of shape** *phr.* 身材走样

Tiger Woods, Golf Player

No, no. Not at all.

Don Riddell, Living Golf

That's just shattered[16] the illusion[17] for everyone.

Tiger Woods, Golf Player

No, no, no, no—I'm just like you and me ... we're all the same, we're all human.

高尔夫球员　泰格·伍兹

当然不是。

"高球俱乐部"唐·里德尔

这粉碎了大家心中的幻想。

高尔夫球员　泰格·伍兹

不，我就和你们大家一样，我们都
一样，都是凡人。

Notes & Vocabulary

golf course 高尔夫球道

读高尔夫球新闻时常搞不清高尔夫术语吗？一起来看看常用的
术语：

高尔夫球术语：

par 标准杆

gross 总杆数

even par 平标准杆

birdie 低于标准杆一杆，也可译成"小鸟"

bogey 高于标准一杆，也可译成"柏忌"

eagle 低于标准杆两杆，也可译成"老鹰"

double bogey 高于标准杆两杆

double eagle 低于标准杆三杆

hole in one 一杆进洞

O.B.(out of bound) 出界

高尔夫球场（golf course/links）：

bunker 沙坑、障碍物

green 果岭、球穴区

out course / in course 前 / 后 9 洞

tee / teeing ground 发球区

动作及球具：

address 击球的准备

drive 发球

tee off 开球

club 球杆

....

16. shatter [ˈʃætə] v. 粉碎

17. illusion [ɪˈluʒən] n. 幻想；幻觉

Rebuilding Lives
Brad Pitt Talks about Home Life and Efforts to Save New Orleans

CNN 专访布拉德·皮特投身灾区重建的心路历程

Step 1 请浏览下方提示的关键问题后，仔细听录音。

1. What is the purpose of the charity that Brad Pitt is representing?
2. Why do they want to start work in the Ninth Ward?
3. What does Brad say that the community was like in New Orleans?
4. What does Brad say about being a father?

Step 2 如果你还听不太懂的话，请浏览下方的关键词汇后再听一次。

debut 首次登台	ward 行政区
parish （美）郡	nucleus 核心；起点
rewarding 有报酬的	fulfillment 满足感

Step 3 试着回答下列听力测验题目。

True or False 是非题

_____ 1. The area along the Gulf Coast is as bad or worse than the Ninth Ward.

_____ 2. After working in the Ninth Ward, the charity will move on to other areas.

_____ 3. When Brad is at home, he sits on the front porch and talks to his neighbors.

_____ 4. Brad denies getting involved with Angelina while they were working together.

名人小档案

布拉德·皮特（1963-）是知名当红演员，与前妻詹妮弗·安妮斯顿（Jennifer Aniston）及现任伴侣安吉丽娜·朱莉（Angelina Jolie）的关系常为演艺界的热门话题。布拉德·皮特亦十分关注社会问题，如支持艾滋病研究及协助重建新奥尔良等。

_____ 5. Brad agrees that being a father is the hardest job in the world, but also says it's rewarding.

Multiple Choice   选择题

_____ 1. Why is the charity Brad talks about starting in the Ninth Ward?
   a. The government asked them to start there.
   b. The Ninth Ward is the largest.
   c. It has been the slowest to recover.
   d. It is the center of New Orleans.

_____ 2. What is the goal of the charity, as stated by Brad?
   a. To rebuild the churches in the Ninth Ward.
   b. To preserve the front porch culture.
   c. To make sure houses are built safely.
   d. To bring America together.

_____ 3. Which does Brad not say is one of Angelina's qualities?
   a. Challenging.
   b. Hard working.
   c. Protective.
   d. Creative.

Step 4 试着用较慢的速度，再仔细听一遍，并检查答案是否正确。

Step 5 核对答案、检验成果，并详读原文，若仍有不懂的地方，可反复多听几次。

（答案请见 p.228）

Larry King, Host

[It's a] great pleasure to welcome to *Larry King Live* Brad Pitt.

Finally, after all these years, we have obtained[1] the services of Mr. Britt ... Mr. Pitt on a very important occasion, by the way. This is the debut[2] of an extraordinary[3] charity to help a much-needed project. Thank you so much for doing this.

Brad Pitt, Movie Star

Yeah. Thanks for having me, having all of us here.

Larry King, Host

OK. So, what ... first of all, isn't it a blight on somebody—city, state, federal—that this Ninth Ward ain't any better?

Brad Pitt, Movie Star

Well, no question. I mean but it, you know, the Ninth Ward is [has] got a lot of attention, and we're starting here because it seems to have the least—or the most difficulty of coming back. But this is, this is everywhere. You, to see the extents[4] of the damage and the extents of the people, the extents of the lack of movement is—I mean, this goes on for parish[5] after parish after parish.

We're hoping we can take—start here as a nucleus,[6] but we can keep expanding on this throughout New Orleans and the Gulf Coast itself.

主持人 拉里·金

很高兴与邀请到布拉德·皮特来"拉里·金直播现场"。

经过这么多年，我们终于获得皮特先生的帮助，而且还是一个非常重要的场合。这场揭幕活动将拉开一场非常特别的慈善活动，目的在于帮助一项非常需要帮助的项目。非常感谢你这么做。

电影明星 布拉德·皮特

是啊，谢谢你们让我来，让我们所有人都能够参与。

主持人 拉里·金

好的，那么……首先，第 9 区到现在都没有任何改善，是不是等于打击了一些人——包括市政府、州政府，以及联邦政府？

电影明星 布拉德·皮特

没错，可是现在第 9 区已经获得许多关注了。我们之所以从这里开始，原因是这里似乎最不容易改观。不过，其实到处都是如此。看看毁损的程度、那么多的人，还有缺乏进展的状况——我是说，这种现象在每个行政区都是一样。

我们希望这里能够是个开端，然后进一步扩展到整个新奥尔良，整个墨西哥湾沿岸。

Notes & Vocabulary

a blight on 打击；扼杀

blight 原本指破坏植物的天然因素，例如阴冷的天气、虫害、枯萎病等。广义延伸为使士气溃散、希望落空、甚而导致毁灭的"破坏性因素"。

• The rise in violent crime was a blight on a once safe city.
暴力犯罪率的增加对这个曾一度安全的城市来说是一大打击。

Ninth Ward 新奥尔良飓风重灾区

2005 年 8 月底，5 级（Category 5）飓风卡里特娜（Hurricane Katrina）登陆美国南方路易斯安那州，横扫墨西哥湾（Gulf Coast）沿岸各州。此飓风引发海水倒灌、堤防冲毁，上千人丧生，损失超过 812 亿美元，是美国有史以来最惨重的"世纪天灾"。

路易斯安那州的新奥尔良市成了水患之国，几乎成为废墟，停水停电、卫生条件恶劣、治安混乱，居民最后不得不全部撤离。新奥尔良市共分 17 个行政区，称之为 ward。受创最严重的 Ninth Ward 就是该市第 9 行政区，位于下城区，临近密西西比河。

灾后除了重建公共设施和堤防之外，政府特别设立 Road Home 计划，提供新奥尔良住户申请贷款 15 万美元。由于资金短缺近 500 万美元，节目播出时仍有数千人还住在政府的临时收容拖车。

....

1. obtain [əbˋten] v. 获得；得到

2. debut [ˋdeˌbju] n. 首次登台

3. extraordinary [ıkˋstrɔrdəˌnɛrı] adj. 特别的；非常的

4. extent [ıkˋstɛnt] n. 程度；范围

5. parish [ˋpɛrıʃ] n. (美) 郡

6. nucleus [ˋnuklıəs] n. 核心；起点

Larry King, Host

And now we have MakeItRightNola.org.

Brad Pitt, Movie Star

Right.

Larry King, Host

Now, that's all one word—MakeItRight. Nola is New Orleans, Louisiana. MakeItRightNola.org is the Web site you go to.

Brad Pitt, Movie Star

That's right. OK, so we're …

Larry King, Host

For anything, right?

Brad Pitt, Movie Star

That's right. We're trying to send people to the Web site, because what we now have here are—we can get families into homes by the end of summer. You're going to see this community[7] start to come back, and where we need help is we need America to come together like they did at … directly after the storm and help, help the families here meet that financing gap to build properly, to build safely.

Larry King, Host

What … what defines home for you?

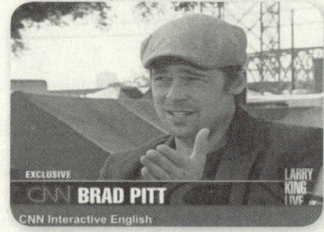

主持人 拉里·金

现在我们又有了"重建新奥尔良"这个网站。

电影明星 布拉德·皮特

没错。

主持人 拉里·金

网址中的"重建"：MakeItRight 是把三个词全部连在一起，Nola 则是指路易斯安那州新奥尔良。大家都可以到"重建新奥尔良"这个网站上。

电影明星 布拉德·皮特

没错。好的，所以我们……

主持人 拉里·金

不论任何需求，都可到这个网站上，对不对？

电影明星 布拉德·皮特

没错。我们尽量请人到这个网站上，因为我们现在能够——我们能够在夏天结束前让一家家的人住进房子里。你将会看到这个社区慢慢恢复。我们需要帮助的地方，就是需要全国人民像当初风暴灾难刚结束后那样同心协力，帮助这里的家庭筹措资金，建造适当的房屋、安全的房屋。

主持人 拉里·金

对你来说，家的定义是什么？

Notes & Vocabulary

meet the gap 填补缺口；凑足（金额）

gap 是指"缺口、差距"，这个短语原本应为 bridge the gap，表示"填补缺口；弥补差距"，在本文指的是"筹足重建资金的差额"。

· The government was able to bridge the budget gap to fund a new hospital.
政府终于凑足了兴建新医院的经费。

....

7. community [kə`mjunəti] *n.* 社区

Brad Pitt, Movie Star

A family. It's all family. You talk to the people here and they'll talk about a ... they'll tell you about a front porch culture, where neighbor helped neighbors, a lot of barbecues, sitting on the front porch and stories and music, and that's it. It's family and friends, period.

Larry King, Host

What is Angelina like as a mother? She's been on this program a lot. I've known her a long time.

Brad Pitt, Movie Star

It's the ... I think it's the greatest gift I can give my kids is that she is ... they have such a fantastic[8] mother—dedicated, kids first, really inventive[9] and great fun for them and very, very protective.[10]

Larry King, Host

What was it like to work with her?

Brad Pitt, Movie Star

Well, apparently[11] it was great fun.

Larry King, Host

You met ...

Brad Pitt, Movie Star

We got on all right.

Larry King, Host

But what was it like? When you're getting emotionally[12] involved with someone you're working with ...

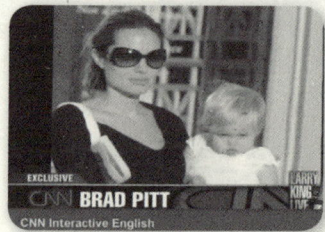

电影明星 布拉德·皮特

家人。家就是家人。只要和这里的人谈话，他们就会告诉你这里的门廊文化，邻居们会彼此照应，一起烤肉聚餐，坐在门廊里讲故事听音乐，就是这样。就是家人和朋友，就这样。

主持人 拉里·金

安吉丽娜是什么样的妈妈？她经常上这个节目，我认识她很久了。

电影明星 布拉德·皮特

我认为，我能够给我儿女最珍贵的礼物，就是这么一位了不起的母亲——全心投入，把孩子放在第一位，非常有创意，能够为他们带来许多欢乐，而且非常保护他们。

主持人 拉里·金

和她一同工作是什么感觉？

电影明星 布拉德·皮特

充满了乐趣。

主持人 拉里·金

你们相遇……

电影明星 布拉德·皮特

我们相处得很愉快。

主持人 拉里·金

可是那是什么感觉呢？你和一同工作的人产生了感情……

Notes & Vocabulary

front porch culture 门廊文化

front porch culture 原本形容的是美国乡村中街坊邻居坐在门廊闲聊、打发午后休闲时间，后来衍生指与左邻右舍及社区频繁互动、保持和谐关系的意思，也可称作 small town culture。随着社会演变，越来越多人住在公寓大厦里，这种有着浓厚人情味的 front porch culture 也渐渐只能在乡村小镇里才能体会得到了。

....

8. fantastic [fæn`tæstɪk] *adj.* 极好的

9. inventive [ɪn`vɛntɪv] *adj.* 有创造力的

10. protective [prə`tɛktɪv] *adj.* 对（人）关切的；保护别人的

11. apparently [ə`pɛrəntlɪ] *adv.* 明显地

12. emotionally [ɪ`moʃənlɪ] *adv.* 感情上地

Brad Pitt, Movie Star

Well, that came after, Larry. That came after, but she is a woman of strong opinion and very specific beliefs and a great voice. I respect it. A great intelligence.[13]

Larry King, Host

You fight a lot?

Brad Pitt, Movie Star

No, not really. Challenge each other a lot. [I'm] having good fun with that.

Larry King, Host

And how do you like being a father? It's [the] hardest job in the world.

Brad Pitt, Movie Star

The hardest job in the world? The most rewarding[14] job in the world. There's something to—you know, we'll put long days in here, we're up here soon as the sun comes up and to go home and have dinner with your kids and have to discipline[15] one of them who's out of line and still have the energy for that is, is … I can't explain the fulfillment[16] of that, but it is … it is everything.

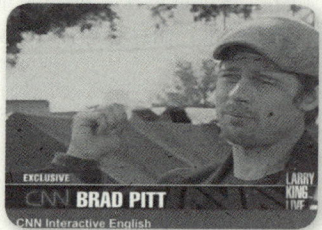

电影明星 布拉德·皮特

那是后来才发生的，拉里。那是后来才发生的。她是个很有主见的女人，有很明确的信仰，而且会强烈表达自己的意见。我尊重这样的特质。她是个很聪明的人。

主持人 拉里·金

你们常吵架吗？

电影明星 布拉德·皮特

不会，但是常常会挑战对方。我乐在其中。

主持人 拉里·金

你喜欢当爸爸吗？这可是世界上最困难的工作了。

电影明星 布拉德·皮特

世界上最困难的工作吗？我觉得是世界上最值得的工作。你知道的，我们每天都花很长的时间在这里，我们天一亮就到这里来，晚上才回家和孩子一起吃晚餐，还必须有精力教育他们要守规矩，实在是……我说不出那种满足感，可是那实在是……那实在就是一切。

Notes & Vocabulary

out of line 越界；不守规矩

字面上的意思就是"超出界线"。当一个人的行为过当、不守规矩、失控的时候，都可以说他 out of line。前面动词常用 be、get 或 step。

· The player was out of line when he disputed the referee's call.
那名球员质疑裁判的判决，这样的行为越界了。

· ·

13. intelligence [ɪn'tɛlədʒəns] *n.* 智慧；智力

14. rewarding [rɪ'wɔrdɪŋ] *adj.* 有报酬的

15. discipline ['dɪsəplən] *v.* 教导；管教

16. fulfillment [fʊl'fɪlmənt] *n.* 满足感；成就感

NOTES

实战应用篇
Part II

Faith and Vision

Taiwanese Entrepreneur Cher Wang Pushes Gadgets[1] to the Cutting Edge[2]

在危机中坚持——专访宏达电子董事长王雪红

Step 1 ◉ 请浏览下方提示的关键问题后，仔细听录音。

1. What did Wang think the PDA would replace?
2. What did Wang do when the business had problems?
3. What companies are HTC's customers now?
4. What is the next step that HTC plans to take?

Step 2 🎧 如果你还听不太懂的话，请浏览下方的关键词汇后再听一次。

cutting edge 尖端；最前沿	converge 整合
big seller 畅销商品	persistent 坚持不懈的
turnaround 形势扭转	sit on the shelf 滞销

Step 3 💡 试着回答下列听力测验题目。

True or False 是非题

_____ 1. Wang wanted to make a device that would replace cell phones and notebooks.

_____ 2. When HTC started, most people agreed that PDAs would become popular.

_____ 3. When the business had problems, Wang found inspiration in the Bible.

_____ 4. HTC is now one of the biggest smart phone manufacturers in the world.

_____ 5. HTC will launch its own brand, which most analysts think is a good idea.

名人小档案

王雪红（1958–）是台塑企业王永庆的三女儿，现任威盛电子、宏达电子、建达国际、全达国际董事长。曾获选年度"亚洲十大女性企业家"，为台湾女首富，也是首位入选美国《福布斯》杂志全球富豪榜的台湾女性富豪。

Multiple Choice 选择题

_____ 1. Why was producing a PDA in 1997 a bad choice?
　　a. There was too much competition.
　　b. There wasn't enough customer interest.
　　c. Taiwanese electronics were unpopular.
　　d. The devices were too heavy.

_____ 2. When the company sank into debt, what did Wang do?
　　a. She let the product sit on the shelves.
　　b. She cut her losses.
　　c. She watched more television.
　　d. She invested money in the company.

_____ 3. What for Wang would be the best PDA?
　　a. One that lets her check her e-mail.
　　b. One that acts like a phone and an MP3.
　　c. One that acts like a normal computer.
　　d. One that acts like a personal secretary.

Step 4 试着用较慢的速度，再仔细听一遍，并检查答案是否正确。

Step 5 核对答案、检验成果，并详读原文，若仍有不懂的地方，可反复多听几次。

（答案请见 p. 229）

James McDonald, Entrepreneurs Only

Success in the tech industry usually means keeping ahead of industry trends. Well, one Taiwan firm was way ahead, in fact, almost too far ahead for its own good.

A busy production day for one of Taiwan's hottest tech companies. The state-of-the-art facility[3] is capable of creating a fully functioning PDA[4] in two hours. It's a high-tech approach suitable for a company called High Tech Computer, or HTC.

Cher Wang, HTC Founder and Chairperson

HTC's product is always very cutting-edge.

James McDonald, Entrepreneurs Only

At one point, perhaps a little too cutting-edge. One of its early innovations[5] almost doomed[6] the company to failure. Here's the story. Cher Wang founded HTC in 1997. The daughter of Taiwan's richest man, her own busy life provided inspiration[7] for her fledgling company's first big project.

Cher Wang, HTC Founder and Chairperson

And I was dreaming that people should not carry so many devices[8] like telephone[s], like MP3[s], like notebook[s]—was still very heavy at that time. And I believed that we should have some devices that converge[9] together.

"企业家特写"詹姆斯·麦克唐纳

在科技行业中，成功往往意味着必须在产业趋势上保持领先。有一家台湾公司就是一直保持在领先地位，事实上，有些领先过度，甚至反而对自己不利。

这是台湾一家著名科技公司忙着制造产品的一天。这里最先进的设备可以在 2 个小时内制造出一部功能齐全的个人掌上电脑。而这种运用高科技的方式，与这家名为"宏达国际电子"（宏达电子）的公司名称相得益彰。

宏达电子创始人兼董事长 王雪红

宏达电子的产品永远都承载尖端科技。

"企业家特写"詹姆斯·麦克唐纳

曾经一度还过于先进了。该公司早期的一项创新差点让公司倒闭。故事是这样的。王雪红在 1997 年创立宏达电子，身为台湾首富的女儿，王雪红本身忙碌的生活为她刚创立的公司提供了第一个大项目的灵感。

宏达电子创始人兼董事长 王雪红

我当时在想，大家不应该携带这么多电子产品，比方像电话、MP3、笔记本电脑等等，当时的重量还很重。我认为我们应该有一些将这些功能结合在一起的电子产品。

Notes & Vocabulary

state-of-the-art 最先进的；最尖端的

名词为 state of the art，指"某种技术的最新发展或最高层次"，加上连字符作形容词使用，常用来形容科技、艺术、科学等。

• The company has some state-of-the-art inventions.
那家公司有一些最尖端的发明。

fledgling 刚开始的；无经验的

动词 fledge 是指"小鸟长羽翼"，也就是开始学飞的阶段，fledgling 当形容词用时比喻某事物"刚开始、刚起步"，也可指某人"缺乏经验"。fledgling 也可作名词，原本是指"刚会飞的小鸟"，可比喻为"缺乏经验者"或"涉世不深的年轻人"，类似网络用语的"菜鸟"。

1. gadget [ˈgædʒət] n. 小装置；小玩意儿
2. cutting edge [ˈkʌtɪŋ] [ɛdʒ] 尖端；最前沿
3. facility [fəˈsɪlətɪ] n. 设备；设施
4. PDA 个人掌上电脑（= personal digital assistant）
5. innovation [ˌɪnəˈveʃən] n. 创新；改革
6. doom [dum] v. 注定（毁灭、失败、死亡等）
7. inspiration [ˌɪnspəˈreʃən] n. 灵感；启发
8. device [dɪˈvaɪs] n. 装置；仪器
9. converge [kənˈvɜdʒ] v. 汇集；整合

James McDonald, Entrepreneurs Only

Wang and her business partners saw the potential for PDAs and smart phones—an essential accessory[10] for today's executives,[11] but uncommon a decade ago, and hardly a big seller.[12]

Cher Wang, HTC Founder and Chairperson

Nobody ~~can~~ [could] see these type[s] of devices would be popular. And so, it is very difficult, once we get out the product OK, it becomes something that people think is just going to sit on the shelves.

James McDonald, Entrepreneurs Only

The company was in debt[13] and appeared to be sinking. But instead of cutting her losses, Wang stayed with her vision. She poured her own money into research and development and kept the faith.

Cher Wang, HTC Founder and Chairperson

I'm a Christian. *The Bible* told us in *Proverbs* that "If my people don't have vision, ~~and~~ [then] my people perish."[14] So when we have a vision, we should be more consistent[15] and persistent[16] to conquer[17] the difficulty.

James McDonald, Entrepreneurs Only

The result was a complete turnaround.[18] HTC has since become the world's largest maker of smart phones using Microsoft operating systems, manufacturing[19] PDAs for some of the industry's top carriers.[20]

"企业家特写"詹姆斯·麦克唐纳

王雪红和她的生意伙伴看到了个人掌上电脑和智能手机的潜力，这些都是当今高层主管的必要配备，但在 10 年前却并不常见，更算不上是畅销商品。

宏达电子创始人兼董事长 王雪红

没有人认为这类产品会受到欢迎。所以很困难，当我们把产品做出来的时候，很多人认为这种东西会卖不掉。

"企业家特写"詹姆斯·麦克唐纳

当时的宏达电子债台高筑，似乎就危在旦夕。但王雪红并没有停止损失，反而坚持她自己的看法。她自筹经费投入研发工作，并坚持她的信念。

宏达电子创始人兼董事长 王雪红

我是基督徒，《圣经》里的《箴言》告诉我们："若我的子民没有梦想，那么我的子民便要灭亡。"，因此当我们有远见时，我们就应该不断地持续地去克服困难。

"企业家特写"詹姆斯·麦克唐纳

结果是彻底的逆转。宏达电子自此成为采用微软操作系统的全球第一大智能手机制造商，专为科技行业大厂制造个人掌上电脑。

Notes & Vocabulary

sit on the shelf 滞销

sit 在此是指"搁着不用"，这个短语字面上的意思是"搁置在架子上"，用来表示物品卖不出去，只能堆在货架上，也可以说 sit on a shelf。

• The proposal has sat on the shelf for years.
  那项提案被搁置多年。

cut one's losses 减少损失；停止损失

cut loss 是投资领域的专有名词，即所谓的"停止损失"，指投资失利造成损失时，要及时认输停止，才不会亏得更严重。cut one's losses 就是指"减少某人的损失"，从对自己不利的境中抽身。

• You should try to cut your losses when the situation doesn't look promising.
  情况看来不乐观的时候，你就该设法减少自己的损失。

10. accessory [æk`sɛsərɪ] n. 配件；附加物件
11. executive [ɪg`zɛkjətɪv] n. 高级主管；行政官员
12. big seller n. phr. 畅销商品
13. in debt phr. 负债
14. perish [`pɛrɪʃ] v. 消灭；死去
15. consistent [kən`sɪstənt] adj. 持续的；始终如一的
16. persistent [pə`sɪstənt] adj. 不断的；坚持不懈的
17. conquer [`kɑŋkə] v. 征服；克服
18. turnaround [`tɜnə,raʊnd] n. 突然好转；形势扭转
19. manufacture [,mænjə`fæktʃə] v. 大量制造；加工
20. carrier [`kɛriə] n. 电信行业企业；电子通信服务公司

Cher Wang, HTC Founder and Chairperson

Well, it excites me to see what, you know, our teamwork has accomplished. But I think our goal is to improve all the time.

James McDonald, Entrepreneurs Only

Just this year, HTC has launched its own brand. Some analysts[21] have questioned this strategy,[22] but the company believes the market will continue to grow. For Wang, who only uses a computer to check e-mail and surf the Web, it's part of a quest to design the ultimate[23] PDA.

Cher Wang, HTC Founder and Chairperson

Because I believe the device is ~~not~~ still not good enough here for me. Yeah, I believe that a device that I will really use is a device like a personal secretary.

宏达电子创始人兼董事长　王雪红

看到我们团队的成就使我感到振奋，但我认为不断进步才是我们的目标。

"企业家特写"詹姆斯·麦克唐纳

就在今年，宏达电子推出了自己的品牌。有些分析师对于这项策略表示质疑，但是该公司认为市场还会继续成长。对于将电脑只用来查看电子邮件和上网的王雪红而言，她所追求的目标则是要设计出顶级的个人掌上电脑。

宏达电子创始人兼董事长　王雪红

因为我相信这个产品对我而言还不够好。我相信我真正会用的产品必须要像是一位私人专属秘书。

Notes & Vocabulary

quest 追求；探索

quest 在此为名词，也可作动词用。

quest 作名词用，常见的短语用法有：

a. on a quest　寻找
  - Peter traveled to France and Spain, on a quest for the perfect wine.
    彼得去了法国和西班牙寻找最好的红酒。

b. in one's quest to　在某人寻求……的过程中
  - In his quest to become a champion swimmer, he broke many records.
    在他努力成为游泳冠军的过程中，他打破了许多纪录。

c. in quest of　为了寻求
  - Sam came to Hollywood in quest of fame.
    山姆为了成名来到了好莱坞。

21. **analyst** [ˈænəlɪst] *n.* 分析师

22. **strategy** [ˈstrætədʒɪ] *n.* 策略；计谋

23. **ultimate** [ˈʌltəmət] *adj.* 极限的；终极的

In Step with Puma CEO Jochen Zeitz

How He Brought the Sportswear Company Back from the Brink[1] of Bankruptcy[2]

Puma CEO 谈令企业起死回生的秘诀

Step 1 请浏览下方提示的关键问题后，仔细听录音。

1. What changes did Zeitz make when restructuring Puma?
2. What elements did Puma use to create its style?
3. How does Zeitz manage and encourage creativity in his staff?
4. How does Zeitz describe himself? What qualities make him a leader?

Step 2 如果你还听不太懂的话，请浏览下方的关键词汇后再听一次。

trend setting 引领潮流	raison d'etre 存在的理由、目的
roadblock 路障	restructure 重整
functionality 功能性	benchmark 以标准衡量
instinct 本能；直觉	elaborate 详尽地陈述

Step 3 试着回答下列听力测验题目。

True or False 是非题

_____ 1. Zeitz's family has had a long tradition of managing companies.

_____ 2. It did not take a long time for Zeitz to restructure Puma.

_____ 3. Zeitz made Puma a sports-fashion brand like other major brands at the time.

_____ 4. Zeitz says he will use any creative idea that his staff will come up with.

名人小档案

约亨·蔡茨（1963–）于 1990 年回到德国担任 Puma 鞋业部的营销与销售经理，不到两年便升为行政总裁，年仅 30 岁即成为德国上市公司最年轻的总裁。他上任后不久便让 Puma 转亏为盈，成功地将运动与时尚结合，并将 Puma 打造成国际知名的运动品牌。

_____ 5. Zeitz says most Germans like to analyze before taking action, but he doesn't.

Multiple Choice 选择题

_____ 1. What was not one of the changes Zeitz made when restructuring Puma?

a. He made it very Germanic.

b. He cut out layers of management.

c. He focused on being a global brand.

d. English was made the corporate language.

_____ 2. Which elements were combined to create Puma's style?

a. Performance and functionality.

b. Lifestyle and performance.

c. Sport, lifestyle and fashion.

d. Fashion and performance.

_____ 3. What does Zeitz say is important if someone wants to rise to the top?

a. Doing things quickly.

b. Being able to reorganize.

c. Being curious.

d. Being creative.

Step 4 试着用较慢的速度，再仔细听一遍，并检查答案是否正确。

Step 5 核对答案、检验成果，并详读原文，若仍有不懂的地方，可反复多听几次。

（答案请见 p. 229）

CNN Anchor

Each week, we get to know the business leaders behind the world's largest companies. CNN's financial editor, Todd Benjamin, goes one-on-one with Jochen Zeitz, CEO of Puma.

Todd Benjamin, CNN Financial Editor

Trend setting[3] is Puma's raison d'etre. Its focus on sports and fashion has made it one of the world's most desirable brands. But that hasn't always been the case. When Chief Executive and Chairman Jochen Zeitz took over in 1993, the company was in financial crisis. He turned it around.[4] Zeitz's move into business was perhaps a surprising one, given his family's 400-year-old tradition of studying medicine. I caught up with him at his German headquarters.[5]

When you took over Puma it was bankrupt on paper. It had several years of losses and, in your words, it was run by people who thought, "Germany was the center of the universe and that everything could be exported to the world. No one thought about the consumer."

Jochen Zeitz, CEO of Puma

That's how it was, yes. It was very Germanic, as we would say back then. And, well, we changed that very quickly. We just took out[6] management layers;[7] we took out roadblocks[8] and restructured[9] the company from top to bottom.

Todd Benjamin, CNN Financial Editor

But this was Germany.

MP3 原声 Track 61 / 慢速朗读 Track 62

CNN 主播

我们每周都会为您介绍全球大公司背后的商业领袖。CNN 金融主编托德·本杰明与彪马 CEO 约亨·蔡茨进行一对一访谈。

CNN 金融主编 托德·本杰明

引领潮流是彪马存在的理由。彪马致力于开发运动与时尚产品，如今已是世界上炙手可热的品牌。不过，彪马并不是一直都这么热门。CEO 兼董事长约亨·蔡茨在 1993 年接管彪马的时候，公司正处于财务危机当中，是他扭转了公司的处境。蔡茨的家族 400 年来一向从医，因此他从商不免令人惊讶。我在德国的公司总部与他见了面。

你接管彪马的时候，公司账面早已呈现破产状态，不但连年亏损，而且你还说当时的经营者自以为"德国是宇宙的中心，所有产品都可以销售到世界各地。没有人在乎消费者的想法。"

彪马 CEO 约亨·蔡茨

当时确实是这样没错。用我们那时候的说法，这家公司在当时非常以德国为中心。我们很快改变了这种情况，减少管理层级，消除障碍，把公司从上到下彻底重整一番。

CNN 金融主编 托德·本杰明

可是这里是德国啊。

Notes & Vocabulary

raison d'etre　存在的理由、目的

这个短语是法语的用法，raison 就是英文的 reason，etre 就是 be 动词，翻成英文就是 the reason of being，就是"存在的理由"或"存在的目的"。

• The company's raison d'etre is to provide inexpensive meals to low-income families.
这家公司经营的目的就是提供低收入家庭低价的餐点。

- -

1. brink [brɪŋk] *n.* 边缘

2. bankruptcy [ˈbæŋkrʌpsɪ] *n.* 破产

3. trend setting *n. phr.* 引领潮流

4. turn around　使……好转

5. headquarters [ˈhɛdˌkwɔrtəz] *n.* 总部

6. take out　扣除；除去

7. layer [ˈleə] *n.* 层面；层

8. roadblock [ˈrodˌblɑk] *n.* 路障

9. restructure [riˈstrʌktʃə] *v.* 重整；重建

Jochen Zeitz, CEO of Puma

Well, but I didn't look at it that way. I just said that our focus has to be from the outside in rather than from the inside out. I never felt that, although we were based in Germany, Puma was and should be considered as a German brand. And so we restructured it in a way that positioned us as a global brand with English being the corporate language, rather than us looking at it from a German perspective.[10]

Todd Benjamin, CNN Financial Editor

The most important thing was to stabilize[11] the company financially, because it was bankrupt on paper. Once you got the company stable, then what became important?

Jochen Zeitz, CEO of Puma

We decided that sport, lifestyle and fashion were three elements that could be mixed together to a very unique formula.[12] And that's what we did; make Puma a sports-fashion brand when at the times everybody talked about sport, and sport performance and functionality.[13] We said, well it's about more.

Todd Benjamin, CNN Financial Editor

How do you encourage your staff to be as creative as possible?

彪马 CEO 约亨·蔡茨

但是我不从这样的角度看事情。我只说过我们必须由外往内看，而不是由内往外看。我从不认为单单因为彪马设立在德国，就应该视其为德国品牌。因此，我们重整公司，自我定位为全球品牌，以英语为企业语言，而不是从德国的视角来看待这家公司。

CNN 金融主编 托德·本杰明

最重要的事情就是稳固公司的财务状况，因为当时公司账面上已经呈破产状态。财务状况稳定之后，接下来最重要的事情是什么？

彪马 CEO 约亨·蔡茨

运动、生活方式和时尚，我们认为这 3 项要素能够以非常独特的方式混合在一起。于是我们就这么做，把彪马塑造成一个运动时尚品牌。当时大家都还只是重视运动、运动方面的表现与功能性，我们认为运动产品还有其他的东西。

CNN 金融主编 托德·本杰明

你怎么鼓励员工尽量发挥创意？

Notes & Vocabulary

on paper 在统计中；理论上

字面意思是在纸上，引申有"账面上；表面上"的意思，其中暗指所呈现出来的可能不是实际的情况。

- Lisa's business plan looked good on paper.
  莉莎的企业计划表面上看起来还是不错的。

另一个与 paper 相关的财经用语是 paper profit，指"账面盈利"。

- Paper profits were better than initial projections.
  账面盈利比预期的要好。

. . . .

10. perspective [pəˋspɛktɪv] n. 观点；看法
11. stabilize [ˋstebəˌlaɪz] v. 使稳定
12. formula [ˋfɔrmjələ] n. 方程式；准则
13. functionality [ˌfʌnʃəˋnælətɪ] n. 功能性

Jochen Zeitz, CEO of Puma

Well, we allow people to be creative. We set a direction, we set the vision, we set the strategy, but within that framework[14] we allow our people to be as creative as they want to be. And there's not an idea that can be crazy enough. We just allow that. Of course, we always benchmark[15] it and check if we think it's in line with what Puma as a brand wants to stand for. But, nurturing[16] creativity, creating creative freedom is important to us.

Todd Benjamin, CNN Financial Editor

What advice would you have for anyone who wants to try to rise to the top?

Jochen Zeitz, CEO of Puma

Follow your instincts,[17] follow what you think is right and then implement[18] as quickly as you can because if you drag things out,[19] that can be very difficult.

Todd Benjamin, CNN Financial Editor

Jochen, clearly you're a very driven[20] man. Where does that drive come from?

Jochen Zeitz, CEO of Puma

I'm a curious person and I always like to test new waters and I've always jumped into the cold water and then started to think about how to swim. And I never did it the traditional German way where you would say well let's elaborate[21] on that and let's analyze the situation all the way through before you make a decision. You know, if I felt that my chances to succeed were about 50 percent, I, you know, went for it.

彪马 CEO 约亨·蔡茨

我们允许大家有创意。我们设定方向，确立愿景，拟定策略，而在这个框架里面，就让大家尽情发挥创意，再怎么天马行空的点子都不为过。我们容许这样的空间存在。当然，我们还是会用标准加以审视，看看这种想法是否符合我们认为彪马品牌所代表的形象。不过，培养创意以及开创创意空间，对我们来说仍然是很重要的。

CNN 金融主编 托德·本杰明

对于想要爬上巅峰的人，你有什么建议？

彪马 CEO 约亨·蔡茨

追随你的直觉，朝着你心中认为正确的方向走，并且尽快采取行动，因为事情越拖就越难处理。

CNN 金融主编 托德·本杰明

约亨，你显然非常有冲劲。你的冲劲是从哪里来的？

彪马 CEO 约亨·蔡茨

我的好奇心很强，喜欢尝试新事物。我总是先跳进水里，再开始思考该怎么游泳。我从不采取传统的德国做法，先阐述一番，彻底分析情况，然后再做决定。如果我觉得差不多有五成的成功几率，就会立即动手去做。

Notes & Vocabulary

in line with　与……一致

in line 本身是"成一条线"的意思，说彼此的意见成一条线，就是意见一致的意思，也可以说 in accordance with、correspondent with/to。

- The stock's performance was in line with expectations.
  股市的表现和预期的一样。

其他与 line 连用的常见短语有：

a. hold the line　坚守岗位；坚守立场
  - The soldiers were told to hold the line until reinforcements arrive.
    长官命令士兵们在后援到达前要坚守阵地。

b. read between the lines　了解到言外之意
  - Jack read between the lines and realized that his girlfriend was breaking up with him.
    杰克终于了解女友的言外之意是要跟他分手。

14. framework [ˈfremˌwɜk] n. 构架；框架

15. benchmark [ˈbɛntʃˌmɑrk] v. 以标准审视

16. nurture [ˈnɜtʃə] v. 培养；培育；教养

17. instinct [ˈɪnˌstɪŋkt] n. 本能；直觉

18. implement [ˈɪmpləˌmɛnt] v. 实施；履行

19. drag out　拖延

20. driven [ˈdrɪvən] adj. 有冲劲的

21. elaborate [ɪˈlæbəˌret] v. 详尽地陈述

Architect[1] of Change

ING CEO and Corporate Restructuring Guru Michel Tilmant

ING 集团 CEO 蒂尔曼特谈企业重整的魄力

Step 1 请浏览下方提示的关键问题后，仔细听录音。

1. What services does ING provide?
2. Why did Tilmant order the restructuring of ING?
3. What qualities does Tilmant say a great leader needs?
4. What does Tilmant say is a CEO's biggest mistake?

Step 2 如果你还听不太懂的话，请浏览下方的关键词汇后再听一次。

befit 适合于	acquisition （公司）收购
accountable 负责任的；可说明的	portfolio 投资组合；全部有价证券
energize 激励；使精力充沛	impatience 没耐心；不耐烦

Step 3 试着回答下列听力测验题目。

True or False 是非题

_____ 1. After a year as CEO of ING, Tilmant ordered a restructuring of the group.

_____ 2. Before Tilmant became CEO, ING had acquired many businesses and was not well organized.

_____ 3. Tilmant thinks a great leader is someone who follows their vision.

_____ 4. Tilmant says what a manager says should match what his employees believe is true.

_____ 5. Tilmant says that his greatest concern right now is his impatience.

名人小档案

米歇尔·蒂尔曼特 (1952–) 毕业于比利时鲁汶大学企业管理系。他原本任职比利时 BBL 银行总裁，后因荷兰 ING 集团并购该银行而加入 ING 集团，并于 2004 年接任总裁一职。ING 集团提供银行、保险及资产管理等金融服务，2008 年由《福布斯》杂志评比为全球排名第九大公司。

Multiple Choice 选择题

_____ 1. Which field is ING not involved in?
a. Banking.
b. Accounting.
c. Insurance.
d. Asset management.

_____ 2. Why does Tilmant say decisions should be made quickly?
a. They will hurt less to make.
b. That is how you learn.
c. So one can focus on important things.
d. So you can move around the world.

_____ 3. What does Tilmant say is easy for a manager to do?
a. Stay connected with reality.
b. Lose touch with the real situation.
c. Build ivory towers.
d. Go back on the work floor.

Step 4 试着用较慢的速度，再仔细听一遍，并检查答案是否正确。

Step 5 核对答案、检验成果，并详读原文，若仍有不懂的地方，可反复多听几次。

（答案请见 p. 229）

Todd Benjamin, CNN Financial Editor

With more than 60 million customers, ING is obviously doing something right. It's one of the world's largest insurance companies. It's also in banking and asset management.[2] The company's ultramodern[3] headquarters befits[4] a leader who's not afraid of taking bold[5] steps.

Less than a month into the job, Michel Tilmant announced a major restructuring. Shaking things up isn't new to him. ING is his third restructuring.

We met up in Amsterdam, and I began by asking him about the reorganization.[6]

Michel Tilmant, CEO of ING

First of all, ING developed itself by a number of acquisitions[7] over the years to become this large international group, and I thought that it was necessary to simplify[8] the organization and to make sure that things were more transparent[9] and more accountable.[10] The organization was more accountable. So that was the objective of my reorganization. I think also that, after so many years of acquisition, it was time to take a step back and say "OK, what is really necessary in this portfolio?[11] What is not necessary? And are we going to concentrate ourselves?"

CNN 金融主编 托德·本杰明

ING 集团的客户超过 6 000 万，虽然一定有什么妙方。其规模在全球保险公司当中数一数二，也涉足银行业与资产管理。这个超级现代化的企业总部，正符合这位企业领导人敢于冒险的个性。

米歇尔·蒂尔曼特接掌 ING 集团不到 1 个月就宣布进行大规模重整。整编组织对他而言并非新鲜事，ING 集团是他重整的第三家公司。

我们在阿姆斯特丹见面，我一开始先问他组织重整的情况。

ING 集团 CEO 米歇尔·蒂尔曼特

首先，ING 集团在过去几年来通过多次并购（注）而成为今天这个庞大的国际集团。我认为有必要简化组织以确保运作透明化，同时把责任划分清楚。现在组织的责任划分已经比较明确，而这也是我重整公司的目标。我也认为，经过这么多年的购并之后，现在该要后退一步，问问自己：“我们的所有产品当中，有哪些是真正必要的？哪些是不必要的？我们是不是要集中火力在某个领域冲刺？”

注：ING Group（荷兰国际集团）于 1991 年由 Nationale-Nederlanden（荷兰国民人寿保险公司）与 NMB Postbank Group（NMB 邮政银行集团）合并组成，此后不断通过并购扩充业务规模。包括：1995—Barings（巴林集团）、1997—Equitable of Iowa Companies 保险公司、1998—比利时 BBL 银行、1999—德国 BHF 银行、2000—美国 Aetra 全球金融服务公司、2001—波兰 Slaski 银行、墨西哥 Seguros Comercial America 保险公司、2002—德国 DiBa 银行。

Notes & Vocabulary

take steps 采取措施

step 作名词有“脚步；措施；台阶”等意思，take steps 即指“采取措施”。

另外，文中出现了 take a step back，字面是指“后退一步”，引申为“暂缓一下，好好想想”的意思。

- After several failures, the scientist took a step back to see if the project was flawed.
  经过数次失败，那位科学家停下来回头想想这个计划是否存在缺陷。

shake sth up （组织）重整

shake up 用于表示对组织等做出重大改变，通常目的是为了使其更好，例如进行改组、裁并部门、人事调动等。shake-up 为名词，表示“重组；大整顿”的意思。

- The government is poised for a major shake-up.
  政府准备进行大规模重组。

....

1. architect [ˈɑrkəˌtɛkt] *n.* 建筑师；创造者

2. asset management [ˈæˌsɛt] [ˈmænɪdʒmənt] *n. phr.* 资产管理

3. ultramodern [ˈʌltrəˈmɑdən] *adj.* 超级现代化的（ultra- 为词首，表示“超……”）

4. befit [bɪˈfɪt] *v.* 适合于；对……适当

5. bold [bold] *adj.* 果断的；冒险的；无畏的

6. reorganization [riˌɔrgənəˈzeʃən] *n.* 整顿；改组

7. acquisition [ˌækwəˈzɪʃn] *n.* （公司）收购；并购

8. simplify [ˈsɪmpləˌfaɪ] *v.* 简化；使精简

9. transparent [trænsˈpɛrənt] *adj.* 透明的

10. accountable [əˈkaʊntəbəl] *adj.* 负责任的；可说明的

11. portfolio [portˈfolɪˌo] *n.* 投资组合；文件夹；作品集；全部有价证券

Todd Benjamin, CNN Financial Editor

But when you do your restructuring, tough decisions need to be made. What did you learn from the process?

Michel Tilmant, CEO of ING

Well, I think when you have to make decisions, you have to make them and make them fast, and I think that's what I learned. I think that you cannot wait, because the world moves around you and you have to basically take those measures as quickly as you can, so that you can concentrate [on] what is essential.

Todd Benjamin, CNN Financial Editor

What separates a good leader from a great leader?

Michel Tilmant, CEO of ING

Well, I think what makes a difference is that a great leader can inspire and can energize[12]—two fantastic qualities.

Todd Benjamin, CNN Financial Editor

Biggest mistake most CEOs make?

CNN 金融主编 托德·本杰明

可是在重整过程中必需要做出艰难的决策，从这个过程中您学到了什么？

ING 集团 CEO 米歇尔·蒂尔曼特

我想，你一旦必须做决策，就不能逃避，而且要立刻做决定。这就是我学到的东西。我认为你不能慢慢等待，因为周围的世界不断变动，你必须尽快采取各种措施，才能专注于真正重要的事物上。

CNN 金融主编 托德·本杰明

优秀的领导人和卓越的领导人有什么不同？

ING 集团 CEO 米歇尔·蒂尔曼特

我想，关键的差别在于卓越的领导人能够激励人心，并唤起实际行动——这是两项很棒的特质。

CNN 金融主编 托德·本杰明

大多数 CEO 所犯的最大错误是什么？

Notes & Vocabulary

make a difference 造成差异

make a difference 字面上是指"造成差异"，引申指"改善"的意思，后面可接 to sth/sb。

- Getting a good education makes a difference when you're starting to work.
  当你开始工作时，有没有接受过良好的教育就有区别了。
- Winning the lottery will make a difference to a poor man not a millionaire.
  中彩票可改变一个穷人的生活，但对百万富翁却没有影响。

12. energize [ˈɛnɚˌdʒaɪz] v. 激励；使精力充沛

Michel Tilmant, CEO of ING

Well, I think that if you are a chief executive, the big risk is you start distancing yourself from[13] reality because you run the risk to work in an ivory tower. And, no, you have to go back to the floor, to the work floor, trying to understand what's going on and make sure that you get connected with the reality.

That's very, very important. And I think that you [also] have ~~also~~ to make sure that what you say and the motivation[14] you give to your people is also connected with that reality, that you don't start believing in a story that is completely disconnected from what the people in the company believe.

Todd Benjamin, CNN Financial Editor

Your greatest strength as a manager?

Michel Tilmant, CEO of ING

Common sense.

Todd Benjamin, CNN Financial Editor

Greatest weakness?

Michel Tilmant, CEO of ING

Impatience.[15]

Todd Benjamin, CNN Financial Editor

Your biggest concern right now?

Michel Tilmant, CEO of ING

I'd like to know what I don't know.

ING 集团 CEO 米歇尔·蒂尔曼特

我认为担任 CEO 的一大危险，就是会把自己关在象牙塔里而与现实脱节。不能够这样，你必须脚踏实地，亲自了解基层的情况，设法了解实际情况，确认自己能够不脱离现实。

这是非常非常重要的事情。我认为，你自己说的话以及给予下属的奖励也都必须合乎实际情况。不要让自己的想法与公司里大多数人的想法完全脱钩。

CNN 金融主编 托德·本杰明

你认为自己身为经理人最大的长处在哪里？

ING 集团 CEO 米歇尔·蒂尔曼特

常识判断。

CNN 金融主编 托德·本杰明

最大的缺点呢？

ING 集团 CEO 米歇尔·蒂尔曼特

缺乏耐性。

CNN 金融主编 托德·本杰明

你目前最关切的事情是什么？

ING 集团 CEO 米歇尔·蒂尔曼特

我想知道自己所不知道的事情。

Notes & Vocabulary

ivory tower 象牙塔

ivory tower 一词最早出现在《旧约全书》中，将新娘子美丽的颈项喻为象牙塔。19 世纪时法国的文艺批评家圣勃夫（Charles Augustin, Sainte-Beuve）以此语批评浪漫派诗人维尼（Alfred Victor, Vigny），指其忽视了现实社会的丑恶悲惨面，自隐于理想中的美满情境而从事创作，此后英语中便常用 ivory tower 比喻与世隔绝的世外桃源或是不食人间烟火的文艺家或学者自我构筑出的小天地；中文里"象牙塔"一词则少了"世外桃源"这层解释，和英语 ivory tower 的外延意义有一点区别。

- Scholars seem to live in ivory towers, cut off from reality.
  学者们似乎住在象牙塔里，与现实社会脱了节。

---

13. **distance oneself from . . .**
    使自己与……保持距离

14. **motivation** [ˌmotəˈveʃən] *n.* 刺激；推动

15. **impatience** [ɪmˈpeʃəns] *n.* 没耐性；不耐烦

Rock 'n' Roll Original[1]
TalkAsia Exclusive Interview with Sting
CNN 专访摇滚乐传奇人物斯汀

Step 1 ◉ 请浏览下方提示的关键问题后，仔细听录音。

1. How did Sting get the nickname "Sting"?
2. How did the members of The Police feel about the fame they got?
3. What does Sting say a band needs to become popular?
4. What sort of things does Sting say he is intrigued by?

Step 2 如果你还听不太懂的话，请浏览下方的关键词汇后再听一次。

croon 低声吟唱	**dabble** 涉猎；涉足
vigor 体力；活力	**suspicion** 猜疑；怀疑
signature 识别标志	**intrigue** 引起强烈兴趣、好奇心

Step 3 💡 试着回答下列听力测验题目。

True or False 是非题

_____ 1. Sting grew up in the suburbs of London.

_____ 2. Sting played in jazz band before joining The Police.

_____ 3. According to Sting, The Police were surprised by the fame they achieved.

_____ 4. Sting says that everyone expected him to leave The Police when he did.

_____ 5. Sting thinks that human beings are impressive and miraculous.

◉ *MP3 原声 Track 65 / 慢速朗读 Track 66*

名人小档案

斯汀（1951–）是近代流行音乐史上罕见的巨星，能唱、能写、能制作并精通多种乐器。曾与鼓手 Stewart Copeland 及吉他手 Andy Summers 组成警察乐队（The Police），是英国最成功的乐团之一。斯汀单飞后的成绩依然不俗，在乐坛表现优异。

Multiple Choice 选择题

_____ 1. Why did Sting wear the yellow sweater that gave him his nickname?

　　a. He wanted to make people laugh.

　　b. His band mates thought it was cool.

　　c. He thought it made him look special.

　　d. It was very cold where he was.

_____ 2. What does Sting say a band has to do to become popular?

　　a. Not sound like any other band.

　　b. Have a good name, like U2.

　　c. Have people argue about who they are.

　　d. Sign their name in a special way.

_____ 3. What does Sting say is important in his life now?

　　a. Making music.

　　b. Meeting people.

　　c. Taking care of rabbits.

　　d. Learning about miracles.

Step 4 试着用较慢的速度，再仔细听一遍，并检查答案是否正确。

Step 5 核对答案、检验成果，并详读原文，若仍有不懂的地方，可反复多听几次。

（答案请见 p. 229）

Lorraine Hahn, TalkAsia

Welcome to *TalkAsia*. I'm Lorraine Hahn. British music icon Sting is our guest this week. The 52-year-old rocker[2] has been at the top of the music industry for over two decades. There are few other songwriters who've composed as many hits or croon[3] as beautifully as Sting.

Born Gordon Matthew Sumner, Sting grew up in a rough[4] neighborhood in northern England. He says he always loved music and dabbled[5] in it a bit, but it was the formation[6] of The Police in 1977 that changed his life forever. The group was considered one of the most progressive[7] and sophisticated[8] of its time.

Well let me ask you, how did your name "Sting" come about?

Sting, Songwriter and Musician

Where did it come from? I was 18. I was playing in a trad jazz[9] group, the traditional jazz group, with people much older than myself, people about my age now, and to define my youth and vigor[10] I would wear this sweater with black and yellow hoops[11]—I looked like a wasp.[12] And I probably looked terrible but I thought it was really cool, and the band all laughed at this sweater and they started to call me Sting as a joke, and I thought, OK, very funny. Next night they called me the same name and it went on all week until it was my name.

Lorraine Hahn, TalkAsia

Talk to you about [The] Police, did the fame of the band catch you by surprise? The fame that you got?

"亚洲名人聊天室" 韩玉花

欢迎收看"亚洲名人聊天室"，我是韩玉花。本周来宾是英国乐坛偶像斯汀。这位 52 岁的摇滚歌手雄踞音乐界龙头地位逾 20 年。很少有其他歌曲创作者能像斯汀一样写出这么好歌金曲，或者歌声和他一样优美。

本名戈登·马修·萨姆纳的斯汀，在英格兰北部一个不时发生暴力事件的社区长大。他说他向来热爱音乐，并略有涉猎，但 1977 年"警察乐队"的成立才彻底改变了他的一生。这个乐队被认为是当时最前卫且最有深度的乐队。

我想问问，你的名字"斯汀"是怎么来的？

作曲家兼音乐人 斯汀

它是怎么来的呢？我当时 18 岁，在一个传统爵士乐队里演奏，成员的年纪都大我一大截，差不多是我现在这个年纪。为了表现我的青春活力，我会穿上一圈圈黄黑相间的毛衣，看起来就像一只大黄蜂。或许我当时的样子很糟，但我自己却觉得很酷，整个乐队都在嘲笑这件毛衣，他们开始开玩笑地叫我"斯汀"，我心想，一点都不好笑。隔天晚上他们又这么叫我，连续叫了一个星期，直到这成了我的名字。（编注：sting 亦有"蜂刺"之意）

"亚洲名人聊天室" 韩玉花

来聊聊"警察乐队"，这个乐队迅速走红是否让你们感到意外？你们成名的感觉如何？

Notes & Vocabulary

catch by surprise 使感到意外或吃惊

sth catch sb by surprise 是表示"某事出乎某人意料；某人在无准备情况下遇到某事"的意思，也可以说 sth take sb by surprise。

• The success of their latest product caught the company by surprise.
那家公司最近推出的产品销量很好让他们大感意外。

• The number of people that showed up at the concert took us completely by surprise.
出席音乐会的观众人数完全出乎我们意料。

1. **original** [əˈrɪdʒənl̩] *n.* 有独创性的人；原著；原型

2. **rocker** [ˈrɑkɚ] *n.* 摇滚歌手

3. **croon** [krun] *v.* 低声吟唱

4. **rough** [rʌf] *adj.* 秩序混乱的；常发生暴力和犯罪事件的

5. **dabble** [ˈdæbəl] *v.* 涉猎；涉足

6. **formation** [fɔrˈmeʃən] *n.* 形成；组成；设立

7. **progressive** [prəˈɡrɛsɪv] *adj.* 先进的；革新的；进步的

8. **sophisticated** [səˈfɪstɪˌketəd] *adj.* 精致的；有深度的

9. **trad jazz** [træd] [dʒæz] *n. phr.* 传统爵士乐
(= traditional jazz)

10. **vigor** [ˈvɪɡɚ] *n.* 体力；活力

11. **hoop** [hup] *n.* 箍；圈；环

12. **wasp** [wɑsp] *n.* 黄蜂

Sting, Songwriter and Musician

Well I think we achieved everything we set out to achieve a hundredfold if not a thousandfold. We had a sneaking[13] suspicion[14] that we had something original and something to offer the world, but we had no idea it would happen so big. [I'm] very grateful for that. [I'm] very proud of that group. But once we'd achieved all of that, I decided that to keep repeating it would just give me diminishing returns and so against all logic I left the band and started again, and here I am.

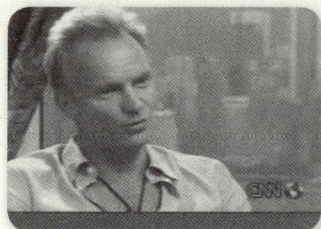

Lorraine Hahn, TalkAsia

When you look at good bands, great bands, whatever, popular bands, [The] Police was obviously a great band. What do you think was the main ingredient[15] to make it such a hit internationally?

Sting, Songwriter and Musician

I think that what happens in the bands that have made it and made it big and stayed in the public perception[16] is that they have an instantly recognizable signature.[17] As soon as you hear a record by R.E.M. or U2 or The Stones or The Police, you instantly know who it is. There's no, there's simply no argument that that is, that's that band.

Lorraine Hahn, TalkAsia

What is it about life for you that is important to you now?

作曲家兼音乐人 斯汀

我想我们所取得的，就算没有当初所想要达成目标的一千倍，起码也有一百倍。我们当时心中隐约觉得我们有原创性，有真材实料要展现给全世界，但我们没想到会这么成功。我对此心存感激，我以这个乐队为荣。但是一旦我们达成了所有的目标，我觉得如果继续重复这样做，只会让我得到的回报越来越少，于是我反其道而行，离开乐队重新出发，一直到现在。

"亚洲名人聊天室" 韩玉花

若谈起乐队、一流的乐队、受欢迎的乐队，警察乐队显然是支一流的乐队，您认为之所以能享誉全球的主要因素是什么？

作曲家兼音乐人 斯汀

我觉得那些成功的、名号响亮的，会被大家一直记得的乐队之所以成功，是因为他们都有显而易见的独特风格。你一旦听到一张"R.E.M."、"U2"、"滚石"或"警察乐队"的唱片，你马上就知道是谁，毋庸置疑就是那个乐队。

"亚洲名人聊天室" 韩玉花

现在您认为人生中有哪些事情对你来说是重要的？

Notes & Vocabulary

diminishing returns
报酬递减；收益递减

收益递减法则 (law of diminishing returns) 是传统经济学上的一种假说，主要的含义是：当技术与某些生产要素固定不变时，若只增加使用可变要素，其产量最终会下降且比平均产量低。

本文中，由于斯汀觉得"警察乐队"已达到当初所设定目标的千百倍，因此再怎么投入，其报酬或成就终究还是会递减，并不会有所突破。于是毅然决定离开"警察乐队"，独自单飞。

....

13. **sneaking** [ˈsnikɪŋ] *adj.* 暗中的；偷偷摸摸的

14. **suspicion** [səˈspɪʃən] *n.* 猜疑；怀疑

15. **ingredient** [ɪnˈgridiənt] *n.* 成分；构成要素

16. **public perception** [ˌpʌblɪk] [pəˈsɛpʃən] *n. phr.* 公众认知；公众对……的认识与理解

17. **signature** [ˈsɪgnəˌtʃə] *n.* 识别标志；签名

Sting, Songwriter and Musician

I'm kind of intrigued[18] more and more about what a miracle it is, you know, what a miracle human beings are and meeting human beings and actually having, you know, meeting with them and contacting these very impressive[19] beings. And the more you get into that the more rewarding it is. You know, I'm not one of these people that likes to sort of shut themselves away from people because I think people are my lifeblood,[20] you know, I tell stories, I have to hear them. And so I'll sit in a pub and I'll listen to people rabbit on about something but . . . I think communication.

Lorraine Hahn, TalkAsia

Well, Sting, thank you. Thank you for sharing that, appreciate it.

Sting, Songwriter and Musician

It's a pleasure. Thanks for listening to me rabbit on.

作曲家兼音乐人 斯汀

我越来越觉得这实在是个奇迹，人类实在很奇妙，去认识不同的人，和他们……与这些令人感动的人实际接触。你投入越深，得到的回报就愈大。我不是那种喜欢离群独处的人，因为我觉得人是我灵感的源泉，我会讲一些故事，也要听听他们的故事。所以我会坐在一间酒吧里，我会听人们喋喋不休说一些事……我想是沟通吧。

"亚洲名人聊天室"韩玉花

斯汀，谢谢您。谢谢您和我们分享这些，感谢您。

作曲家兼音乐人 斯汀

这是我的荣幸，谢谢你听我闲聊这么多。

Notes & Vocabulary

shut oneself away 离群索居

此语常指因某种缘故而刻意避开人群独处，也许是因为心情不好或想一个人专心做事、读书等，文中的 shut themselves away from people 则是单纯地指不喜欢热闹的人群、喜欢"离群索居"。

- After retiring, Jacob shut himself away in a mountain cabin.
  雅各布退休后，在山上的小木屋过着离群索居的生活。

rabbit on 唠叨；喋喋不休

这是英式押韵俚语（rhyming slang）的一种衍生用法，原本是以 rabbit and pork（兔肉和猪肉）与 talk 押韵的情形，而衍生出"唠叨；说个不停"的意思。rabbit and pork（闲聊）除了作动词用外，也可作名词用，如 have a rabbit and pork with（与……闲聊）。文中的 rabbit 则是 rabbit and pork 的简略说法，因此 rabbit on 即"唠叨；喋喋不休"之意。

- Marcy's sister can rabbit on about any subject.
  玛西的姐姐对什么话题都能喋喋不休讲一大堆。

....

18. intrigue [ɪnˋtrig] *v.* 引起强烈兴趣、好奇心

19. impressive [ɪmˋprɛsɪv] *adj.* 令人印象深刻的；让人刮目相看的

20. lifeblood [ˋlaɪfˏblʌd] *n.* (维持生命所必需的)血液；活力之源

Micro-Finance Magician

Nobel Laureate[1] Muhammed Yunus Turns Tiny Loans into Big Opportunities

穷人银行家尤努斯——小贷款创造大改变

Step 1 ◉ 请浏览下方提示的关键问题后，仔细听录音。

1. What does the correspondent say a person needs to make money?
2. What did Yunus do before starting Grameen Bank?
3. What does Yunus help beggars to do?
4. What didn't Yunus realize at first?

Step 2 如果你还听不太懂的话，请浏览下方的关键词汇后再听一次。

laureate 获得殊荣者	rural 乡村的
famine 饥荒	equivalent 等同物；等价物
merchandise 商品；产品	pick up 改善；有起色

Step 3 💡 试着回答下列听力测验题目。

True or False 是非题

_____ 1. Yunus feels good being able to help even just one person for one day.

_____ 2. Yunus finds economic theories that he teaches to be elegant.

_____ 3. Seeing the famine in Bangladesh caused Yunus to become an economics professor.

_____ 4. Yunus was surprised at how small the amounts of money were that were being loaned.

_____ 5. Yunus's loans help some beggars become businesspeople.

名人小档案

穆罕默德·尤努斯（1940-）是孟加拉的银行家和经济学者，2006 年与其所创立的乡村银行共同获得诺贝尔和平奖。他早年与大学里的研究项目合作，以"微型贷款"协助贫民。乡村银行成立后，更扩大了对该大学附近村落的贫民的帮助，并获得政府协助拓展到首都达卡及全国各地乡村，而后更将这种成功的模式扩展至其他国家，使许多穷人受惠。

Multiple Choice 选择题

_____ 1. Who wouldn't want Grameen's clients?
   a. Beggars.
   b. Conventional banks.
   c. Economic theorists.
   d. Small businessmen.

_____ 2. What made Yunus feel terrible?
   a. Teaching elegant theories.
   b. Not being able to help people.
   c. Not being repaid his loans.
   d. Working at a university.

_____ 3. What does Yunus suggest beggars do?
   a. Sell things door to door.
   b. Start working at universities.
   c. Learn about economic theories.
   d. Become moneylenders.

Step 4 试着用较慢的速度，再仔细听一遍，并检查答案是否正确。

Step 5 核对答案、检验成果，并详读原文，若仍有不懂的地方，可反复多听几次。

（答案请见 p.229）

Jonathan Mann, CNN Correspondent

To make money you have to have something to make money with. You have to start with something. Millions of people are trapped in poverty² because they don't have even the smallest something. For more than 30 years, Muhammed Yunus and the Grameen Bank he founded have been lending money to clients no conventional³ banker would want, in amounts so small no conventional banker would bother. *Gram* means village, and Grameen bankers go to rural⁴ villages to offer loans from a few dollars to a few hundred dollars to start a small business. As each borrower pays it back, the money is loaned out to ~~other~~ [others].

Jonathan Mann, CNN Correspondent

You are an economics professor.

Muhammed Yunus, Nobel Peace Prize Winner

That's right.

Jonathan Mann, CNN Correspondent

Was this an idea straight out of the text book?

CNN 特派记者 乔纳森·曼恩

想要赚钱，就必须有赚钱的工具。你总得要先有些资本才能开始。数百万的人受贫穷之苦，就是因为他们连最基本的资本都没有。30 多年来，穆罕默德·尤努斯和他所创立的乡村银行一直贷款给一般银行不愿接受的客户，而且借贷款项常常是一般银行不屑一顾的金额。Gram 是指乡村，乡村银行的职员会到各个村庄，提供村民几美元至数百美元的贷款，好让他们做点小生意。只要借款人偿还借款，这些钱就可以再贷给别人。

CNN 特派记者 乔纳森·曼恩

您是经济学教授。

诺贝尔和平奖得主 穆罕默德·尤努斯

是的。

CNN 特派记者 乔纳森·曼恩

这个构想是直接从教科书里而来的吗？

Notes & Vocabulary

straight out of 直接出自于

straight 在这里作副词，表示"直接地"，这个短语是指直接出自某处，未经修改搬过来照用。此外，straight out 还有"坦白；直说"的意思。

- The idea came straight out of the research and development department.
  这个想法直接出自于研发部门。
- Jack could tell straight out that the restaurant would be too expensive for his budget.
  杰克大可直说那家餐厅对他的预算来说太贵了。

1. laureate [ˈlɔriət] *n.* 获得殊荣者
2. poverty [ˈpɑvətɪ] *n.* 贫穷；贫困
3. conventional [kənˈvɛnʃənl] *adj.* 传统的；一般的
4. rural [ˈrurəl] *adj.* 乡村的

Muhammed Yunus, Nobel Peace Prize Winner

No. I had no idea. I was actually teaching economics at the university and Bangladesh was going through a famine[5] situation at that time in [the] early '70s—1974 actually. And I felt terrible that I teach such elegant[6] theories of economics in the classroom and outside the classroom people go hungry and I have nothing that I can do. So I thought maybe I shouldn't carry ~~this~~ [these] elegant theories with me, just be a human being and go out there and be with people. If I can help one person, even for one day, I will feel I did something.

Jonathan Mann, CNN Correspondent

But you didn't go out to give the money. You went out to lend the money. How much was the first loan and who did it go to?

Muhammed Yunus, Nobel Peace Prize Winner

I was confronted with this money lending business in that little village that I was working next to the campus and I made a list of people who borrowed from money lenders. There were 42 people on my list. Total money was $27. [I] said, my god this [is] so easy to solve this problem. I didn't realize that [there's] such a tiny little amount of money involved.

Jonathan Mann, CNN Correspondent

It's half a dollar. Now, I take it the smallest loan that's available through the Grameen Bank is 500 taka, the equivalent[7] of about US$9, and it goes to beggars.

诺贝和平奖得主 穆罕默德·尤努斯

不是，我本来一点概念都没有。我原本在大学教经济学，当时孟加拉正遭遇饥荒，那是 70 年代早期，确切时间是 1974 年。我觉得很惭愧，因为我在课堂上讲授这些冠冕堂皇的理论，但是课堂外的民众连饭都没得吃，我却一点办法也没有。于是，我觉得自己也许不该死守着这些理论不放，而应该以普通人的身份走到民众当中。只要我能够帮助一个人，就算只是帮助一天也好，那么我就会觉得自己做了点事。

CNN 特派记者 乔纳森·曼恩

可是你不是给钱，而是借钱。你第一笔借款借出多少钱，借给了谁？

诺贝和平奖得主 穆罕默德·尤努斯

我到校园附近的小村庄去帮忙，碰到了借贷的问题。我把所有向别人借钱的居民列入一份名单，共有 42 个人，借贷总额为 27 美元。我心想：天啊，这个问题实在太容易解决了。我原本不知道涉及的金额竟然这么少。

CNN 特派记者 乔纳森·曼恩

每个人借半美元。据我所知，乡村银行的最低贷款额度是 500 塔卡，约等于 9 美元，而且这笔钱是借给乞丐的。

Notes & Vocabulary

be confronted with sth 碰到；面临

confront 有"面临；与……冲突"的意思，常用被动形式 be confronted with sth。另外，confront sb with sth 则是指向某人质问某事，通常是关于不好的事，或是让对方对某事加以解释。

- Greg was confronted with making the decision of which workers to lay off.
  格雷格面临要决定解雇哪一位员工的难题。
- Mr. Jefferies confronted his secretary with a phone bill showing all the personal calls she made.
  杰弗里斯先生质问秘书那些她打的私人电话的账单是怎么一回事。

5. famine [ˈfæmən] *n.* 饥荒
6. elegant [ˈɛləgənt] *adj.* 讲究的；优雅的
7. equivalent [ɪˈkwɪvlənt] *n.* 等同物；等价物

Muhammed Yunus, Nobel Peace Prize Winner

Beggars.

Jonathan Mann, CNN Correspondent

And the beggar turns into a businessman? What kind of business can a beggar do?

Muhammed Yunus, Nobel Peace Prize Winner

What we are suggesting as we talk to the beggars, you go house to house begging and it's a very hard life. Since you go house to house anyway, would you like to carry some merchandise[8] with you? Little snacks, what the kids would love or housewives would love, or some household items or some toys for the kids, simple things that you can carry with you.

So you give people [the] option whether they will give you something free or want to buy something from you. And it's up to them. If they support you, your business picks up[9] and you could close down your begging kind of division[10] of your work and concentrate[11] on the business division. And you become a door-to-door business person.

诺贝尔和平奖得主 穆罕默德·尤努斯

乞丐，没错。

CNN 特派记者 乔纳森·曼恩

然后乞丐就成了生意人？乞丐能够做什么生意？

诺贝尔和平奖得主 穆罕默德·尤努斯

我们对这些乞丐说，你挨家挨户乞讨其实很辛苦。既然一样是挨家挨户拜访，你何不带点商品在身上呢？像是小孩或家庭主妇喜欢的小点心，或者居家用品，或者小孩子的玩具，总之是能够带在身边的小东西。这么一来，你所乞讨的对象就可以选择是要施舍给你，还是向你买东西。完全由他们自己决定。他们如果支持你，你的生意能做得起来，那么你就可以不再做乞丐的事情，专心在生意这一块。这么一来，你就成为挨家挨户推销商品的生意人了。

Notes & Vocabulary

house to house 挨家挨户

字面解释为"从这家到那家"，即"挨家挨户"的意思，和 door to door 的意思一样。形容词则写作 house-to-house (= door-to-door)。

- Police conducted a house-to-house search for the suspect.
  警察挨家挨户搜寻该名嫌犯。

be up to sb 由某人决定

口语中是指某事"让某人决定"、"依某人的意思"，也用来表示某事是某人的责任或义务。

- It's now up to the judge whether the defendant will be sentenced to prison.
  现在被告要不要被判刑由法官决定。

up to 的其他常见意思还有：

a. 直到……（时间、数量等），与 up until 意思相同。
  - Up to now, Steve has been working in the company's mail room.
    到目前为止，史蒂夫一直都在公司的收发室工作。

b. up to sth 指正在做某事，通常是违法的、秘密的事或坏事。
  - What have you been up to?
    你最近在忙什么？

....

8. **merchandise** [ˈmɜtʃənˌdaɪz] *n.* 商品；产品

9. **pick up** 改善；有起色

10. **division** [dəˈvɪʒən] *n.* 部门；分部

11. **concentrate** [ˈkɑnsənˌtret] *v.* 专注于；集中于；浓缩

Galaxy[1] Star

Soccer Celebrity[2] David Beckham Hopes to Shine In L.A.

贝克汉姆旋风袭卷美国足坛

Step 1 请浏览下方提示的关键问题后，仔细听录音。

1. Why didn't Beckham's transition to the new team go smoothly?
2. What did Beckham consider to be an added bonus?
3. What is Beckham like when he isn't able to play soccer?
4. Why has the attention Beckham received surprised him?

Step 2 如果你还听不太懂的话，请浏览下方的关键词汇后再听一次。

parade 展览；展示	superstardom 明星地位
nagging 烦人的；唠叨的	pitch 足球场
lad 伙伴；家伙	profile 曝光率

Step 3 试着回答下列听力测验题目。

True or False 是非题

_____ 1. Beckham spent much time on the bench instead of playing because of an ankle injury.

_____ 2. Beckham scored a goal with a free kick against L.A. Galaxy.

_____ 3. The interview took place five weeks after Beckham was introduced in Southern California.

_____ 4. Beckham feels he is terrible to be around when he's not playing soccer.

_____ 5. Beckham is no longer passionate about playing soccer.

名人小档案

大卫·贝克汉姆（1975–）是英国著名的足球明星，曾任英国国家代表队队长。在职业生涯中，最早效力于曼联队（Manchester United），帮助曼联囊括三大足球赛（英超联赛、英格兰足总杯及欧洲杯）冠军，后来加入西班牙皇家马德里队（Real Madrid），现为美国洛杉矶银河队（L.A. Galaxy）的一员。

Multiple Choice 选择题

_____ 1. Where was Beckham interviewed?
   a. Southern California.
   b. Los Angeles.
   c. Madrid.
   d. New York.

_____ 2. Why was the attention Beckham received in California surprising?
   a. He is considered a sex symbol.
   b. Soccer is not very popular in America.
   c. It has lifted soccer's profile in America.
   d. He has never played in America before.

_____ 3. What does Beckham say he hates?
   a. The treatment room.
   b. Goals from free kicks.
   c. Being called a sex symbol.
   d. Playing in MLS.

Step 4 试着用较慢的速度，再仔细听一遍，并检查答案是否正确。

Step 5 核对答案、检验成果，并详读原文，若仍有不懂的地方，可反复多听几次。

（答案请见 p.229）

CNN Anchor

But back to Beckham. A few weeks ago, the icon was paraded[3] before the lights, the cameras and the fans in Southern California, but the transition[4] from Real Madrid superstardom[5] to life in Major League Soccer didn't go exactly smoothly. A nagging[6] ankle injury meant that he spent more time on the bench than on the pitch.[7] But in his first start for the Los Angeles Galaxy, Beckham eased the pressure by scoring his first goal[8] for the club. *World Sport*'s Mark McKay caught up with Beckham in New York to find out about his life in America.

Mark McKay, World Sport

David, how big was that free kick goal against D.C. United?

David Beckham, Soccer Superstar

It was big in the sense of everybody was sort of getting impatient[9] obviously with my ankle, and impatient with the fact that I wasn't playing. And it was just, I was happy for myself just to actually get onto the field and start playing again. Scoring the goal was an added bonus,[10] and scoring the goal like it was was, of course, you know, an added bonus for myself and for the fans. But I'm just happy to be back playing and happy to be around the lads[11] actually on the field and hopefully it continues.

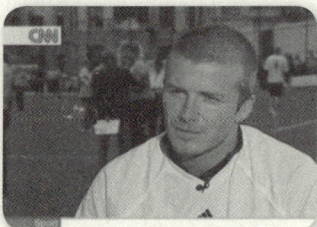

CNN 主播

回来再谈贝克汉姆。几星期前，这位偶像被置于南加州的镁光灯、照相机和球迷面前，但是从皇家马德里超级巨星到美国职业足球大联盟（注）的生活，其中的转换过程并非一帆风顺。脚踝的旧伤意味贝克汉姆待在板凳区的时间要比在球场上还久。但是在为洛杉矶银河队出场的第一场比赛中，贝克汉姆为球队射入第一分而舒缓了不少压力。"世界体育"的记者马克·麦凯在纽约找到了贝克汉姆，想知道他在美国的生活。

"世界体育" 马克·麦凯

大卫，你在对阵华盛顿联队时踢进的那一记任意球有多重要？

足球巨星　大卫·贝克汉姆

那一球很重要，因为大家显然对我脚踝的伤势已感到有点不耐烦了，还有事实上我没有上场踢球。我很高兴自己能够真的重回赛场踢球。能踢进那一球是锦上添花，踢进那一球感觉就像……你知道的，对我自己和对球迷而言都是一种额外收获。我很高兴能够再度踢球，而且是在场上和那群年轻人一起，希望能继续这样下去。

注：美国职业足球大联盟（Major League Soccer）是美国最高等级的职业足球联赛，成立于 1996 年，主要队伍来自美国与加拿大，具有独特的美式风格。

Notes & Vocabulary

on the bench　坐冷板凳；无法出场

bench 是指"长凳；板凳"，on the bench 照字面解释是坐在板凳上，在体育用语中则引申为"坐在替补球员席"，也就是"无法出赛"的意思。on the bench 另外可以表示"担任法官职位"。

- Jimmy spent the whole football season on the bench.
  吉米整个足球赛季都待在替补球员区。
- Judge Parker served for 20 years on the bench.
  帕克法官当了 20 年法官。

in the sense of　就某种意义而言

sense 有"意识；意义；判断力"等解释。文中的 in the sense of 应改为 in the sense that + 从句，等同于 because of the fact that。

- Mark was a failure in the sense that he never finished what he started.
  马克真是个没出息的家伙，因为他做事从不有始有终。

....

1. galaxy [ˈgæləksɪ] *n.* 银河
2. celebrity [səˈlɛbrətɪ] *n.* 名人；名流
3. parade [pəˈred] *v.* 展览；展示
4. transition [trænˈzɪʃən] *n.* 转换；变迁
5. superstardom [ˈsupəˌstɑrdəm] *n.* 明星地位
6. nagging [ˈnægɪŋ] *adj.* 烦人的；唠叨的
7. pitch [pɪtʃ] *n.* (英式用法) 足球场
8. goal [gol] *n.* 得分；(足球等运动的) 球门
9. impatient [ɪmˈpeʃənt] *adj.* 没耐性的
10. bonus [ˈbonəs] *n.* 额外的好处；红利；奖金
11. lad [læd] *n.* 伙伴；家伙 (苏格兰口语)

Mark McKay, World Sport

Now, of course, you've got the ankle that is healing now, what about when you were sitting on that bench? How badly did you want to be out there?

David Beckham, Soccer Superstar

I think I'm a terrible person to be around when I'm not playing soccer. When I'm injured or when I'm out of the team, you can ask my wife, she knows exactly how I am and how passionate[12] I am about being on the field. And when I'm not on the field, then it affects me on and off the pitch. So, yeah, it's been frustrating.[13] It's been frustrating being in the treatment room every day, because, again, I hate the treatment room.

Alexei Lalas, L.A. Galaxy General Manager

The newest member of the L.A. Galaxy, Mr. David Beckham.

Mark McKay, World Sport

David, we're speaking five weeks to the day that you were introduced in Southern California. Has all the attention drawn[14] to you surprised even you?

"世界体育"马克·麦凯

当然，你的脚踝正在痊愈中，但是当你坐在板凳上的时候呢？你有多想上场踢球？

足球巨星 大卫·贝克汉姆

我想我不踢球的时候是个很讨人厌的人。我受伤的时候，或是没跟球队在一起的时候，你可以去问我太太，她完全了解我是个什么样的人，她理解我有多渴望上场比赛。我没上场踢球的时候，在各方面都会受到影响。所以，那的确让人很沮丧。每天待在治疗室里很令人泄气，因为我讨厌治疗室。

洛杉矶银河队总经理 阿莱克西

洛杉矶银河队最新的队员：大卫·贝克汉姆。

"世界体育"马克·麦凯

大卫，你来到南加州至今不过 5 周的时间，大家对你的关注是否连你自己都感到意外？

Notes & Vocabulary

field 足球场地

field 可解释为"原野；场地；野外"，也可指抽象的"（知识）领域；（专业）范围"。但 field 在本文特指"足球运动场地"。

其他运动场地的英文说法有：

足球场 soccer/football pitch/field（英式用法可直接说成 pitch）

美式足球场 football field

冰上曲棍球场 ice hockey rink

高尔夫球场 golf course/links

篮球场 basketball court

棒球场 baseball diamond/field

网球场 tennis court

拳击场 boxing ring

赛车场 race track

板球场 cricket pitch

保龄球馆 bowling alley

----

12. passionate [ˈpæʃənət] *adj.* 热情的；激昂的

13. frustrating [ˈfrʌsˌtreɪtɪŋ] *adj.* 令人感到受挫折的

14. draw [drɔ] *v.* 吸引；招来

David Beckham, Soccer Superstar

It has, because to a certain extent, you know, we all know that soccer's not the biggest sport in America, and there are so many other great sports. But, you know, the attention that I have received has been great in a way because it lifts the profile[15] of the MLS and soccer in the States. So I think that's been the great thing about the attention I have received since I arrived.

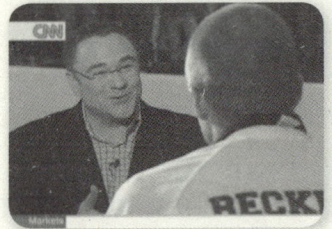

Mark McKay, World Sport

Now some of the attention, of course, and this might make you blush,[16] has to do with the fact that you are regarded by many as a sex symbol.

David Beckham, Soccer Superstar

Right.

Mark McKay, World Sport

Can that be used to improve the image of soccer in the United States?

David Beckham, Soccer Superstar

Er, I'm not sure about that. You know, I've never looked at that in that way, but, you know, the image of soccer in the States is very good. It just needs a bit more worldwide publicity.[17]

足球巨星　大卫·贝克汉姆

的确，因为就某种程度而言，我们都知道足球并非美国最热门的运动，美国还有很多其他伟大的运动，但是我受到关注却是件好事，因为这样可以让美国足球大联盟和足球在美国的曝光率提高。所以我觉得来了之后受到的注意，对足球来说是很棒的事。

"世界体育"马克·麦凯

当然，有些对于你的关注，我这么问你可能会不好意思，和你被很多人视为性感偶像有关。

足球巨星　大卫·贝克汉姆

是的。

"世界体育"马克·麦凯

这点可以用来提升足球运动在美国的形象吗？

足球巨星　大卫·贝克汉姆

嗯，这点我不太确定。我从来没有从这个角度看这件事，但是你知道的，足球在美国的形象相当好，只不过还需要更多全球性的宣传。

Notes & Vocabulary

to a certain extent 到达某种程度

extent 意思是"程度；限度；范围"，to a certain extent 则解释为"到达某种程度"，与 to some extent 意思相同。

- Safety inspectors investigated the extent of the damage caused by the storm.
  安全人员调查了暴风造成损害的程度。
- To a certain extent, Robert was the architect of his own downfall.
  就某种程度来说，罗伯特本身是造成失败的主要原因。

....

15. profile [ˈprəʊˌfaɪl] *n.* 曝光的程度
16. blush [blʌʃ] *v.* 脸红
17. publicity [pʌˈblɪsətɪ] *n.* （公众的）注意力；名声

Finishing on a High Note
TalkAsia Exclusive Interview with
Luciano Pavarotti
CNN 专访世纪男高音帕瓦罗蒂

Step 1 🔘 请浏览下方提示的关键问题后，仔细听录音。

1. How did Pavarotti get started in opera?
2. What are some of Pavarotti's accomplishments?
3. How does Pavarotti feel about singing with the Three Tenors?
4. How does Pavarotti respond to the idea that opera is too intellectual?

Step 2 🎧 如果你还听不太懂的话，请浏览下方的关键词汇后再听一次。

amateur 业余爱好者	accolade 赞誉之词；奖项
curtain call 谢幕	snobbish 自视甚高的；势利的
indispensable 不可或缺的	renowned 著名的

Step 3 💡 试着回答下列听力测验题目。

True or False 是非题

_____ 1. Pavarotti made 45 curtain calls in Berlin.

_____ 2. Pavarotti's father was a baker who introduced him to singing.

_____ 3. Pavarotti's debut was at New York's Metropolitan Opera.

_____ 4. The Three Tenors got together after Pavarotti got sick.

_____ 5. Pavarotti's barber is an opera connoisseur.

名人小档案

鲁契亚诺·帕瓦罗蒂（1935–2007）自幼热爱音乐，曾任小学教师。1961 年首度登台，出演歌剧《波希米亚人》(*La Bohéme*) 男主角鲁道夫，正式开始职业演唱生涯。1972 年在纽约大都会歌剧院演出时，于高潮处轻松唱出了 9 个高音 C，令观众如痴如醉，创下谢幕 17 次的纪录，自此声名大振。

Multiple Choice 选择题

_____ 1. What embarrassed Pavarotti?
   a. Winning so many awards.
   b. Having to take so many curtain calls.
   c. Singing with the other two tenors.
   d. Singing at the Metropolitan Opera.

_____ 2. What is compared to a super group in the classical world?
   a. *TalkAsia*.
   b. *La Bohéme*.
   c. The Three Tenors.
   d. The Metropolitan Opera.

_____ 3. Where is Pavarotti being interviewed?
   a. New York.
   b. Hong Kong.
   c. Modena, Italy.
   d. Berlin.

Step 4 试着用较慢的速度，再仔细听一遍，并检查答案是否正确。

Step 5 核对答案、检验成果，并详读原文，若仍有不懂的地方，可反复多听几次。

（答案请见 p.229）

Lorraine Hahn, TalkAsia

Hello and welcome to *TalkAsia*, I'm Lorraine Hahn. My guest today is a man who's been charming audiences for more than four decades with his rich tenor and beautifully expressive phrasing.[1] Luciano Pavarotti was born in Modena, Italy in October 1935. He was close to his father, an amateur[2] tenor who introduced him to singing through the local choral group.[3] Young Pavarotti made his debut[4] in 1961 with *La Bohéme*, but it was at New York's Metropolitan Opera a few years later that he achieved true superstardom. Since then, he's received accolades[5] from around the world, including Emmy and *Gramophone*[6] awards, and is the best-selling classical recording artist of all time. Now aged 70, Pavarotti is in the midst of his farewell tour, 40 performances that will take him around the world for the last time.

Welcome to Hong Kong. Thank you very much for speaking with us. It has been a long journey for you since your debut in 1961, 44 years. How would you describe those years?

Luciano Pavarotti, Tenor Opera Singer

[Marvelous],[7] sensational,[8] challenging, but almost always winning the battle. In fact, you would not be there for 44 years if you don't win the battle.

"亚洲名人聊天室" 韩玉花

大家好，欢迎收看"亚洲名人聊天室"，我是韩玉花。今天的来宾风靡乐坛 40 余年，以浑厚的男高音和精彩生动的唱法而广受乐迷喜爱。鲁契亚诺·帕瓦罗蒂于 1935 年出生于意大利的摩德纳，他和身为业余男高音的父亲感情很好，并在父亲介绍下加入了当地的合唱团。年轻的帕瓦罗蒂在 1961 年首度登台演出的是歌剧《波希米亚人》，但直到数年后登上纽约大都会歌剧院的舞台，他才真正名扬天下。此后他获得了来自世界各地的赞美与肯定，其中包括艾美奖与英国《留声机》杂志唱片大奖（注），他也是古典乐坛有史以来唱片销售量最高的艺人。如今年至古稀的帕瓦罗蒂正在各地举行告别巡回演唱会，这一系列 40 场的演出将带他最后一次周游世界。

欢迎莅临香港，非常感谢您来我们的节目。自从您 1961 年出道以来，在这一行度过了漫长的 44 年，您会如何来形容这段时光？

歌剧男高音 鲁契亚诺·帕瓦罗蒂

美妙、精彩、富挑战性，而我几乎一直在打胜仗。老实说，要是你打不赢这场仗，也不可能在这一行待上 44 年。

注：The Gramophone 是英国一本古典音乐杂志，而 The Gramophone Awards 则可堪称古典乐中的奥斯卡金像奖。

Notes & Vocabulary

finish on a high note 华丽收场

note 除了可作"笔记；钞票"解释之外，还可表示"音符"。finish on a high note 字面上指"以一个高音作结尾"，即"在高潮处结束"、"风光落幕"之意。帕瓦罗蒂纵横古典乐坛数十年，年至 70 高龄仍然为乐迷带来高水准的告别演出，的确称得上 finish on a high note，而这个源自于音乐术语的用法用在这位"高音 C 之王"的身上也显得格外贴切。

- Morris finished his inspirational speech on a high note.
莫里斯在高潮中结束了他的精彩演说。

in the midst of 在……中

in the midst of 通常是指正处于某种情况、活动或事件当中，也可以说 in the middle of。

- In the midst of storm, the power in our house went out.
暴风雨的时候，家里停电了。
- Kevin left in the middle of the concert to go meet his friend at the airport.
凯文在音乐会中途离席去机场见朋友。

---

1. phrasing [ˈfrezɪŋ] n. 断句
2. amateur [ˈæmətʃʊr] n. 业余人士
3. choral group [ˈkɔrəl] [grup] n. phr. 合唱团
4. debut [ˈde.bju] n. 首次演出
5. accolade [ˈækə.led] n. 赞誉之词；奖项
6. gramophone [ˈgræmə.fon] n. 留声机
7. marvelous [ˈmɑrvələs] adj. 美妙的；神奇的
8. sensational [sɛnˈseʃənl] adj. 引起轰动的

Lorraine Hahn, TalkAsia

There is one performance in 1972 that I read where you had 17 curtain calls[9] at the Met, at the Metropolitan Opera.

Luciano Pavarotti, Tenor Opera Singer

Yes, but it was beaten [by] around 49 call[s] in Berlin. They applaud[ed][10] for 45 minutes. I was embarrassed. Yes, I was embarrassed. You have to finish the opera singing with a piano on the stage. It was something very special.

Lorraine Hahn, TalkAsia

Very, very special. I wanted to also ask you about the Three Tenors. They seem to be like a super group in the classical world.

Luciano Pavarotti, Tenor Opera Singer

We are.

Lorraine Hahn, TalkAsia

How did that idea take shape[11] and how did you all bond[12] so well?

Luciano Pavarotti, Tenor Opera Singer

Many, many people would like to have the Three Tenors together. I was the only one to say no. To say no because there is no reason that we go there to see who is the best of us. We are three different personality [ies]. But at that time, Mr. Carreras was very sick and he become [came] back. He survived. And we celebrated with the concert in Rome.

"亚洲名人聊天室" 韩玉花

我在资料中读到，1972 年你在大都会歌剧院的一场演出谢幕多达 17 次。

歌剧男高音 鲁契亚诺·帕瓦罗蒂

没错，但那项纪录已被打破，我在柏林的一场演出大约谢幕了 49 次。听众鼓掌长达 45 分钟之久，让我都觉得不好意思。真的，我都觉得不好意思。一部歌剧唱到最后连钢琴都搬上舞台，变得像独唱会一样才收场。真是一次很特别的经历。

"亚洲名人聊天室" 韩玉花

实在很特别。我还想请教关于三大男高音的问题，三位在古典乐坛似乎是个超级组合。

歌剧男高音 鲁契亚诺·帕瓦罗蒂

我们的确称得上超级组合。

"亚洲名人聊天室" 韩玉花

这个构想从何而来？你们的感情又为什么这么好？

歌剧男高音 鲁契亚诺·帕瓦罗蒂

很多人都希望我们三人联合演出。我是唯一持反对意见的人，因为让我们三人同台竞技根本毫无意义，我们是三个不同个性、不同类型的男高音。但当时由于卡雷拉斯大病初愈，我们为了庆祝他战胜病魔，才决定在罗马举行联合演唱会。

Notes & Vocabulary

The Three Tenors 三大男高音

tenor 一词可以指文章或演说的"要旨"或"大意"，也可指事件发生的"趋势；倾向"。在音乐中是指"男高音的音色"或"男高音歌手"。

英文中不同音域的歌手称呼如下：soprano "女高音"、mezzo-soprano "女中音"、alto "女低音"、tenor "男高音"、baritone "男中音"、bass "男低音"。

在古典乐坛中，三大男高音指的是意大利的鲁契亚诺·帕瓦罗蒂以及同属西班牙籍的普拉西多·多明戈（Plácido Domingo）与何赛·卡雷拉斯（Jose Carreras）。三人原本单独演唱，并未合作，直到 1990 年为庆祝卡雷拉斯战胜血癌复出，才在经纪人穿针引线下于世界杯足球赛期间首度同台演出，风靡全球。此后"三大男高音"还在 1998 年和 2002 年的世界杯足球赛中再度联袂登场。

· ·

9. curtain call [ˈkɜtn̩] [kɔl] *n.* 谢幕

10. applaud [əˈplɔd] *v.* 鼓掌

11. take shape *v. phr.* （计划；想法）成形

12. bond [bɑnd] *v.* 建立关系；培养感情

Lorraine Hahn, TalkAsia

Classical music, to a lot of people always has this, I don't know, reputation[13] as being intellectual,[14] maybe even a little bit snobbish. But for you, for the Three Tenors, you have almost made it so that everybody, the mass[es][15] can appreciate. Is that important to you?

Luciano Pavarotti, Tenor Opera Singer

It is indispensable.[16] Music . . . I always say that you don't need to be a professor to understand music. My barber is one of the greatest connoisseurs[17] of music, of opera especially. Purity[18] is the good performance. Purity. Because, if you made bad performance for [a] few people it's not purity. To make [a] beautiful performance for many people is purity.

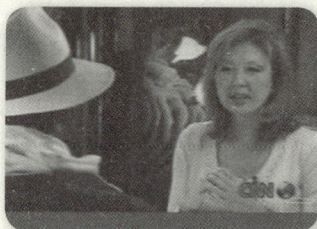

Lorraine Hahn, TalkAsia

Mr. Pavarotti, thank you very, very much for spending time with us and of course the four decades of wonderful music. Thank you. We wish you all the very, very best.

And you'd been watching *TalkAsia*, my guest has been world renowned[19] tenor, Luciano Pavarotti. I'm Lorraine Hahn. Let's talk again next week.

"亚洲名人聊天室"韩玉花

对许多人而言，古典音乐似乎总给人一种——我不知该怎么说——属于知识分子的形象，听古典乐的人甚至有一点居高自傲的味道。但对于你和三大男高音而言，你们却让一般大众也得以欣赏古典音乐。这一点对你而言很重要吗？

歌剧男高音 鲁契亚诺·帕瓦罗蒂

再重要不过。谈到音乐……我一直认为你不一定非得是教授才有能力欣赏音乐。我的理发师就是一位音乐行家，对歌剧尤其有研究。好的演出就是纯粹艺术，如果你为少数人做了不佳的演出，便谈不上纯粹，为许多人带来精彩的表演才叫纯粹。

"亚洲名人聊天室"韩玉花

帕瓦罗蒂先生，非常感谢您今天来上节目，当然也要感谢您带给我们40多年的美妙音乐。谢谢！我们衷心祝福您！

您刚才收看的是"亚洲名人聊天室"，今天的来宾是世界知名男高音鲁契亚诺·帕瓦罗蒂，我是韩玉花，我们下周见！

Notes & Vocabulary

snobbish 自视高人一等的；势利的

snobbish 为 snob（自负傲慢的人；势利鬼）的形容词形式，其中 -ish 为形容词词尾，其常见的含义有四种：

a. 表示"……族的；……语的"，如：

　　Finnish 芬兰人的；芬兰语的

　　Spanish 西班牙语的

　　Danish 丹麦语的；丹麦人的

b. 表示"有……特征的"，如：

　　snobbish 势利的

　　childish 幼稚的

　　selfish 自私的

c. 表示"大约……"，常加在数字后，如：

　　fortyish 大约四十的

　　sevenish 大约为七的

d. 表示"稍微……的；有点……的"，加在形容词后，如：

　　darkish 有点暗的

　　coldish 有点冷的

　　oldish 有点老旧的

．．．．．．．．．．．．．．．．．．．．．．．．．．．．．．．．．．．．

13. **reputation** [ˌrɛpjəˈteʃən] *n.* 名声；名誉

14. **intellectual** [ˌɪntəˈlɛktʃəwəl] *adj.* 聪明的

15. **mass** [mæs] *n.* 社会大众；一般民众

16. **indispensable** [ˌɪndɪˈspɛnsəbəl] *adj.* 不可或缺的

17. **connoisseur** [ˌkɑnəˈsɜ] *n.* (源自法语) 行家

18. **purity** [ˈpjʊrətɪ] *n.* 纯粹；纯洁

19. **renowned** [rɪˈnaʊnd] *adj.* 著名的

King of the Courts
Talking Tennis with World Champion Roger Federer
无敌的滋味——专访网球球王费德勒

Step 1 请浏览下方提示的关键问题后，仔细听录音。

1. How did Federer feel about his playing throughout the year?
2. When did Federer start playing tennis?
3. Why does Federer like playing tennis so much?
4. What other sport does Federer follow, and why does he like it?

Step 2 如果你还听不太懂的话，请浏览下方的关键词汇后再听一次。

set foot on 到达某地	tournament 比赛；锦标赛
forehand 正手击球	backhand 反手击球
position 身份	come so far 一直努力

Step 3 试着回答下列听力测验题目。

True or False 是非题

_____ 1. Federer's favorite shot has always been his backhand.

_____ 2. Federer gave his rating as excellent for the year.

_____ 3. The problem with soccer for Federer was that he knew it was his fault if his team lost.

_____ 4. Federer does not like the atmosphere in a soccer stadium.

_____ 5. Federer loved to watch Wimbledon in his bedroom at home.

名人小档案

罗杰·费德勒（1981-）1998 年开始闯入职业网坛，次年便已名列全球男网前一百名。2001 年在温布尔登公开赛中击败前球王桑普拉斯，2003 年便在温布尔登赢得生平首个大满贯赛冠军，后来更分别在澳大利亚、温布尔登及美国三项大满贯赛封王，稳居世界网球球王宝座。

Multiple Choice 选择题

_____ 1. Whose record did Federer tie?
   a. Edberg's.
   b. Becker's.
   c. Borg's.
   d. Rao's.

_____ 2. What is Federer's forehand?
   a. His weakness.
   b. His favorite shot.
   c. His greatest happiness.
   d. His future goal.

_____ 3. Why did Federer choose to play tennis?
   a. He could blame himself if he lost.
   b. He could play it much better than soccer.
   c. He knew he would win the majors.
   d. He knew he could blame the goalkeeper.

Step 4 试着用较慢的速度，再仔细听一遍，并检查答案是否正确。

Step 5 核对答案、检验成果，并详读原文，若仍有不懂的地方，可反复多听几次。

（答案请见 p. 229）

Anjali Rao, TalkAsia

Our guest today is widely regarded as the greatest player ever to set foot on the tennis court. He's Roger Federer. I'm Anjali Rao and this is *TalkAsia*.

Roger, welcome back to *TalkAsia*. It's marvelous to have you with us again.

Roger Federer, Tennis Champion

Thank you. It's my pleasure. Thank you.

Anjali Rao, TalkAsia

It's been quite a year for you, hasn't it? How would you rate[1] it?

Roger Federer, Tennis Champion

Well, excellent. It couldn't almost be any better. I really played great, you know, in the big, big tournaments[2] this year. This is really what my big focus is, obviously. At the moment, that I can play well at the majors[3] and hopefully finish the year off nicely in Shanghai, and I won four of the five big ones and was in the finals of the French Open, which was just great, and protected my number-one rank again, won Wimbledon for a fifth straight [time], which was really important to me, equaling[4] Bjorn Borg's record. So it's great now, looking ahead to 2008, obviously.

Anjali Rao, TalkAsia

So show me some of your signature moves, then.

"亚洲名人聊天室" 安姿丽

今天的来宾是公认的网坛有史以来最伟大的选手。他是罗杰·费德勒。我是安姿丽，欢迎收看"亚洲名人聊天室"。

费德勒，欢迎回到"亚洲名人聊天室"，能再次请到您真是太棒了。

网球球王　费德勒

谢谢，这是我的荣幸。谢谢你。

"亚洲名人聊天室" 安姿丽

你今年的表现非常好，不是吗？你怎么评价自己今年的表现？

网球球王　费德勒

棒极了，几乎不可能更好了。我真的打得很棒，我是指今年的几场大比赛。我的确是把重心放在这里，毋庸置疑。目前我在大赛中打得不错，希望今年能在上海画下完美句号。我在 5 场大赛中赢了 4 场，并且打进了法国公开赛的决赛，这点实在很棒，我再度保住了世界第一的头衔，在温布尔登写下 5 连胜，这对我而言真的很重要，追平了伯格的纪录。所以现在真的很棒，我很期待 2008 年的到来。

"亚洲名人聊天室" 安姿丽

请露几手你的招牌打法让我瞧瞧。

Notes & Vocabulary

set foot on　到达某地

set foot on 后面加上地点，是指"踏上个某地点"，即"到达"的意思。文中的 set foot on the tennis court 表示"踏入网坛"。介词 on 可因地点不同而改变。

- Ben has never set foot on foreign soil.
  本从来没出过国。
- The moment Jack set foot in the office, he had to deal with a crisis.
  杰克一进办公室就得处理一桩紧急事件。

finish off　结束；解决；完成

常用来表示"完成某事；终结某事"，或将某人或事物"彻底打败、破坏"的意思，另外也有把食物"吃完、喝完"的意思，宾语可放在 off 前面或之后。

- As soon as he finished off the sky bridge project, he got a new assignment.
  他一完成天桥那个项目马上就接到了新任务。
- Vanessa finished off all the pizza in the refrigerator.
  瓦内萨把冰箱里的比萨全吃光了。

1. rate [reɪt] *v.* 对……评价、估价
2. tournament [ˈtɜːnəmənt] *n.* 比赛；锦标赛
3. major [ˈmeɪdʒə] *n.* 重要的人或事物（比赛、公司等）
4. equal [ˈiːkwəl] *v.* 等于；比得上

Roger Federer, Tennis Champion

Well my favorite shot is always going to be the forehand.[5] It used to be always be my favorite shot when I was young, so it's always been the one I've won all the points with. Backhand[6] used to be my weakness.

Anjali Rao, TalkAsia

Yeah.

Roger Federer, Tennis Champion

The serve,[7] I was too young and too small and too, you know, not ~~enough~~ powerful [enough] to have a good serve, and when I was young, so my forehand was always my signature shot. So I always used to run around my backhand, you know, use my forehand as much as I could, and so that's why I think it's my strength also today, you know. But, what's your strength today?

Anjali Rao, TalkAsia

I don't have a strength, today!

Roger Federer, Tennis Champion

You've got to have one.

Anjali Rao, TalkAsia

If we go way back to the start then of your tennis days, you were what, two, three, four years old when you picked up a racket?[8]

Roger Federer, Tennis Champion

Young, yeah.

网球球王 费德勒

我最喜欢的打法一直是正手击球。年轻的时候，我总是最爱打正手击球，所以我都是靠正手击球来拿下分数。反手击球曾经是我的弱点。

"亚洲名人聊天室"安姿丽

没错。

网球球王 费德勒

至于发球，以前我太年轻，个头太小，力量不够，发出来的球威力不够，所以我的正手击球一直都是我的招牌打法。所以我以前打反手球都会绕到正手位去打，尽量多用正手击球来打，所以这也是为何现在我会认为正手击球是我的强项。你现在的强项是什么？

"亚洲名人聊天室"安姿丽

我现在没有强项！

网球球王 费德勒

你一定要有才行。

"亚洲名人聊天室"安姿丽

我们回到当初您开始学网球的那段日子，你拿起球拍时才二、三、四岁吧？

网球球王 费德勒

是啊，那时很小。

Notes & Vocabulary

run around backhand 绕过反手击球位置

run around 原本是指"忙着做一堆事"，run around (one's) backhand 在本文中是网球术语，较常见的用法是 run around (one's) forehand，名词则写作 run-around forehand "跑到正手球位击球"，意思是指对方来球明明是在反手击球位，但为了能击出有利的球，或是因为正手击球较强劲，而刻意跑到正手击球位回击来球。

下面介绍一些网球击球术语：

approach shot 上网球

chip shot 削球

crosscourt shot 对角线球

drop shot 过网急坠球

flat shot 平击球

lob 高吊球

passing shot 穿越球

volley 截击

. . . .

5. forehand [ˈfɔrˌhænd] *n.* 正手击球

6. backhand [ˈbækˌhænd] *n.* 反手击球

7. serve [sɜv] *n.* 发球

8. racket [ˈrækət] *n.* （网球或羽毛球的）球拍

Anjali Rao, TalkAsia

Really little. Why tennis? What was it about this game that took you?

Roger Federer, Tennis Champion

I enjoyed the position[9] I was in as a tennis player—I was to blame when I lost, I was to blame when I won—and I really like that, you know, because I played soccer a lot too, and I couldn't stand it when I had to blame it on the goalkeeper.[10] For me that was just something that was the worst, for me to go into the locker room[11] saying I had played a great match, but we lost. Even though it's still my number one sport I follow, because I really like, you know, the atmosphere[12] in the stadium[13] and the game of soccer.

But tennis for me was always what did it to me, you know. I used to follow it in the living room, watching Wimbledon, seeing Becker and Edberg win or lose and, you know, crying if they lost, happy if they won, and it's always something that was very close to my heart, and I realized this is really the sport I always wanted to do, and it's just a great feeling I could come so far. Honestly, today, I still can't believe how far I've come.

"亚洲名人聊天室"安姿丽

是真的还很小。为什么会是网球？
网球比赛有什么地方吸引你？

网球球王 费德勒

对于身为网球选手的身份我乐在其
中。输了球怪我自己，赢了球也是
我自己的本事。我真的很喜欢这
样，因为我也常踢足球，我无法忍
受问题出在守门员身上。对我而
言，走进更衣室里说我这场比赛踢
得真棒，但我们还是输了，这是最
糟的情况。但足球依然是我最喜爱
的运动，因为我真的很喜欢体育场
上足球比赛的气氛。

但是对我而言，网球是真正打动我
的运动。以前我会在客厅里看网
球，看温布尔登，看贝克尔和埃德
柏格赢球或输球，如果他们输了我
就哭，赢了我就开心，网球在我心
里一直占有很重的分量，我明白网
球是我真正一直想要从事的运动，
能有今天的成绩感觉实在很棒。说
真的，直到今天，我都不敢相信自
己竟有这样的成就。

Notes & Vocabulary

be to blame 责怪；归咎

blame 是"责怪；将……归咎于"，be to blame 前面可用人
或事物当主语，为某件事发生的原因。

- A mysterious virus was to blame for hundreds of
  deaths.
  导致数百人死亡的原因是一种未知的病毒。

come so far 一直努力

字面上的意思是"走了这么远"，比喻已经为某事辛苦奋斗了很
久，常用在表达一直努力，刚看到一点成绩的意思。

- Beth has come so far since she got out of rehab.
  贝思离开康复中心之后已经保持清醒很久了。

9. position [pəˈzɪʃən] *n.* 身份；地位；立场

10. goalkeeper [ˈgolˌkipə] *n.* 守门员

11. locker room [ˈlɑkə] [rum] 更衣室；衣帽间

12. atmosphere [ˈætməˌsfɪr] *n.* 气氛

13. stadium [ˈstediəm] *n.* 体育场；运动场

One Hop Ahead of the Competition
In *The Boardroom* with Qantas CEO Geoff Dixon
稳健领航——**CNN** 专访澳航 **CEO** 杰夫·迪克森

Step 1 请浏览下方提示的关键问题后，仔细听录音。

1. What characterized the years after Dixon took over as CEO of Qantas?
2. What does Dixon say about the airline he inherited?
3. What is Dixon's attitude toward work?
4. What does Dixon say about getting a university degree?

Step 2 如果你还听不太懂的话，请浏览下方的关键词汇后再听一次。

agonize 痛苦；苦恼	turbulence 波动；动乱
aftermath 后续的影响；余波	privatization 私营化
viability 生存能力	cadet 实习生

Step 3 试着回答下列听力测验题目。

True or False 是非题

_____ 1. Qantas is an airline that has been losing money.

_____ 2. Dixon started out as a journalist in Australia.

_____ 3. Dixon earned a degree from a university.

_____ 4. Dixon has always been suited for a nine to five job.

_____ 5. Dixon has found that living for the moment works for him.

名人小档案

杰夫·迪克森（1940–）于 1994 年进入澳大利亚航空公司。1995 年澳航成为全世界最大航空公司之一，含子公司在内共有 130 架飞机，每年运送多达 1 400 万旅客。2001 年时杰夫被推选为总裁及总经理，带领澳航顺利度过航空业的低迷时期。

Multiple Choice 选择题

_____ 1. Which was something that didn't happen since Dixon became CEO?
   a. The aftermath of 9/11.
   b. SARS.
   c. The millennium computer bug.
   d. Record oil prices.

_____ 2. What were there doubts about?
   a. Dixon's ability to lead the airline.
   b. The viability of a lot of airlines.
   c. Dixon's lack of a university degree.
   d. The changes after privatization.

_____ 3. What did journalism give Dixon?
   a. A wide view of the world.
   b. An interest in regular jobs.
   c. A radical shake-up.
   d. A feeling of tremendous satisfaction.

Step 4 试着用较慢的速度，再仔细听一遍，并检查答案是否正确。

Step 5 核对答案、检验成果，并详读原文，若仍有不懂的地方，可反复多听几次。

（答案请见 p.229）

Andrew Stevens, The Boardroom

Geoff Dixon says he deals well with stress.

Geoff Dixon, CEO of Qantas

I agonize[1] over decisions when I've made them and I wonder about the consequences[2] but I can move on.

Andrew Stevens, The Boardroom

It's a good quality to have when you're the head of an airline, given all the turbulence[3] in the industry over the past several years. Dixon has served as CEO of the Australian flag carrier Qantas since 2001. He's piloted[4] the flying kangaroo through just about everything, from the aftermath[5] of 9/11, to SARS, to record oil prices. To do that, he's radically[6] shaken up Qantas, and today it's one of the world's most profitable airlines. *The Boardroom* caught up with Dixon in Sydney.

You've been the chief executive officer of Qantas for six years, probably the six toughest years the industry has ever seen. What keeps you going, what keeps you interested?

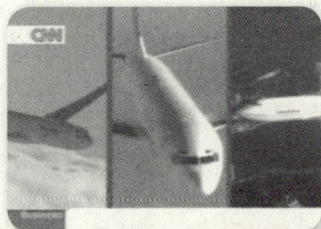

"董事会"安德鲁·史蒂文斯

杰夫·迪克森说他能从容应对压力。

澳航 CEO　杰夫·迪克森

我做了决策后会辗转反侧，反复思索后果会如何，不过我还是可以继续前进。

"董事会"安德鲁·史蒂文斯

就航空业在过去几年间经历的风风雨雨而言，拥有这种特质对于一个航空公司负责人来说是件好事。迪克森从 2001 年起即担任这家代表澳大利亚航空公司的 CEO。他可以说带领这个"飞跃的袋鼠"（注）渡过了一切，从"911 事件"、SARS，到创历史新高的油价。为了渡过难关，迪克森彻底改造了澳航，如今澳航成为全球获利最高的航空公司之一。"董事会"在悉尼专访了迪克森。

您担任澳航 CEO 已经 6 年了，这或许是航空业有史以来最艰难的 6 年。是什么动力令您能继续下去，令您对航空业持续感兴趣？

注：澳航成立于 1920 年，其绰号为一只"飞跃的袋鼠"，澳航为澳航集团的一员，其所经营的航空业务尚包括捷星（Jetstar）、捷星亚洲（Jetstar Asia）和 QantasLink 等。

Notes & Vocabulary

given　鉴于；由于

given 原为 give 的过去分词，可以作形容词用，指"特定的；作为前提的"，在本文中则作介词用，表示"鉴于；由于"，也可用 in view of、considering 来表示。

- Thomas has accomplished a lot, given the difficulties he's had.
  虽然托玛斯遇过不少困难，他仍然成就不凡。

flag carrier　国家航空公司

原本是指国营（state-owned, state-run）的航空公司，因机身上通常会以国旗为标志，故得此名。即使后来转为私营（privatized）或半私营，甚或机上没有了国旗图案，只要是该国最具代表性的航空公司，就可称为 flag carrier。

----

1. **agonize** [ˈægəˌnaɪz] v. 痛苦；苦恼
2. **consequence** [ˈkɑnsəˌkwɛns] n. 结果
3. **turbulence** [ˈtɜbjələns] n. 波动；动乱
4. **pilot** [ˈpaɪlət] v. 引领；带领
5. **aftermath** [ˈæftəˌmæθ] n. 后续的影响；余波
6. **radically** [ˈrædɪkəlɪ] adv. 彻底地；完全地

Geoff Dixon, CEO of Qantas

Ah, the excitement of the chase I suppose. I enjoy the job and the board[7] asked me to stay on and I like it, so it's no more simple than that. As a matter of fact, I like what I am doing. While they want me to work, I'll continue to work. I inherited[8] a very good airline where a lot of change had been made after privatization,[9] but then everything seemed to happen at once, and obviously there were real doubts about the viability[10] of a lot of airlines, not just Qantas. And I've got tremendous[11] satisfaction about how the management team and the board and indeed the people, despite all the change, have come along with us, and that we've been able to really be one of the very few airlines in the world that's consistently made decent money.

Andrew Stevens, The Boardroom

You started off your career as a journalist[12] in country Australia, a cadet[13] journalist. Do you think that has shaped you at all in your future career?

Geoff Dixon, CEO of Qantas

Journalism[14] makes you think very, very quickly. I believe it gives you a very wide view of the world. You see a lot of different things. And it gave me a sense of excitement which I've carried through into jobs. I've always wanted jobs that were a bit different. I obviously would not be suited for a normal ~~five~~ nine to five job. And, by the way, I've never ever sat down and said, "Now what should I be doing in five years time?" I've generally said, "well, I'll see what comes up."

澳航 CEO 杰夫·迪克森

我想是追求刺激感吧。我很享受这份工作，董事会要我留任，而我也愿意，事情就是这么简单。事实上，我喜欢我做的工作。只要他们要我，我就会继续做。我接管了一家很优秀的航空公司，私营化之后进行了很多改变，但似乎所有事都在同一时间发生。很显然很多家航空公司都怀疑是否还能存活下去，并不只有澳航。尽管变化如此之大，我对于公司管理团队、董事会和员工们一路来的表现，以及对于我们能够成为全球少数几家一直很盈利的航空公司仍然感到非常满意。

"董事会"安德鲁·史蒂文斯

您最早的一份工作是在澳大利亚当一名实习记者，您认为这是否成就了您日后的事业？

澳航 CEO 杰夫·迪克森

新闻工作会让你脑筋动得很快。我相信从事新闻工作会拓展你对世界的看法，你会看到很多不一样的事物。它给我一种兴奋感，而我把它运用到了工作上。我一直想要从事一些不太一样的工作。显然我不适合一般的朝九晚五的工作。顺便提一下，我从没有坐下来说："这5年中我应该做些什么？"我通常会说："先看看情况怎么样再说。"

Notes & Vocabulary

decent 可观的；相当好的

用来形容金钱（如薪资、收益、营业额等）时，是指金额"令人满意"、"很不错"的意思。decent 还可表示"适当的；得体的；体面的"。

- Jan had a decent meal on her flight home.
  珍在回程的飞机上吃了很棒的一顿饭。
- Students are expected to behave in a decent manner.
  人们希望学生举止要合乎礼节。

另外，Are you decent? 意思是"你衣服穿好了吗？"，常用在要开门进某人房间时，先问对方是否已穿好衣服，免得因为衣衫不整而造成尴尬。

7. board [bɔrd] n. 董事会
8. inherit [ɪnˈhɜrɪt] v. 继承；承接
9. privatization [ˌpraɪvətəˈzeʃən] n. 私有化；民营化
10. viability [ˌvaɪəˈbɪlətɪ] n. 可行性；生存能力
11. tremendous [trɪˈmɛndəs] adj. 极大的；极好的
12. journalist [ˈdʒɜnəlɪst] n. 记者
13. cadet [kəˈdɛt] n. 实习生
14. journalism [ˈdʒɜnəˌlɪzəm] n. 新闻业

Andrew Stevens, The Boardroom

Live the moment?

Geoff Dixon, CEO of Qantas

Yeah, and that's obviously worked for me.

Andrew Stevens, The Boardroom

You don't have a university degree. Do you think, in the 21st century, someone could get to where you are now without a degree?

Geoff Dixon, CEO of Qantas

Yeah, I think they can, but it's more than likely to be more difficult. I think that it's difficult when you're going up the ladder perhaps. But when you get to a certain level I think, you're then competing and you're being judged by people who are going to hire you on your performance and on your intellect,[15] not on a piece of paper. Although, I would advise[16] everybody to get out there and get that piece of paper.

"董事会" 安德鲁·史蒂文斯

活在当下?

澳航 CEO 杰夫·迪克森

对，这显然很适合我。

"董事会" 安德鲁·史蒂文斯

您没有学士学位。您认为在 21 世纪，有人可以在没有学历的情况下，达到像您现在这样的成就吗？

澳航 CEO 杰夫·迪克森

我觉得做得到，但是很可能会比较困难。我认为在升迁的过程中会有困难。但是当你升到了某个级别后，你就会与人竞争，而那些评判你的人会根据你的表现和才智来决定是否雇用你，而非根据一张纸。不过，我还是会建议大家去获取一张文凭。

Notes & Vocabulary

live the moment 活在当下

有时会写成 live in the moment 或 live for the moment，都是 "把握现在；珍惜此刻" 的意思，表示注重实际、不好高骛远的态度。类似的说法还有 live for today、live in the present、no day but today、seize the day。

- Robert decided to live the moment and took the afternoon off to enjoy the perfect weather.
  罗伯特决定把握眼前时光，于是下午请假去享受好天气了。

up the ladder 升迁；晋升

字面上的意思是 "沿着楼梯向上"，用来比喻级别或职位 "步步高升"，即 "升迁"、"晋级" 的意思。

- Lola hopes to move up the ladder in her company this year.
  罗拉希望今年在公司里能获得升迁。

....

15. intellect [ˈɪntəˌlɛkt] n. 智力；出众的才华

16. advise [ədˈvaɪz] v. 建议；忠告

Making Her Own Way

BUPA CEO Valerie Gooding Discusses Success and Gender in Business

BUPA CEO 瓦莱莉·古丁畅谈职场女性成功之道

Step 1 请浏览下方提示的关键问题后，仔细听录音。

1. What does Gooding say women don't do that holds them back?
2. What does Gooding say women should do if they want to get ahead?
3. How does Gooding define good leadership?
4. What does Gooding say about the differences between men and women?

Step 2 如果你还听不太懂的话，请浏览下方的关键词汇后再听一次。

glass ceiling 无形障碍；限制	hang back 畏缩；踌躇不前
inclusive 面面俱到的	autocratic 专制的；独裁的
dictatorial 独裁者的；自大的	buzz 狂热

Step 3 试着回答下列听力测验题目。

True or False 是非题

_____ 1. Gooding is one of the top five most powerful women in the world.

_____ 2. Gooding says it is important that you enjoy the work you do.

_____ 3. Gooding says producing good results is not enough to get promoted.

_____ 4. Gooding has seen many clear differences between male and female leaders.

名人小档案

瓦莱莉·古丁（1950–）于 1996 年加入英国保柏集团 (BUPA, British United Provident Association Ltd.)，1998 年当上 CEO。BUPA 为英国最大的医疗保险公司，提供老年人健康保险及医疗保健等服务，其业务更拓展至海外各大洲。

_____ 5. Gooding says she loves business because she's constantly being challenged.

Multiple Choice 选择题

_____ 1. Which is not a reason Gooding gives for a lack of female business leaders?

    a. Men won't accept women as bosses.

    b. They aren't considered for promotion.

    c. There are no role models for women.

    d. Women don't make the effort.

_____ 2. What quality does Gooding see that women might have and men don't?

    a. Consulting with everyone on decisions.

    b. Being dictatorial and autocratic.

    c. Talking about their accomplishments.

    d. Lack of confidence.

_____ 3. How does Gooding say great leaders should be described?

    a. They transformed the business.

    b. They help everyone feel victorious.

    c. They upped company performance.

    d. They exceeded expectations.

Step 4 试着用较慢的速度，再仔细听一遍，并检查答案是否正确。

Step 5 核对答案、检验成果，并详读原文，若仍有不懂的地方，可反复多听几次。

（答案请见 p.229）

Todd Benjamin, CNN Financial Editor

Valerie Gooding is in the top five most powerful businesswomen in Europe as named by the *Financial Times*.

She runs global health and care organization BUPA. Under her leadership it has grown to over 8 million customers in over 190 countries and record[1] revenues.[2]

I caught up with her in London and began by asking her why there are so few women at the top. She said it goes beyond[3] family issues.

Valerie Gooding, CEO of BUPA

Women sometimes don't put themselves forward for things. And one of the things I think about and talk about a lot is that women often lack confidence to go for the next job, the top job. They sometimes don't wish to compete[4] or they think they're not good enough for the next thing or whatever.

Todd Benjamin, CNN Financial Editor

Why do you think that is?

Valerie Gooding, CEO of BUPA

Partly a lack of role models, partly maybe conditioning[5] from a very early age about what the role of women is in society and the family, in work. But also I think there is still—I don't like to call it a glass ceiling, but I think there is still an unseen barrier[6] for women, which is that, if you ask most business people, would they like to promote more women, they all say yes, they'd love to: "Where are these women, I want to promote them," will be the answer. But often they don't really automatically[7] think of a woman first for a top job.

CNN 金融主编 托德·本杰明

瓦莱莉·古丁被《财经时报》称为欧洲最有权力的五大商界女性。

她经营一家全球性的健康护理机构 BUPA，在她领导下，这家企业在 190 多个国家已拥有超过 800 万客户，创下空前的收益。

我和她在伦敦见面，一开始就问她居于高职位的女性为什么这么少。她回答并不只是家庭因素。

BUPA CEO 瓦莱莉·古丁

女性有时并不会主动提出对事情的看法。我常在想也常在谈的一件事就是女性常常缺少争取下一份工作、高层工作的信心。她们有时并不希望竞争或她们认为自己没有优秀到可以争取下一份职务之类的。

CNN 金融主编 托德·本杰明

你认为为什么会这样呢？

BUPA CEO 瓦莱莉·古丁

部分原因是缺少可以作为榜样的角色，部分或许是社会、家庭和职务对女性的角色该怎么样在她们幼年时就决定了。但我还认为仍然有——我不喜欢称之为无形障碍，但我认为对女性还是有看不见的障碍，也就是说，如果你问大部分的商界人士，他们是否愿意提拔更多的女性，他们一定全都回答是的、他们愿意。"这些女性在哪里呢？我想要提拔她们"则是他们的答案。不过对于高层工作，他们往往不会主动想到女性。

Notes & Vocabulary

put forward 提出；推荐

put forward 意思是"提出（建议、主意、想法等）"，也可说 put forth。提出的若是"人"（put sb forward），意即"推荐（某人）"。

- Steven put forward the idea of opening a second store to his boss.
  史蒂文向老板提出开第二家店的想法。
- The election for class president was coming up, and Jake put himself forward for the post.
  班长的选举活动即将到来，杰克毛遂自荐担任该职。

glass ceiling 无形障碍；藩篱

glass ceiling 字面上指"玻璃天花板"，表示你看得见天花板上面的景象，却又无法穿越那层透明的障碍而更上一层楼，通常用来比喻少数民族或女性在职场上所面对的无形阻碍。

- Many minorities feel there is a glass ceiling preventing them from getting the top jobs.
  许多少数民族认为有道无形的阻碍使他们无法获得高层的工作。
- When the old law firm made Jane a partner, many felt she had broken the glass ceiling.
  那家历史悠久的律师事务所让简成为合伙人，许多人认为她打破了那道藩篱。

1. record [ˈrɛkəd] *adj.* 创纪录的

2. revenue [ˈrɛvəˌnu] *n.* 收入；收益

3. go beyond 超出……的范围

4. compete [kəmˈpit] *v.* 为……竞争

5. condition [kənˈdɪʃən] *v.* 约定；作为……的条件

6. barrier [ˈbɛriə] *n.* 障碍；阻碍

7. automatically [ˌɔtəˈmætɪklɪ] *adv.* 自动地

Todd Benjamin, CNN Financial Editor

And what advice would you give to women who want to try and make it to the top?

Valerie Gooding, CEO of BUPA

Well, first of all, to learn as much as you can and to make sure you've got the right experience, the right qualifications,[8] and to enjoy each job for its own interest and job satisfaction.

But I think another piece of advice I would give to women is not to be afraid to put themselves forward and say what it is they want, because I think one thing that happens with women, which perhaps is a gender difference, is that women often hang back[9] and think "I will be noticed for my results. Everybody will see how great I am because I've delivered[10] these exceptional[11] outcomes."[12] But actually life isn't like that, you have to tell people about your results and your achievements,[13] and men are often better at doing that than women are.

Todd Benjamin, CNN Financial Editor

What do you think separates[14] good leadership from great leadership?

Valerie Gooding, CEO of BUPA

Well, I think good leaders should be judged on their results. And I think of a good leader you should be able to say "she transformed[15] the business" , "she upped the performance",[16] "she exceeded[17] the expectations of the stakeholders".[18] I think of a great leader I think I would go to that old Chinese saying, "of a great leader the people will say 'we did it ourselves.'"

CNN 金融主编 托德·本杰明

你会给那些想要尝试升到高层的女性什么样的建议呢?

BUPA CEO 瓦莱莉·古丁

嗯,首先,尽可能多去学习,并确保你得到适用的经验、适当的资格,并享受每一份工作的趣味和工作上的满足感。

但我想给女性的另一个建议是不要害怕表现自己,害怕表达自己的需要,因为我认为女性常常会踌躇不前,这或许是性别差异,且认为"我会因为工作表现而受到注意,大家会看到我有多棒,因为我取得了卓越的成果。"但事实上人生并不是如此,你得要告诉别人你的成果及成就,男性这部分做的往往比女性好。

CNN 金融主编 托德·本杰明

你认为好的领导力和卓越的领导力要如何区分?

BUPA CEO 瓦莱莉·古丁

嗯,我认为好的领导者应该由他们的工作成果来判定。我认为对好的领导者你可以说"她改造了企业"、"她提升了绩效"、"她超越了股东的期望"。而我认为卓越的领导者则可用一句中国古话来说:"对卓越的领导者,人们会说:'这些都是我们自己做的。'"(注)

注:源自老子的《道德经》第 17 章:功成事遂,百姓皆谓:"我自然"。

Notes & Vocabulary

up 提升

up 最常见的用法是作副词或介词使用,在本文中作动词用,意思是"提升"。

· The company upped the budget for online advertising to twice the previous amount.
那家公司把网上广告的预算提高了一倍。

英语中其他介 / 副词也可作动词用的包括:

a. out 揭露(秘密等)
· The politician had problems when he was outed as a gambling addict.
那位政治人物因遭人揭露沉迷赌博而陷入困境。

b. down 喝下;吞下
· After jogging, Stan quickly downed two glasses of water.
斯坦慢跑完后立刻喝了两杯水。

8. qualification [ˌkwɑləfəˈkeʃən] n. 资格

9. hang back 畏缩;踌躇不前

10. deliver [dɪˈlɪvə] v. 实现;履行

11. exceptional [ɪkˈsɛpʃənəl] adj. 杰出的;优秀的

12. outcome [ˈautˌkʌm] n. 结果

13. achievement [əˈtʃivmənt] n. 成就

14. separate [ˈsɛpəˌret] v. 区分;区别

15. transform [trænsˈfɔrm] v. 改变

16. performance [pəˈfɔrməns] n. 表现;绩效

17. exceed [ɪkˈsid] v. 超越;超出

18. stakeholder [ˈstekˌholdə] n. 股东

Todd Benjamin, CNN Financial Editor

Do you think that women in general as managers are more inclusive[19] than men?

Valerie Gooding, CEO of BUPA

No, I don't. In fact, I sometimes find these gender differences, when sort of represented[20] in the business environment, are actually just not very useful. I think men and women have very different styles of leadership as individuals and I don't think it goes down to straightforward[21] gender divide. Because I have seen women who are more autocratic[22] and more leading from the front and more dictatorial,[23] and I've equally seen men who are very consultative.[24] So, I don't just think it divides that way.

Todd Benjamin, CNN Financial Editor

You clearly love what you do. What is it about business that you think is such a buzz?[25]

Valerie Gooding, CEO of BUPA

It's the constant challenge. There's always something new, there's a new competitor, there's a new pressure, there's a new opportunity, there's a new challenge, I think that's what keeps us all going. I think it's the thrill[26] of the chase, basically.

CNN 金融主编 托德·本杰明

你认为一般来说女性管理者会比男性更加面面俱到吗？

BUPA CEO 瓦莱莉·古丁

不，我不这么认为。事实上，我有时会发现这些性别差异，职场中多少会出现，其实不是非常有用。我认为男性和女性每个人都有非常不同的领导风格，但并不是直接以性别来区分。因为我看过更为强势、更勇往直前、更独裁的女性，我同时也看过事事征求意见的男性。所以，我认为不是以性别来区分。

CNN 金融主编 托德·本杰明

你显然热爱你的工作。关于企业，是什么让你一直都这么精力充沛？

BUPA CEO 瓦莱莉·古丁

是不断的挑战。总是有新的事情、新的竞争对手、新的压力、新的机会、新的挑战，我想那就是让我们继续向前的原因。基本上我认为那是一种追寻的快乐。

Notes & Vocabulary

go down to 直接关乎；追根究底

go down to 也可写作 come down to，后者为较常用的说法，意思是指"直接关于"，另外也有"论及本质；追根究底"的意思。

- Every decision he made came down to a question of whether he could afford it.
  他所做的每项决定都直接关乎他是否承担得起。

- When it comes down to it, John didn't invite Amy because he's still mad that she wouldn't go out with him.
  追根究底，约翰没邀请艾米是因为仍对她不肯跟他约会感到气愤。

lead from the front 带头领导

front 指"前线"，lead from the front 即是指"带头领导"。

- The manager usually led from the front. He didn't like to delegate unless he had to.
  那位经理常带头前进，除非必要，否则他不喜欢委托他人。

. . . .

19. inclusive [ɪnˋklusɪv] *adj.* 包含在内的；面面俱到的

20. represent [ˌrɛprɪˋzɛnt] *v.* 呈现

21. straightforward [ˌstretˋfɔrwəd] *adj.* 直接的

22. autocratic [ˌɔtəˋkrætɪk] *adj.* 专制的；独裁的

23. dictatorial [ˌdɪktəˋtorɪəl] *adj.* 独裁者的；自大的

24. consultative [kənˋsʌltətɪv] *adj.* 咨询的

25. buzz [bʌz] *n.* 狂热

26. thrill [θrɪl] *n.* 刺激；兴奋

听力测验解答

实战应用篇 Part I

Unit 1
是非题：1.T 2.F 3.F 4.T 5.F
选择题：1.d 2.b 3.c

Unit 2
是非题：1.F 2.F 3.T 4.F 5.T
选择题：1.d 2.d 3.a

Unit 3
是非题：1.F 2.T 3.F 4.F 5.F
选择题：1.a 2.c 3.d

Unit 4
是非题：1.F 2.T 3.T 4.F 5.T
选择题：1.c 2.d 3.b

Unit 5
是非题：1.T 2.F 3.T 4.T 5.F
选择题：1.c 2.b 3.d

Unit 6
是非题：1.T 2.F 3.F 4.T 5.T
选择题：1.d 2.b 3.c

Unit 7
是非题：1.T 2.T 3.F 4.F 5.F
选择题：1.c 2.c 3.b

Unit 8
是非题：1.T 2.F 3.T 4.F 5.T
选择题：1.c 2.b 3.d

Unit 9
是非题：1.T 2.F 3.F 4.F 5.F
选择题：1.a 2.d 3.b

Unit 10
是非题：1.F 2.F 3.F 4.T 5.T
选择题：1.d 2.b 3.c

Unit 11
是非题：1.F 2.T 3.F 4.F 5.F
选择题：1.a 2.d 3.b

Unit 12
是非题：1.F 2.T 3.F 4.F 5.T
选择题：1.c 2.b 3.b

Unit 13
是非题：1.F 2.F 3.T 4.T 5.F
选择题：1.b 2.c 3.b

Unit 14
是非题：1.F 2.T 3.T 4.T 5.F
选择题：1.c 2.c 3.b

实战应用篇 Part II

Unit 1
是非题：1. T　2. F　3. T　4. T　5. F
选择题：1. b　2. d　3. d

Unit 2
是非题：1. F　2. T　3. F　4. F　5. T
选择题：1. a　2. c　3. a

Unit 3
是非题：1. F　2. T　3. F　4. T　5. F
选择题：1. b　2. c　3. b

Unit 4
是非题：1. F　2. T　3. T　4. F　5. T
选择题：1. c　2. a　3. b

Unit 5
是非题：1. T　2. T　3. F　4. T　5. T
选择题：1. b　2. b　3. a

Unit 6
是非题：1. T　2. F　3. T　4. T　5. F
选择题：1. d　2. b　3. a

Unit 7
是非题：1. F　2. T　3. F　4. F　5. T
选择题：1. b　2. c　3. b

Unit 8
是非题：1. F　2. T　3. F　4. F　5. F
选择题：1. c　2. b　3. a

Unit 9
是非题：1. F　2. T　3. F　4. F　5. T
选择题：1. c　2. b　3. a

Unit 10
是非题：1. F　2. T　3. T　4. F　5. T
选择题：1. a　2. d　3. b

美式英语与 英式英语和澳大利亚英语的 发音区别

世界上有不少国家以英语为母语，但因地域不同，口音也有所差异，甚至于在一个国家之中，不同的地区、不同的社会阶层都会有不同的口音。这里我们就美式英语、英式英语和澳大利亚英语中最常见的差异作出说明。

一、英式发音

虽然英音及美音有一些差异，但也有大致的规则可循。美语是含卷舌音的语言，即 [r] 音会完整发出来。而英国人会把 bigger 去除卷舌音，意思就是词尾的 r 通常不发出来，或者是会弱化成非重音的元音 [ə]，即 bigger 读成 [ˈbɪɡə]、near 读成 [nɪə]、artist 读成 [ˈɑtɪst]，而美国人则读成 [ˈbɪɡər]、[nɪr] 及 [ˈɑrtɪst]。

这两种音调的发音，词尾音常会发得不一样，词尾为 y 的词就是其中一例。标准英语发音会把词尾 y 发成 [ɪ]，而美语发音则会发成 [i]。例如：英国人读 quickly 会读成 [ˈkwɪklɪ]，但美国人读成 [ˈkwɪkli]。请注意 KK 音标系统对词尾 y 用的音标是用英式发音 [ɪ]，而不是美式发音 [i]。

标准英音与美音之间另一个区别是元音 a 的发音区别。通常，美国人会发 [æ]，而英国人会发 [ɔ] 或 [ɑ]。例如，美国人把 can 读成 [kæn]，而英国人读成 [kɑn]。但也不是全部如此，例如 pasta 这个词，美国人读成 [ˈpɑstə]，而英国人则读成 [ˈpæstə]。

这里有一段来自英国的饭店前台人员与美国人 Tom 之间的对话，您可仔细听听两种发音的区别。(请听 MP3 Track 79)

F.D.: Globetrotters Hotel front desk. May I help you?

Tom: Yes, I'd like to know why there is a man standing in my bedroom.

F.D.: There's a **man standing** in your bedroom?

Tom: Yes, he seems like a nice man, but he's staring at me very strangely.

F.D.: What does he look like?

Tom: He is tall and thin. He has gray hair on the sides of his head and on top . . . nothing.

F.D.: Is he **smiling**?

Tom: No, he's just quietly standing there, doing and saying nothing. It seems so strange.

F.D.: What's he wearing?

Tom: A bathrobe. He looks like he's been using my shower.

F.D.: Using your **shower**? That's unusual.

Tom: I know. I also think it's pretty strange. That's why I called you.

F.D.: Shall I call the police?

Tom: Maybe you'd better. I don't think he should just stand there all night with nothing to do. He'll get bored, and I don't think I can sleep well with him watching me like that.

F.D.: I'll call the police. What's your room **number**?

Tom: It's 1004.

F.D.: 1004? Let's see. So you are Mr. Johnson?

Tom: No, this is Tom Smith.

F.D.: Are you **sure** Mr. Smith? I have a Mr. **Johnson** registered at that room number.

Tom: Yeah, I'm sure my name is Mr. Smith—Tom Smith.

F.D.: Mr. Smith, your room number is 1006. **You're** looking at Mr. Johnson. You're in his room!

Tom: Oh . . . Thanks, good-bye.

二、澳大利亚英语

澳大利亚英语源于英国伦敦的伦敦 (Cockney) 腔，如果大家看过电影 *My Fair Lady*《窈窕淑女》就会有印象，典型澳大利亚发音中有两个元音与英音及美音明显不同，一是 [e] 发成 [ai] 并拉长；一是 [o] 发成 [ɔi] 并拉长。而词尾及词中的 r 跟其他的英音相同，通常不会读出来。

> 例如：
>
> emergency, car, sir, heart, prefer, hurt 中的 r 不卷舌。
>
> male, pain 的音近似 [ai]
>
> side, fine 的音近似 [a]，又带一点 [ɔ] 音，比美音的 [ai] 短。
>
> car, heart 的音比美音 [ɑ] 更长。
>
> bad, allergy 的音比美音 [æ] 口形扁，近似 [ɛ]。
>
> technician 的音比美音的 [ɛ] 口形更扁。
>
> shock, hospital, doctor 的音介于 [ɑ] 与 [ɔ] 之间。

这里，虽用 KK 音标来说明澳大利亚英语的特色，但实际上并非能完全用 KK 音标标出，在此只是供读者参考。请仔细听下面这一段澳大利亚人 Sam 与美国人 Tom 之间的对话，以了解这两种发音的差别。(请听 MP3 Track 80)

Sam: We have an **emergency**! We have a young **male**, approximately 25 years old, who has been hit by a **car**.

Tom: I've been hit by a car?

Sam: Just **lie** still. Don't **move**. The subject is bleeding from his **side** and is in **shock**.

Tom: I'm bleeding? Where's the blood? Oh, there it is.

Sam: Please **Sir**, stay here until the ambulance **arrives** to take you to the **hospital**.

Tom: Who are you?

Sam: I am an EMT, Emergency Medical Technician. I **saw** the accident and I called it in to the hospital.

Radio: This is the Sydney Hospital. Does the subject have insurance?

Sam: Do you have insurance?

Tom: Yes, I have insurance.

Sam: He has insurance. Have you ever had a **heart** attack or have a history of heart disease?

Tom: No, and no history of heart disease. Am I going to be OK?

Sam: You're **going** to be **fine**.

　　对学习者来说，没有哪一种发音有正确或错误之分，可以参考的只有某一地区的标准发音（如标准英语、标准美语）。因此，如果您想更多地了解不同地区口音的异同，您可以利用自己的听力材料，多接触各种不同的英语媒体，从中发现其中的区别。

LiveABC互动英语系列

数字化换代产品
超强多功能光盘震撼登场!

抢救上班族英语

简报英语篇
定价：48.00元

求职英语篇
定价：48.00元

商务词汇精选1000
定价：48.00元

会议英语篇
定价：48.00元

商业写作篇
定价：48.00元

商务书信篇
定价：42.00元

商业会话篇(第二版)
定价：48.00元

办公室会话篇(第二版)
定价：48.00元

美语会话全集

衣食住行
定价：65.00元

观光旅游(第二版)
定价：68.00元

上班族必备口袋书系列

商业会话
定价：25.00元

职场会话
定价：25.00元

CNN互动英语系列

Step by Step
听懂CNN
定价：58.00元

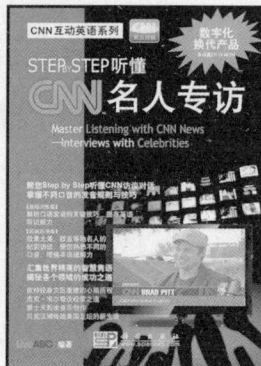

Step by Step听懂
CNN名人专访
定价：58.00元

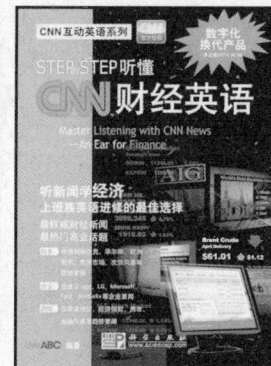

Step by Step听懂
CNN财经英语
定价：58.00元

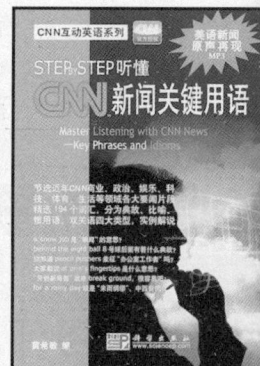

Step by Step听懂
CNN新闻关键用语
定价：45.00元

LiveABC 英语关键力

10步写出好英文
定价：35.00元

易混淆词比较分析篇
定价：49.00元

新托业备考系列

新托业完全热身与实战演练
定价：59.00元

新托业完全攻略
定价：52.00元

新托业高频词汇短语
定价：45.00元

关键句型篇
定价：42.00元

关键词汇篇
定价：45.00元

关键数字篇
定价：40.00元

关键口语篇
定价：42.00元